THE BLIND VICTORIAN
HENRY FAWCETT
AND BRITISH LIBERALISM

THE BLIND VICTORIAN
HENRY FAWCETT
AND BRITISH
LIBERALISM

EDITED BY

LAWRENCE GOLDMAN

DEPARTMENT FOR EXTERNAL STUDIES
UNIVERSITY OF OXFORD

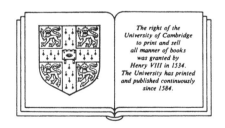

The right of the
University of Cambridge
to print and sell
all manner of books
was granted by
Henry VIII in 1534.
The University has printed
and published continuously
since 1584.

CAMBRIDGE UNIVERSITY PRESS

CAMBRIDGE
NEW YORK   PORT CHESTER
MELBOURNE   SYDNEY

PUBLISHED BY THE PRESS SYNDICATE OF THE UNIVERSITY OF CAMBRIDGE
The Pitt Building, Trumpington Street, Cambridge, United Kingdom

CAMBRIDGE UNIVERSITY PRESS
The Edinburgh Building, Cambridge CB2 2RU, UK
40 West 20th Street, New York NY 10011–4211, USA
477 Williamstown Road, Port Melbourne, VIC 3207, Australia
Ruiz de Alarcón 13, 28014 Madrid, Spain
Dock House, The Waterfront, Cape Town 8001, South Africa

http://www.cambridge.org

First published 1989
First paperback edition 2002

A catalogue record for this book is available from the British Library

Library of Congress Cataloguing in Publication data
The Blind Victorian: Henry Fawcett and British Liberalism / edited by Lawrence Goldman.
p.   cm.
"Henry Fawcett, 1833–1884: a bibliography".
Includes bibliographical references and index.
ISBN 0 521 35032 8
1. Fawcett, Henry, 1833–1884.
2. Statesman – Great Britain – Biography.
3. Economists – Great Britain – Biography.
4. Liberalism – Great Britain – History – 19th century.
5. Great Britain – Politics and government – 1837–1901.
6. Goldman, Lawrence. 1957–   .
DA565.F33B57   1989
941.081'092'4–dc19   88-38762   CIP
[B]

ISBN 0 521 35032 8 hardback
ISBN 0 521 89274 0 paperback

Contents

III POLITICS

Illustrations

vii

Notes on contributors

GIACOMO BECATTINI is Professor of Economics in the University of Florence. He is currently Vice-President of the Society of Italian Economists. He has edited and prefaced works by J. S. Mill and Alfred Marshall, has worked on the theory of value and he is currently interested in problems of economic development.

STEFAN COLLINI is University Lecturer in English and Fellow of Clare Hall, Cambridge. His previous publications include *Liberalism and Sociology. L. T. Hobhouse and Political Argument 1880–1914* (Cambridge, 1979), *That Noble Science of Politics. A Study in Nineteenth-Century Intellectual History* (with Donald Winch and John Burrow) (Cambridge, 1983) and *Matthew Arnold* (Oxford, 1988).

PHYLLIS DEANE was Professor of Economic History in the University of Cambridge and retired in 1983 to pursue research interests in economic history and the history of ideas. She is the author of *The Evolution of Economic Ideas* (Cambridge, 1978).

LAWRENCE GOLDMAN is Staff Tutor in History and Politics at the Department for External Studies, University of Oxford. He was previously a Junior Research Fellow at Trinity College, Cambridge. He has published articles on Victorian political and intellectual history and on the history of social investigation. He is currently working on a book on the history of the Social Science Association.

CHRISTOPHER HARVIE is Professor of British and Irish Studies at the University of Tübingen. He taught previously at the Open University. He is the author of *The Lights of Liberalism. University Liberals and the Challenge of Democracy, 1860–1886* (London, 1976), *Scotland and*

Nationalism (London, 1977) and *No Gods and Precious Few Heroes. Scotland since 1914* (London, 1981). He is presently at work on a study of political fiction in Britain and the mid-Victorian section of *The History of Oxford University.*

BOYD HILTON is University Lecturer in History and Fellow of Trinity College, Cambridge. He is the author of *Corn, Cash and Commerce. The Economic Policies of the Tory Governments 1815–1830* (Oxford, 1977) and *The Age of Atonement. The Influence of Evangelicalism on Social and Economic Thought 1795–1865* (Oxford, 1988).

DAVID RUBINSTEIN is Senior Lecturer in Economic and Social History in the University of Hull. He has written about the history of education, housing, recreation, labour and women in the nineteenth and twentieth centuries. He is the author of *Before the Suffragettes. Women's Emancipation in the 1890s* (Brighton, 1986). He is now working on a biography of Millicent Garrett Fawcett.

DONALD WINCH is Professor of the History of Economics in the University of Sussex. He has written various studies in the history of economic and political thought from the late eighteenth to the mid-twentieth centuries, and more recently books on *Adam Smith's Politics* (Cambridge, 1978) and, with Stefan Collini and John Burrow, *That Noble Science of Politics. A Study in Nineteenth-Century Intellectual History.*

Preface

'Let us now praise famous men': this is the usual justification for historical biography. Why, then, remember Henry Fawcett? In the roll-call of famous and eminent Victorians, Henry Fawcett does not figure. He is not forgotten, certainly: a correspondence in the *Guardian* in June 1985 on the identity of the first blind member of parliament brought him forward as a candidate.[1] But the name Fawcett is as likely to remind people today of his wife, Millicent Garrett, as to remind them of the man himself. In 1874, however, Henry Fawcett's name was, in the judgement of *The Times*, 'a household word throughout the world'.[2] During his lifetime 'it was said that Fawcett's popularity was second only to Mr Gladstone's' and his death in 1884 at the age of fifty-one was 'felt as a national misfortune'.[3] In 1880 it was generally believed that but for the fact that Fawcett was blind he would have been offered a place in Gladstone's second cabinet.[4] As it was, in Gladstone's tribute to him after his sudden, untimely death, 'he acquired a place in the hearts and minds of his countrymen such as is accorded to few; and I believe that he won a place equally high in the esteem and respect of the House of Commons'.[5]

Such tributes often exaggerate – though in Gladstone's case there were so many reasons to downplay the contribution of one of his most effective and persistent critics that they lend credibility to this particular assessment. Indeed, there is little reason to doubt this and similar judgements extolling Fawcett's qualities and popularity; after all, Leslie Stephen's biography of his friend ran through five editions inside two years after its publication in 1885. Fawcett's celebrated triumph over physical disability and his place at the forefront of a developing politics of mass participation

---

[1] *Guardian*, 27 June 1985, p. 12. [2] *The Times*, 27 April 1874, p. 11.
[3] Leslie Stephen, *Life of Henry Fawcett* (London, 1885), pp. 291–2; Leslie Stephen, 'Henry Fawcett. In Memoriam', *Macmillan's Magazine*, vol. 51 (Dec. 1884), p. 130.
[4] Stephen, *Life of Fawcett*, p. 409. [5] *Hansard*, ccxciii, 7 Nov. 1884, 1223.

– the keys to his popularity – are very different claims to fame, but both brought him recognition and celebrity during his life and may be considered sufficient excuses for a more modern assessment of his career. Yet there are many others in addition: indeed, it is the very range and diversity of Fawcett's interests and commitments (if not their depth) which commands attention. From a humble background he secured a Fellowship at a Cambridge college, the Chair of Political Economy there, a seat in Parliament and then a position as Postmaster General in Gladstone's second administration. He was known as a leading proponent of the claims of the organised working class, of women, of colonial subjects, of the blind. He was a prominent university reformer, a supporter of popular education and consistently in favour of widening the franchise. As a radical Liberal who was frequently at odds with the leadership of the Liberal party and Gladstone in particular, he built a reputation for principled independence in politics that won the plaudits of the press and public even as it exasperated his colleagues. Fawcett was all of these things at once, prominent in each separate capacity even if an internally consistent synthesis of these elements was beyond his abilities.

In addition, he had contact with more familiar Victorian figures – contact that expands our understanding of them and adds interest to Fawcett's own career. In early manhood in Cambridge, Fawcett was inseparable from Leslie Stephen in a relationship that points the contrast between the mature and immature Stephen. Later, as a confessed disciple of John Stuart Mill, Fawcett helped consolidate Mill's intellectual ascendancy in mid-Victorian Britain. And in Parliament, as a formidable antagonist to Gladstone, Fawcett did more than any other individual to disrupt the smooth progress of business during Gladstone's first administration and was the cause of one of the great political debacles of the nineteenth century – the loss of Gladstone's Irish Universities Bill in March 1873 with all its attendant effects on the political fortunes of both the Liberals and the Conservatives. In recent years the history of Liberalism in Britain in the mid-nineteenth century has tended to be written in terms of Gladstone's career and priorities. A study of Fawcett may provide a salutary corrective to this particular perspective, providing a quite different view of Liberal ideology and practice in government and reminding us that Gladstone's idiosyncracies were not to all Liberal tastes.

These various claims to historical attention brought together a number of scholars on the occasion of the centenary of Henry Fawcett's death at the end of 1984. The venue was, appropriately enough, Fawcett's own college at Cambridge, Trinity Hall, where he was a Fellow for nearly thirty years. The terms of reference had been drawn broadly and for all the participants the occasion provided an opportunity to examine aspects of the history of political economy, Victorian politics and the Liberal outlook during the mid-nineteenth century. Fawcett's life and work formed a point of departure in all cases, but the issues covered were of more general interest as well, and in consequence, the papers delivered have been collected together and published.

All the contributions to the conference are included in this volume. The three papers by Phyllis Deane, Stefan Collini and Lawrence Goldman are published with the comments of, respectively, Donald Winch, Boyd Hilton and Christopher Harvie who acted as discussants. Giacomo Becattini's paper is the revised text of the 1984 Fawcett Lecture which he delivered and with which the conference began. There are two subsequent additions: an introduction setting out the basic details of Fawcett's life, which has been designed to set the more specialist contributions in context and to provide more information on Fawcett's later political career, and an essay on Fawcett's marriage and feminism from David Rubinstein. At a relatively late stage it was discovered that Dr Rubinstein was at work on a biography of Millicent Garrett Fawcett, and he was invited and kindly consented to write a piece for the collection.

The papers thus fall into three sections: Fawcett's personal life and sensibilities; his place as a political economist in relation to the classical and neo-classical traditions; and his position in politics as a somewhat ambivalent champion of the working class. Fawcett as a professor at Cambridge, as a noted economic populariser and as a member of parliament for twenty years gives access to a range of important historical issues and it is hoped that this collection can provide an insight into a number of related themes in the history of British Liberalism. The relationships between Liberal politics and economic doctrine; between liberal principles and the Liberal Party; between the Liberal Party and the Victorian working class; between the liberal temper and the more general moral and intellectual sensibilities of the age; between Liberalism and feminism; and between the English universities and the politics of the Liberal Party at Westminster are all examined in these papers. And in the process, it is intended that something of the texture and grain of academic and political life in mid-Victorian Britain will be communicated.

Taken together, the papers do not present a single and consistent picture of Henry Fawcett. It was never intended that the original conference and this book growing from it should seek to present a simple biography, not least because Leslie Stephen's *Life of Henry Fawcett* based on intimate personal acquaintance could hardly be surpassed as a narrative. The aim of this collection, rather, is to place Fawcett as a representative figure in various contexts and so illuminate both the life *and* the times. In the process, the differences of authorial approach and interest have resulted in varied interpretations, especially in the treatment of Fawcett as a political economist. To Phyllis Deane, summing the whole of his work, Fawcett is an important populariser without many original insights of his own. Lawrence Goldman, examining Fawcett's economics in relation to his characteristic political postures of the 1860s has isolated inconsistencies that suggest Fawcett's limitations as an economic thinker free from contemporary prejudices. Yet Giacomo Becattini, concentrating on some of Fawcett's very earliest publications, has made a spirited defence of the young Fawcett as an influential innovator in his first discussions of the 'labour question'. The differences between these views may owe something to the type of economist Fawcett was, truly a *political* economist in an intellectual tradition which, as Donald Winch explains, was then coming to a close. He cast his net wide and consequently left historians with plenty of latitude for interpretation. The differences may also owe something to the varied disciplinary backgrounds of each of the authors. But these differences do not need to be excused: Fawcett was involved in so many areas of mid-Victorian life, political, social and intellectual, that only a broadly based approach across a range of historical sub-disciplines could hope to capture the breadth of his engagements. And that broad approach has produced a series of essays marked by differences in tone and emphasis and interpretation that suggests, hopefully, the richness of the sources and the significance of the historical questions at issue.

In editing a collaborative volume like this one incurs many obligations. Thanks must go first to the Master and Fellows of Trinity Hall for hosting the conference and for providing such generous hospitality for all the participants. Dr Jonathan Steinberg of Trinity Hall deserves special mention: he first brought the contributors together; he organised the conference in all its details and he has continued to provide help and advice as this book has been prepared for publication. Mrs Thelma Jeffs, the Tutors' Secretary at Trinity Hall dealt with correspondence and arrangements with her usual cheerfulness. At Cambridge University Press, Richard Fisher's enthusiasm for the project and encouragement have been invaluable. In an individual capacity as a contributor to this volume I would like to thank Dr J. P. Parry and Dr Colin Matthew for their help and advice on the introduction. And, as editor, I would like to acknowledge the good humour of my fellow-contributors. They have had to wait a long time until it was possible for me to edit and collate this book and I must thank them for their patience.

LAWRENCE GOLDMAN

Acknowledgements

We wish to thank the following for their permission to quote from collections and manuscripts in their possession or keeping: Mrs C. G. Williams, St Brelade, Jersey; the Curators of the Bodleian Library, Oxford; the Trustees of the British Library; the British Library of Political and Economic Science, Manuscripts Division; the Syndics of the Cambridge University Library; Department of Palaeography and Diplomatic, University of Durham; the Fawcett Library, City of London Polytechnic; the Mistress and Fellows of Girton Colege, Cambridge; the City of Manchester Archives Department, Manchester Central Library; the Mills Memorial Library, McMaster University; the Marshall Library of Economics, University of Cambridge; the Milton S. Eisenhower Library, the Johns Hopkins University; the Library, University of Sheffield; Lord Shuttleworth and the John Rylands University Library, Manchester; the President and Fellows of St John's College, Oxford; the Master and Fellows of Trinity College, Cambridge; the Master and Fellows of Trinity Hall, Cambridge; the Library, University College, London; Yale University Library.

For permission to reproduce illustrations in this book we are grateful to the Bodleian Library, Oxford; the National Portrait Gallery, London; the Mary Evans Picture Library, London; the Master and Fellows of Trinity Hall, Cambridge.

Introduction *'An advanced Liberal'*
Henry Fawcett, 1833–1884

LAWRENCE GOLDMAN

I

Henry Fawcett was born on 26 August 1833 in Salisbury, Wiltshire, the third of four children. His father, William, a draper, originally from Kirkby Lonsdale in Westmorland, had arrived in Salisbury in 1815. He opened his own shop in the town in 1825, and two years later secured his rising social status by marrying Mary Cooper, a daughter of the solicitor who acted as the local agent for the Whigs. The Fawcetts were staunch Liberals and their strict party loyalty rubbed off: there is no need to look far for the origins of Fawcett's Liberalism.[1] In the year of the Great Reform Act, William Fawcett was Mayor of Salisbury; eleven years later in 1843, when Cobden and Bright visited the town as they took their anti-protection campaign into the heart of rural England, they stayed with the Fawcetts.[2]

Henry was not a precocious child. He was educated first at a dame school, proceeding from there through two other schools until he was sent to King's College School in London in 1849. It was evident that he had a talent for mathematics but not for classics and after a brief spell at King's College itself he entered Peterhouse in Cambridge in October 1852, coming up while the Royal Commission appointed in 1850 to investigate 'the state, discipline, studies and revenues of the University' was still sitting. Leslie Stephen first saw him on the towpath of the Cam, 'a very tall, gaunt figure swinging along with huge strides ... over 6 feet 3 inches in height ... remarkably large of bone and massive of limb'.[3] The pathetic contrast in later life between this powerful frame and physique, full of

---

[1] Millicent Garrett Fawcett, *What I Remember* (London, 1924), p. 58.
[2] Leslie Stephen, *Life of Henry Fawcett* (London, 1885), p. 4.
[3] ibid., p. 18.

1 Henry Fawcett as a student in Cambridge in 1855 before he was blinded, from an engraving by Joseph Brown after a photograph

restless energy, and the dependence caused by blindness, was not lost on contemporaries.

Fawcett determined early that he would aim for a Fellowship. Ever alert to the main chance, he migrated from Peterhouse within a year when he discovered stiff internal competition for a Fellowship there, entering Trinity Hall where standards were not so exacting. He was disappointed to be classed Seventh Wrangler in the Mathematical Tripos – a higher position had been generally expected – but it was enough to secure him election to a Fellowship at Trinity Hall at Christmas 1856. His first objective had been achieved and Fawcett set out on his next – to win a place in politics by the traditional means open to a young man of talent who lacked connections and money: a career at the bar. As he wrote to a friend just before he entered Lincoln's Inn in the autumn of 1856, 'I started life as a boy with the ambition some day to enter the House of Commons. Every effort, every endeavour, which I have ever put forth has had this object in view.'[4] But Fawcett's career at the bar was cruelly short, terminated by the accident that left him totally and permanently blind – yet an accident that paradoxically changed everything and nothing for him.

Ironically, Fawcett had serious problems with his eyes before the accident. In the winter of 1856–7 he was advised to take 'perfect rest' to restore his failing sight, affected by over-work.[5] Then, on 17 September 1858, Fawcett went out shooting with his father, and William Fawcett, with a cataract in one eye failed to see his son in advance of the party. He fired at some partridges and two pellets went through the tinted spectacles that Henry had been advised to wear, blinding him in both eyes.[6] Fawcett apparently once told a friend that it took him just 'one night to decide whether the loss of my sight should make any difference in my life or not; I decided it should not'.[7] Whether or not this is true, it is clear that within a matter of weeks he had come to terms with blindness and determined to continue as before. For the rest of his life he continued to walk vigorously, ride, skate and fish when he could. He rowed at Cambridge in a dons' eight called the 'Ancient Mariners'; he even went roller-skating soon after it was introduced.[8] And his plans to enter Parliament were not altered in intention, though it was evident that the route to politics via the bar was now closed to him. Instead, he struck out on a more individual strategy (and a relatively new one in the 1860s, as Christopher Harvie points out in this volume, though it was to become more common in later years): to

---

[4] Fawcett to Mrs Hodding quoted in ibid., pp. 38–9.   [5] ibid., p. 35.
[6] ibid., pp. 43–5.
[7] Ray Strachey, *Millicent Garrett Fawcett* (London, 1931), p. 23.
[8] Winifred Holt, *A Beacon for the Blind. Being a Life of Henry Fawcett, the Blind Postmaster General* (London, 1915), p. 171.

2 Henry Fawcett in the late 1860s

enter politics on the basis of an academic position and a reputation built up by writing in the journals, speaking on the platform and generally being noticed. Seven years after his accident he had won his seat in Parliament and it is in this sense that blindness changed nothing in his life. He did not allow it to alter his ultimate ambition and sense of purpose.

Fawcett's very success in overcoming such a handicap obscures the many problems he faced. Blindness could only bring sadness and pathos: 'he was always asking his friends how Milly was looking and begging them for descriptions of her face'.[9] And, especially in the early years, there was the difficulty of convincing others of his capabilities and self-reliance. In his first election campaign in Southwark in 1860 the electors of the borough needed reassurance that if returned to the Commons he would be able to catch the Speaker's eye in debate.[10] He was initially blackballed by the committee of the Reform Club and it was only Thackeray's intervention which secured his election.[11] In presenting a testimonial on Fawcett's behalf to the electors of the Chair of Political Economy at Cambridge, Mill felt it necessary to counter the objection arising 'from Mr. Fawcett's inability to read his lectures'.[12] And his blindness was used to explain his exclusion from the cabinet in 1880. It was contended that his reliance on a secretary would breach the necessary confidentiality of cabinet papers, though the suspicion remains that here was a convenient excuse for keeping out such a potentially disruptive force from the inner circles of government.

On the other hand, there was no cynicism in Stephen's judgement that his friend turned blindness 'by his special courage, into something like an advantage'.[13] After all, in urging Fawcett to follow his ambition Mill had expected that his 'misfortune' would tell 'very much in your favour, not only by exciting interest, and neutralising envy and jealousy, but because it will cause you to be much sooner talked about'.[14] He was right, of course. And Fawcett's triumph over handicap was no small benefit to a political economist who sought to instruct the masses that economic and moral improvement could only be obtained by their own efforts and self-reliance. The man on the platform was living proof of the virtues he preached. Indeed, it was on the platform that blindness told most obviously in his favour: his Oxford contemporaries G. C. Brodrick and James Bryce agreed that blindness 'compelled him to concentrate his

---

[9] Strachey, *Millicent Garrett Fawcett*, p. 36.
[10] *Morning Star* (London), 12 Nov. 1860, p. 2.
[11] Holt, *A Beacon for the Blind*, p. 127.
[12] *Collected Works of John Stuart Mill* (25 vols., Toronto, 1963–), vol. 15, p. 860.
[13] Leslie Stephen, 'Henry Fawcett. In Memoriam', *Macmillan's Magazine*, vol. 51 (Dec. 1884), p. 130.
[14] Mill to Fawcett, 26 Feb. 1860, in *Collected Works of John Stuart Mill*, vol. 15, p. 688.

thoughts and train his memory' so that 'he became a master of lucid statement and cogent argument'.[15] There is no doubting the astonishing effect that Fawcett could induce on a hall crowded with hundreds of listeners. The blind M.P., tall and eloquent, could fascinate and mesmerise. As one listener recalled his speeches on behalf of the candidacy of the working man, George Odger, at the Southwark by-election in 1870,

> It was my first experience of hearing a blind person address a crowded audience, and to watch him as he stood close to the platform's edge, a tall commanding figure, and then to realise that he could not *see* the people he was speaking to affected me deeply. At the end of ten minutes the reaction came. Whether he was able to use his eyes no longer interested me; his lips were all that mattered. I saw nothing else, and time and time again I caught myself anticipating half aloud the words that were about to fall from his lips.[16]

II

Fawcett returned to Cambridge early in 1859. If the years before he entered university represent a first phase in his life, and the period up to his accident a second phase, then a third phase now began and lasted until his election to Parliament in 1865. Using Cambridge as his base, Fawcett sallied forth into a series of electoral contests, into various public arena and into the society of Liberal intellectuals and activists. His attitude to the university was a mixture of the progressive and the complacent. In academic matters he was a conservative, admiring mental discipline and the rigorous intellectual gymnastics of the traditional Tripos and decrying 'research' and the development of new subjects and specialisms.[17] His attitude to university studies was thus at one with the intellectual limitations that many of his friends and contemporaries noted in him. An editorial in *The Times* in April 1874 spoke for them all: 'There are, without doubt, more things in heaven and earth than are dreamt of in Mr. Fawcett's philosophy.'[18] And that was just the point: Fawcett showed a 'want of interest in the questions generally called philosophical'.[19] As Bryce put it, his 'was an eminently English intellect' with a 'broad, commonsense way of looking at things'.[20] Leslie Stephen's hilarious *Sketches from Cambridge* in 1865 described the traditional diet there of mathematics and classics as a 'race-course for rival candidates to run'.[21]

[15] G. C. Brodrick, *Memories and Impressions, 1831–1900* (London, 1900), p. 264; Viscount Bryce, 'Preface' to Holt, *A Beacon for the Blind*, p. x.
[16] F. W. Soutter, *Recollections of a Labour Pioneer* (London, 1923), p. 50.
[17] Noel Annan, *Leslie Stephen. The Godless Victorian* (London, 1984), p. 34.
[18] *The Times*, 27 April 1874, p. 11.   [19] Stephen, *Life of Fawcett*, p. 94.
[20] Bryce, 'Preface' to Holt, *A Beacon for the Blind*, p. x.
[21] [Leslie Stephen], *Sketches from Cambridge. By a Don* (London and Cambridge, 1865), p. 42.

Stephen was being ironic, using images of sport and competition to criticise a curriculum of which he disapproved. Fawcett, however, used the same language in a spirit of reverential earnest: 'the race', he wrote, 'is a manly and noble contest'.[22] The prize at the end was the Fellowship, and throughout his life Fawcett hymned the academic contest by which these were secured. Where many, even in an age of university reform, saw privilege and exclusivism, Fawcett saw an intellectual meritocracy allowing poor boys like himself to take their place at the High Table of life. 'What other coveted distinction is there', he asked, 'which wealth and rank have no influence in securing?'[23] Cambridge provided a model of open competition (or so he believed) that Fawcett so admired in all other spheres, and as a university reformer he was committed to opening up the old universities so as to admit, at least in theory, all sects and all classes. In this respect he was squarely representative of a generation graduating in the 1850s and 1860s whose journey into Liberalism and radicalism began with consideration of the role of the university in a changing culture. From 1857, when Fawcett took his place on a committee of young Cambridge dons set up to secure the abolition of celibacy among senior members of the university,[24] this issue was at the head of his concerns, and it was on questions of university reform that Fawcett made his political reputation and achieved notoriety in the later 1860s and early 1870s.

Election to the Chair of Political Economy in November 1863 secured Fawcett's position in the university and doubled his income to around £600 a year – no small consideration for a man bent on a political career. Fawcett had developed a serious interest in political economy after his election to a Fellowship and he began work on his *Manual of Political Economy* – the book by which he was best known – in the autumn of 1861. He had been encouraged to write the *Manual* by his Cambridge friend, the publisher Macmillan. Both men were aware that the Chair of Political Economy, held by the aged Pryme, would probably soon fall vacant and that Fawcett's candidacy would be far more serious with a book behind him.[25] The timing was perfect. The *Manual* was published in early 1863 and Pryme retired that summer. There then followed the election. As Leslie Stephen later wrote to James Russell Lowell, he had been busy

---

[22] Henry Fawcett, 'On the exclusion of those who are not members of the Established Church from Fellowships and other privileges of the English Universities', *Macmillan's Magazine*, vol. 3 (March 1861), p. 414.

[23] ibid.

[24] See Fawcett to R. Potts, 17 May 1857, in 'Memorial, signatures, correspondence, etc. on the celibacy question. Cambridge, 1857', Cambridge University Library, Add. 725(c).

[25] Stephen, *Life of Fawcett*, p. 117.

in securing the election to a professorship of political economy of my blind friend
Fawcett ... As the electors were the resident M.A.s who are almost *ex-officio*
Conservatives and High Churchmen, and as my friend had the reputation of being
an infidel Radical, this wanted skill. However, I did it, or, at least humbly assisted
in it, and very nearly got drunk on the occasion.[26]

Fawcett had been a member of the Political Economy Club since 1861 and
he could point to testimonials from Mill, Herman Merivale, William
Newmarch, W. T. Thornton, J. E. Thorold Rogers, T. E. Cliffe Leslie and
Robert Lowe among others – an impressive clutch. But academic merit
was not the only consideration and the young Liberal was opposed by
many of the most powerful university figures. He only squeaked home
because the St John's vote was split between two candidates from the
college (one of whom, Leonard Courtney, was later to become a very close
friend and an ally of Fawcett's in Parliament). 'I don't think an election
has produced so much excitement at Cambridge for years' wrote Fawcett
on the day following his success.[27]

This was by no means the only election that Fawcett fought in the early
1860s. Indeed, by the time he was elected to the Chair he was already a
veteran of two parliamentary campaigns. In 1860 he began his political
career in audacious style by presenting himself as a candidate at a
by-election at Southwark.[28] In early 1863 he came close to election in
Cambridge itself, beaten by 708 to 627 votes at a cost of some £600.[29]
Then, a year later, he stood for the vacant seat at Brighton, finishing a
creditable second in a field of four and only defeated by a split in the
Liberal ranks. But he had made his mark: 'all my friends at Brighton seem
to think I cannot be defeated there at the next election' he wrote soon
afterwards.[30] And at the general election in 1865 he was elected for
Brighton on a united Liberal vote at a cost of £900.[31] At the age of
thirty-two he had achieved his ambition.

The achievement owed much to the encouragement and practical help
of Fawcett's friends. His talent for conversation, his infectious optimism,
inevitably made him a popular figure in the university and outside, and
many gave of their time and talents to further the career of a blind man. Of
all of these early friendships, that with Leslie Stephen, which is discussed
in Stefan Collini's contribution to this volume, was most important.
Though it cooled once Fawcett had a seat in Parliament and after Stephen

[26] F. W. Maitland, *The Life and Letters of Leslie Stephen* (London, 1906), p. 157 (1 Jan.
1864).
[27] ibid., pp. 117–22; G. P. Gooch, *Life of Lord Courtney* (London, 1920), pp. 58–61.
[28] See p. 153 below.   [29] Stephen, *Life of Fawcett*, pp. 203–6.
[30] Fawcett to Fanny Hertz, 3 Sept. 1864, Marshall Library, University of Cambridge, Misc.
1 (77).
[31] Stephen, *Life of Fawcett*, p. 217.

had left Cambridge in 1867 on his marriage, it sustained Fawcett during these years.[32] Stephen not only masterminded his election to the Chair of Political Economy. In the Cambridge parliamentary election of 1863 he is pictured 'haranguing a Radical crowd from the window of an inn and "properly exciting" his audience'.[33] And in 1864 he led a party down to Brighton to canvas and agitate on Fawcett's behalf to the apparent dismay of the local residents.[34] It was all part of the game: 'we were young men, sanguine, bouyant and sociable' wrote Stephen in 1885.[35] The quotation is from Stephen's celebrated biography of his friend, written at the request of Mrs Fawcett in the months after Fawcett's death. Enlivened with elements of autobiography in its early chapters on Cambridge in the 1850s and 1860s, it was among the most popular of Stephen's books. But as a celebration of the life of a friend it could not be wholly honest. Ten years after it was published Stephen could be more detached:

> He was to the end a very dear friend of mine although the differences between us were so great that I am inclined to think that it was only the accident of our living at the same college during the period most favourable to the formation of friendships that could have brought us together.[36]

The judgement may be unduly harsh, coloured by the melancholy that enveloped Stephen's advancing years and his recognition of the change in his spirit on leaving Cambridge. Noel Annan has contended that 'intellectually, Stephen lost by his attachment to Fawcett nearly as much as he gained'.[37] Certainly there was an obvious imbalance in the relationship. On Fawcett's return to Cambridge in 1859 'Stephen's tender care for him was beautiful to see' and it may have been that Stephen gave of himself so liberally out of sympathy rather than respect and true amity for his handicapped friend.[38] Stephen's impatience with Fawcett in 1874 'talking Mill's "Liberty" of the crudest kind at the top of his voice for an hour or two, till I damned all radicals as heartily as Ruskin', points the contrast between Fawcett's increasing stridency and dogmatism and Stephen's growing scepticism and doubt in the years after Cambridge.[39] It also points to the new friendship that Fawcett made in the 1860s with Mill himself.

Mill's intellectual influence over his young disciple is explored in Stefan Collini's essay. Mill was mentor, model and prophet for Fawcett in one. In his first letter to Mill at the end of 1859 Fawcett explained that 'for the last three years your books have been the chief education of my mind'.[40] In

[32] Maitland, *Life of Leslie Stephen*, p. 386.   [33] ibid., p. 105.   [34] ibid., p. 106.
[35] Stephen, *Life of Fawcett*, p. 76.   [36] Maitland, *Life of Leslie Stephen*, p. 48.
[37] Annan, *Leslie Stephen*, p. 40.
[38] Maitland, *Life of Leslie Stephen*, p. 105.
[39] Stephen to Charles Eliot Norton, 12 Oct. 1874, ibid., p. 246.
[40] Fawcett to Mill, 23 Dec. 1859, in Stephen, *Life of Fawcett*, p. 102.

May 1867, when seconding Mill's amendment to the Reform Bill that
would have extended the franchise to women, Fawcett averred that 'he
had always looked up to the hon. Member for Westminster as his
teacher, and from him he had learnt all his lessons of political life'.[41]
From his own experience Fawcett could attest that 'a constantly increasing number of the young men of the greatest promise at Oxford and
Cambridge' looked up to Mill 'as a master'[42] – he was just the most
ardent and persistent of adulators. For his part, Mill accepted Fawcett as
a disciple and follower: as he wrote to Helen Taylor in February 1860
after reading one of Fawcett's earliest papers, 'I think we may look to
him with great hopes (notwithstanding his misfortune) as one of the
successors'.[43] Mill first heard of Fawcett from his friend Thomas Hare
who had seen him at the Bradford Congress of the Social Science Association in October 1859, and it was Hare who introduced the two men in
February 1860.[44] Their common interest was Hare's scheme for electoral
reform and the fruit of their early collaboration was Fawcett's first
publication, the pamphlet *Mr Hare's Reform Bill, Simplified and
Explained*. Mill gave advice on Fawcett's career, encouraging him in the
strategy of 'making yourself known by well-considered writings' and
reading the resulting pamphlets, papers and books.[45] Later they collabo-
rated in Parliament in support of Hare's plan and in an attempt to
improve the Bribery Bill of 1868, in addition to their support for
women's enfranchisement, but all to no avail.[46] Throughout, it was a
relationship of unequals, recognised as such by both men, that was
cordial but never intimate. Thus Mill only learnt of Fawcett's marriage
from the newspapers, and Millicent regarded an invitation to dinner with
Mill and Helen Taylor 'as a very great honour'.[47] It is unlikely that Mill
reciprocated Mrs Fawcett's sentiments: working with her in the women's
movement of the period led to withering criticism of her 'prosaic, literal
way of looking at things' and of her lack of 'a speculative [and] an
organising intelligence'. Thus, 'even supposing that she were twice her
present age, she is quite unfit to be a leader, though an excellent guerrilla

41 *Hansard*, clxxxvii, 20 May 1867, 835.
42 [Henry Fawcett] 'Mr. Mill's Treatise On Representative Government', *Macmillan's Magazine*, vol. 4 (June 1861), p. 97.
43 J. S. Mill to Helen Taylor, in *Collected Works of John Stuart Mill*, vol. 15, p. 686.
44 Mill to Hare, 30 Oct. 1859; Mill to Helen Taylor, 17, 21 Feb. 1860, in ibid., pp. 642–3, 680, 682. See also p. 155 below.
45 Mill to Fawcett, 24 Dec. 1860, in *Collected Works of John Stuart Mill*, vol. 15, p. 716.
46 On women's suffrage, see *Hansard*, clxxxvii, 20 May 1867, 835–8. On the 'Bribery Bill' (the Election Petitions and Corrupt Practices at Elections Bill) see ibid., cxcii, 21 May 1868, 680, 685; cxciii, 18, 22, 23, 24 July 1868, 1439–58, 1615–51, 1675–92, 1715–33.
47 Mill to Fawcett, 1 May 1867, in *Collected Works of John Stuart Mill*, vol. 15, p. 1266. M. G. Fawcett, *What I Remember*, p. 60.

partisan'.[48] As Millicent's subsequent career showed, even John Stuart Mill could be wrong.

III

Marriage to Millicent, the subject of David Rubinstein's essay in this collection, was another product of this period of Fawcett's life – a period that saw him striking out in various directions from his base in Cambridge. It was the classic Liberal match. They met at a party at the Campden Hill home of the radical M.P., Peter Taylor, in May 1865. It was entirely appropriate that Fawcett should have been attracted by the voice of a young woman expressing in conversation her sense of the tragic sadness of Lincoln's recent assassination.[49] Support for the North in the American Civil War was an article of faith for Fawcett and a defining feature of 'university radicalism' as it emerged in the early 1860s. But Millicent was not his first love: Fawcett had made at least three unsuccessful proposals before his engagement to Millicent, two of them, as befitted a man who was to become known for his feminism, to notable figures in the mid-Victorian women's movement. As David Rubinstein explains, he had proposed unsuccessfully to Bessie Rayner Parkes, whom he had probably met at the Bradford Congress of the Social Science Association in October 1859. Five years later, in the autumn of 1864 he was engaged to the Hon. Miss Eden, almost certainly Eleanor Eden, the daughter of Lord Auckland, the Bishop of Bath and Wells, though the engagement only lasted for a matter of weeks.[50] And before Millicent Garrett there was her older sister, Elizabeth, soon to become famous (as Elizabeth Garrett Anderson) as the first female physician trained and practising in Britain.[51] Fawcett's proposal of marriage on 8 May 1865 was declined immediately by Elizabeth on grounds of her devotion to her career. Yet

[48] Mill to George Croom Robertson, 6, 21 Nov. 1871, in *Collected Works of John Stuart Mill*, vol. 15, pp. 1850, 1921.

[49] M. G. Fawcett, *What I Remember*, p. 21; Strachey, *Millicent Garrett Fawcett*, p. 21.

[50] See *Salisbury Journal*, 27 Aug. 1864, p. 5. The short report on Fawcett's engagement only mentions 'the Hon. Miss Eden'. Lord Auckland had five daughters but only three were unmarried in 1864. And of these three only Eleanor Eden fits the newspaper's description of Fawcett's fiancée as 'an author' of 'several works ... within the last three or four years'. Eleanor Eden, who was born in 1826, wrote several novels and improving tracts for the Society for Promoting Christian Knowledge. She never married and died in 1879. I am indebted to David Rubinstein's thorough investigation for this information.

See also Fawcett to Fanny Hertz, 3 Sept. 1864: 'The report of my engagement to Miss Eden is quite correct – I think when you know her, that you will approve of my choice. She is sensible, very liberal in her opinions, thoroughly unaffected, and a first rate reader; and I believe she warmly sympathises with my tastes and pursuits.' Marshall Library, Misc. 1 (77). See also Fawcett to Fanny Hertz, 29 Nov. 1864, ibid. (78).

[51] See p. 71 below. For an earlier account of this affair, see Jo Manton, *Elizabeth Garrett Anderson* (London, 1965), pp. 156–7.

within a matter of days he was introduced to her younger sister Millicent and a new relationship had begun. They became engaged in October 1866, though they then endured several anxious weeks as Millicent came under familial pressure to break the engagement to a relatively poor, blind man. Objections from Millicent's father, Newson Garrett, a merchant and shipowner from Aldeburgh, Suffolk, who built the Maltings at Snape that is now the home of the annual Aldeburgh Music Festival, and from Elizabeth (who may have been jealous or piqued, or genuinely concerned about Henry's prospects – her motives in this are not clear and her feelings can only be guessed at) were weighed in the balance and found wanting. The couple were married on St George's Day, 1867.[52]

Millicent and Henry Fawcett are among the more renowned marital partnerships of the Victorian period. Mrs Fawcett was an intellectual companion with whom Henry could discuss politics and political economy, his speeches, his books – all the details of his career. For four years after their marriage Millicent served as his secretary, grappling 'with newspapers and blue books'.[53] Initially they kept two modest homes in Cambridge and London, constrained by a professorial salary: apparently the couple were often seen walking arm in arm in Cambridge, forgoing a carriage to save a little.[54] But after 1875 they were able to purchase two more substantial houses – 51, The Lawn, South Lambeth Road, about twenty minutes walk from Westminster, and 18, Brookside, Cambridge. The latter is now home to the university's Department of Education – a fitting change of occupancy given Fawcett's passionate interest in all questions educational. In 1868 their only child, Philippa, was born. They were 'advanced' parents, giving her considerable freedom of expression and movement, and the results, at least if judged in academic terms, were successful.[55] As a student at Newnham, the Cambridge college her parents had worked to found, Philippa achieved what her father had hoped for but failed in: long before women were officially classed, she excelled in the Mathematical Tripos in 1890, emerging considerably ahead of the designated Senior Wrangler.[56] It was a familial triumph and a tremendous coup for the women's movement.

Fawcett's feminism pre-dated his marriage to Millicent as a number of letters from Mill indicate.[57] It was merely confirmed, though also altered in significant ways, by his wife. After 1867 he played a part in a variety of feminist campaigns. The first meeting of the committee to create

[52] Manton, *Elizabeth Garrett Anderson*, p. 181; Strachey, *Millicent Garrett Fawcett*, pp. 27–9.
[53] M. G. Fawcett, *What I Remember*, p. 64.
[54] ibid., p. 55; Strachey, *Millicent Garrett Fawcett*, p. 36.
[55] Strachey, *Millicent Garrett Fawcett*, p. 70.
[56] ibid., p. 143; M. G. Fawcett, *What I Remember*, p. 139.
[57] Mill to Helen Taylor, 21 Feb. 1860; Mill to Fawcett, 21 July 1862, 14 Oct. 1863, in *Collected Works of John Stuart Mill*, vol. 15, pp. 683, 787, 890.

Newnham College was held in the Fawcett's drawing room in Cambridge in late 1869.[58] He was a consistent advocate of women's suffrage – an issue over which he fell foul of Gladstone when a member of the government in 1883–4 – and he took a position on the more radical wing of the movement that favoured enfranchising married women as well as widows and spinsters.[59] As Postmaster General, moreover, he opened a number of positions in the Post Office to women, and after the Married Women's Property Act was passed in 1882 he gave a woman postmistress the option of retaining her appointment in her own name rather than transferring it to her husband – a small but indicative measure. His objection to the special protection of women under the Factory Acts, however, brought controversy and undermined his relationship with the trades union movement. He had favoured the extension of factory legislation in 1867 which had brought the working conditions of large numbers of women under the regulation of statute for the first time. But by 1873, as David Rubinstein shows, he had adopted the view prevalent in the women's movement and espoused by Mrs Fawcett that specific restrictions on the labour of adult women were discriminatory, forcing women out of many trades and lowering their wages.[60] He lost many old friends in the labour movement and was unanimously condemned at the Trades Union Congress in Sheffield in January 1874 for his allegation that proposed legislation to limit the hours of women was the work of male trades unionists seeking to restrict the competition of women's labour.[61] One trades unionist, writing to *The Times*, accused him of 'a stab in the back from a so-called "People's Friend"' and warned him of the difficulty in recovering his place 'in the popular esteem'.[62]

As David Rubinstein conjectures, Fawcett may have come under the influence of his wife on this particular question. But it is doubtful if his feminism owed much in general spirit (as opposed to points of detail) either to Millicent's personal influence or the wider women's movement. Rather, it is best explained as a natural corollary of his Liberalism – an emancipatory creed that fought against all restrictions of opportunity as it fought against unearned privilege. Women were another group, not unlike the nonconformists and the respectable working class in this perspective, whose rights as citizens were being infringed by legal and institutional discrimination. This was a perspective that husband and wife shared (and mutually reinforced) though they had arrived at it by separate

[58] M. G. Fawcett, *What I Remember*, p. 73.

[59] 'Henry Fawcett' in Olive Banks (ed.), *Biographical Dictionary of British Feminists*, vol. 1, 1800–1930 (Brighton, 1985), p. 76.

[60] Stephen, *Life of Fawcett*, p. 176; Ray Strachey, *The Cause. A Short History of the Women's Movement in Great Britain* (London, 1923), pp. 234–5; *The Times*, 19 Jan. 1874, p. 7.

[61] *The Times*, 16 Jan. 1874, p. 12.   [62] ibid., 24 Jan. 1874, p. 5.

routes. Thus, in reply to an enquiry about women in the professions from a member of the Liberation Society, the political vanguard of religious dissent, Mrs Fawcett wrote of the inestimable value 'of the opportunity of free development to the individual ... I think the principal argument is like the argument for Free Trade – train the faculties by a sound and healthy education, and then allow these faculties free scope in whatever direction nature and natural gifts may indicate as the fittest.'[63] This sounds like Henry. But, as recently argued, Mrs Fawcett also derived her feminism from a wider and antecedent Liberalism.[64] In this they were united, for Henry Fawcett's feminism, like that of his wife, was the product of a political philosophy opposed in social as in economic spheres to artificial and unjust restraints.

IV

What sort of Liberal was he? In 1860, Mill had called him a 'man of independent opinions'. Six years later Fawcett explained to the House of Commons that he had been called 'a Radical and a representative of the working classes', and in a letter to the Liberal M.P. Sir William Harcourt in July 1876 he described himself as 'an advanced Liberal'. As Stefan Collini suggests, there were elements in Fawcett's political creed which had their roots in the Philosophic Radicalism of the 1830s and the 'Manchester School' of the 1840s. His watchword, to be heard in several speeches, was 'merit, not birth' and he was committed to the idea 'that a career should be thrown open to all men of ability'.[65] He shared the deep suspicion of Cobden of abuses of government patronage, writing to Gladstone in April 1869 after the passage of the Political Pensions Act for information on 'all the offices which will be entitled to pensions under the new Act which were not entitled previously' and including some stiff remarks on the proliferation of 'sinecure offices'.[66] There was, too, a strong desire for a Liberalism dedicated to the abolition of anomalies and inconsistencies – a rational Liberalism imposing logical consistency by legislation and reform. So he was affronted by the absence of a provision

[63] M. G. Fawcett to J. Carvell-Williams, quoted in Strachey, *Millicent Garrett Fawcett*, pp. 76–7.
[64] Ann Oakley, 'Millicent Garrett Fawcett: duty and determination', in Dale Spender (ed.), *Feminist Theories. Three Centuries of Women's Intellectual Traditions* (London, 1983), pp. 190–2.
[65] Mill to Fawcett, 26 Feb. 1860, in *Collected Works of John Stuart Mill*, vol. 15, p. 686; *Hansard*, clxxxiii, 13 March 1866, 200; Fawcett to Sir William Harcourt, 12 Jan. 1876, Harcourt Papers, Bodleian Library, Oxford, 207, fos. 1–3.; *Daily News*, 25 Jan. 1871, p. 2; Stephen, *Life of Fawcett*, p. 187.
[66] Fawcett to Gladstone, 4 April 1869, Gladstone Papers, British Library, Add. MS 44156, fo. 14. For the passage of the Political Pensions for Civil Offices Bill, see *Hansard*, cxciv, 22 Feb. 1869, 165–9.

for compulsory attendance in Forster's Education Act in 1870, contrasting the situation in the elementary schools with the compulsory education given to the children of paupers.[67]

Above all, in the tradition of Cobden, Fawcett was hostile to 'over-legislation' and staunch in his support for the principle of laissez-faire, for 'the cardinal social maxim that the condition of a people cannot be advanced if self-reliance and prudence are discouraged; and that the policy of the State on all social questions should be guided by the principle that it is no use helping those who show no desire to help themselves'.[68] There were exceptions, of course; most obviously elementary education which was one of Fawcett's chief interests. Here government interference could be justified on two grounds. First, because of the proof in the 1860s that without government action nothing would be done – and Fawcett's political economy could tolerate government interference 'if that which it seeks to do cannot be done without it'. Secondly, because the state could legitimately intervene when the recipient of its aid was a minor who would otherwise be kept in ignorance by a parent.[69] But education was an exception, and from the late 1860s Fawcett was complaining about the drift of legislation. For the first time he had doubts about 'a democratic suffrage' which might coerce the state 'to do for people what they have the power to do for themselves'.[70] 'It seems to me that the tendency to over legislation is rapidly increasing & is fraught with the greatest peril', he wrote to the third earl Grey in July 1872.[71] Six months later in a letter to Harcourt he lamented 'that Radicals are amongst the foremost to propose schemes which must lead to increased expenditure. Thus Dilke began his speech the other night by saying that he was in favour of free education, free lands, free law etc. etc.'[72] Fawcett was a different sort of radical from the young Charles Dilke who was expected at this stage to be a leader of the party in the future: Fawcett's doctrines harked back to the 1840s and 1850s rather than forward to the 1890s and 1900s.[73]

---

[67] Fawcett to A. J. Mundella, 11 Dec. 1873: 'I cannot understand how it is possible for the Government to resist General Compulsion, now that they have guaranteed education to the children of all paupers. If things remain in their present position, a man will have to congratulate himself in after-life on the fact that when he was a child his father was a pauper'. Mundella Papers, Sheffield University Library, GP/6/21/i.

[68] Henry Fawcett, 'To what extent is England prosperous?', Fortnightly Review, vol. 9 (n.s.) (Jan. 1871), p. 52.

[69] See Fawcett's speech delivered in Cambridge and reported in The Times, 8 Jan. 1870, p. 4.

[70] 'To what extent is England prosperous?', p. 51.

[71] Fawcett to Grey, 19 July 1872, Grey of Howick MSS, Dept of Palaeography and Diplomatic, University of Durham.

[72] Fawcett to Harcourt, 16 Jan. 1873, Harcourt Papers 204, fos. 20–1.

[73] Stephen, Life of Fawcett, p. 160. See also Henry Fawcett, State Socialism and the Nationalisation of Land (Cambridge and London, 1883).

Yet it cannot be said that this university radical was close to the radical nonconformity which had inspired and still animated John Bright. Fawcett admitted to little influence with Bright, was openly critical of the stance of political nonconformity on the question of elementary education for its undue emphasis on sectarian details, and he looked askance at the parvenu middle class who were coming to represent Liberal opinion. As he wrote to the economist J. E. Cairnes, the 1868 general election, 'though satisfactory in a party sense, will, I fear, return a House scarcely superior in character to the last. Few good new men are coming out, and more over-rich manufacturers and ironmasters are standing than ever.'[74] The cultural gulf between Cambridge and Manchester could not be bridged, and, in consequence, the term 'radical' had many meanings and denoted many sub-groupings on the left of the Liberal Party. Fawcett's following was certainly different from the new manufacturers and ironmasters: though he frequently acted alone, by 1869–70 he had emerged at the head of a maverick group often called 'Fawcettites' – 'a gaggle of young, rich and educated M.P.s' as they have recently been called.[75] They did not share any clear principles but were united in opposition to an insufficiently radical government (as they saw it) of their own party. They included Dilke, who had encountered Fawcett during his distinguished undergraduate career at Trinity Hall in the early 1860s; the eccentric and extreme individualist, Auberon Herbert, whose brief and controversial four years in the House from 1870 coincided with Fawcett's notoriety; the stiff and reserved Walter Morrison whose extensive wealth in business was offset by his education at Eton and Balliol; and Lord Edmond Fitzmaurice, the second son of the fourth marquess of Lansdowne and a university reformer educated at Trinity College, Cambridge, who had entered Parliament in 1868. Supporting contributions came from G. J. Shaw-Lefevre who held a number of junior offices in Gladstone's first administration and seemed set for a most distinguished political career; G. O. Trevelyan, whose progress through the Liberal ranks was cut short when he resigned from the Admiralty over Forster's Education Bill in 1870; and from Charles Clifford (educated at Christ Church), Sir David Wedderburn (Trinity College, Cambridge) and Andrew Johnston (Rugby and University College, Oxford).[76]

[74] Fawcett to Mundella, 13 Jan. 1875, Mundella Papers, GP/8/3/iv; *Hansard*, ccxvii, 17 July 1873, 578; Fawcett to J. E. Cairnes in Stephen, *Life of Fawcett*, pp. 238–9.

[75] J. P. Parry, *Democracy and Religion. Gladstone and the Liberal Party, 1867–1875* (Cambridge, 1986), p. 250. See Fawcett to Dilke, 20 Nov. 1868, British Library, Add. MS 43909, fo. 101.

[76] For all these, see *Dictionary of National Biography* and M. Stenton and S. Lees, *Who's Who of British Members of Parliament* (4 vols.), vols. 1 and 2, 1832–1918 (Hassocks, Sussex, 1976–8).

These men were independent, difficult for the party managers to deal with, outside the dominant party factions – the whig-liberals and non-conformists – and highly critical of government policy. Several of them, notably Dilke, Herbert and Trevelyan, made no secret of their republicanism. And Fawcett also came under severe public scrutiny when his membership of a Cambridge dining circle, the Republican Club, was divulged by the press in late 1870. Leslie Stephen passed it off as a little harmless fun. But with a definition of republicanism in its rules – 'hostility to the hereditary principle as exemplified in monarchical and aristocratic institutions, and to all social and political privileges dependent upon differences of sex' – it could not fail to create a minor scandal.[77] In genteel Brighton, Fawcett's seat, news of republicanism added to his well-publicised attacks on Gladstone threatened to unseat him. When Fawcett addressed his constituents in January 1871, his exhilarating speech was a clever mixture of honest admission and redefinition. He turned the issue round, focussing on the more anomalous aspects of the aristocratic ascendancy like the House of Lords, and counterposing the hereditary principle with 'intellectual merit and moral worth'. It was one of his finest performances and he won his vote of confidence handsomely.[78] This was the only serious difficulty he encountered in a five-year campaign which must rank as one of the most notable examples of an M.P.'s opposition to government by his own party in modern British history. After the 1868 election Mill had sent him a letter expressing 'great satisfaction ... that you are still in the House to assert great principles and that you are as unlikely as anyone there to be easily discouraged'.[79] Throughout Gladstone's first administration Fawcett was vociferous in assertion of principles great and small and did not seem to know the meaning of discouragement.

V

Understanding Fawcett's opposition involves understanding his relationship with Gladstone – in many ways the dominant political relationship of his career and one that illustrates some important themes in the Liberal politics of the period. Leslie Stephen could not make too much of the hostility between the two in his biography, written to celebrate the life of one of Gladstone's ministers and published while Gladstone was Prime Minister. But Fawcett's opposition to the Liberal government was, to a surprising degree, a hostility to Gladstone – his style of leadership,

[77] Stephen, *Life of Fawcett*, pp. 286–9.   [78] *Daily News*, 25 Jan. 1871, p. 2.
[79] Mill to Fawcett, 7 Dec. 1868, in *Collected Works of John Stuart Mill*, vol. 16, pp. 1511–12.

idiosyncratic preoccupations and his failure to assert what Fawcett
understood to be true Liberal principles. In a letter to Gladstone in April
1872 Fawcett admitted that 'I often have occasion to differ from you.'
Yes, replied the Prime Minister, 'we have differed more frequently than
either of us could wish'.[80]

Yet Fawcett initially admired Gladstone. As Chancellor of the
Exchequer, Gladstone's creative financial statesmanship and growing
rapport with the classes outdoors could not but attract a professor of
political economy with democratic sympathies. 'Since I have known
politics,' wrote Fawcett, 'you have been the only man who has been able
to arouse real popular enthusiasm on financial questions.'[81] He sent
Gladstone the first two editions of the *Manual*; in response, at the end of
1865 Gladstone sent him a pamphlet of speeches from his recent election
campaign in South Lancashire and Fawcett was all praise: 'When I read
them, at the time they were delivered, I thought they were amongst the
happiest and most successful of your many great oratorical achievements.'[82] And Gladstone's performance, replying to Disraeli in the debate
on the first reading of the 1867 Reform Bill on 18 March 1867, drew
appreciation: 'although I have always been one of your most devoted
followers, I shall now place greater confidence than I have ever felt before
in your leadership of the Liberal Party'.[83]

If confidence later seeped away, it had something to do with their
different personalities: as Mrs Fawcett later recalled, 'as regards misun-
derstandings between my husband and Mr. Gladstone, no doubt they
arose from the two men being fundamentally different'.[84] After listening
to the famous Commons debate on British policy towards China in March
1857, Fawcett had commented in a letter that Gladstone's 'mind is too
subtle', and subtlety was not a virtue in Fawcett's plain and direct
approach to politics.[85] Part of the problem may have been the supposed
difference in outlook between Oxford and Cambridge in the mid-
Victorian period. In Stephen's *Sketches from Cambridge*, the 'Oxford
man' was 'not content without a touch of more or less refined philosophy'
and he picked out as his example of the typical Oxford mind 'Mr
Gladstone, with his great abilities somewhat marred by over-acuteness

80 Fawcett to Gladstone, 18 April 1872, B.L., Add. MS 44156, fo. 18; Gladstone to
   Fawcett, 19 April 1872, ibid., 44541, fo. 222. See also Fawcett's speech in Brighton,
   Daily News, 25 Jan. 1871, p. 3: 'no one would suspect him of being too devoted a
   supporter of Mr. Gladstone ... the occasions were not few when he had differed from
   him'.
81 Fawcett to Gladstone, 18 April 1872, B.L., Add. MS 44156, fo. 18.
82 Fawcett to Gladstone, 21 Dec. 1865, ibid., fo. 5.
83 Fawcett to Gladstone, 20 March 1867, ibid., fo. 7. See *Hansard*, clxxxvi, 18 March 1867,
   25–46.
84 M. G. Fawcett, *What I Remember*, p. 111.   85 Stephen, *Life of Fawcett*, p. 42.

and polish'.[86] In comparison, according to the stereotype, 'typical Cambridge men' were claimed to be 'believers in hard facts and figures, admirers of strenuous common sense, and hearty despisers of sentimentalism'.[87] It is a caricature that fits the two personalities in this case if not in others.

But the difference went even deeper than the cast of mind imparted by two different institutions and educations. At the spiritual, philosophical and practical levels, there could be no common ground at all over the issue of religion. For Gladstone it was the mainspring of all secular activity, for Fawcett it meant nothing. In the debate on the second reading of the 1870 Elementary Education Act, Fawcett described himself as 'a moderate Churchman'.[88] In truth, he was no sort of churchman at all but an agnostic whose attachment to the social virtues of industry and endeavour owed nothing to faith.[89] And like other 'rationalist academic agnostics', as they have recently been called, when Fawcett saw religion standing in the way of social progress, as in the case of elementary education, he could be outspoken in condemnation of the waste of time and energy 'in a series of sectarian squabbles'.[90] Given the number of outstanding issues of church and state that had to be resolved between 1868 and 1874, and given Gladstone's evident tenderness for his own and others' religious scruples – even those of the obscurantist Catholic hierarchy in Ireland – a clash was inevitable. And Gladstone's delays over elementary education and university reform in particular brought on Fawcett's sarcasm. 'It is wonderful', he told his Brighton constituents in early 1871, 'with what fondness even those who are called Liberal statesmen cling to the obsolete tatters of ecclesiastical ascendancy.'[91] Fawcett was heard to say of his party leader that 'he would go as far as he dared on the road to economic and fiscal reform, but only as far as he was forced on the road to religious freedom'.[92] Pressure would have to be applied, and it ended in the Liberal defeat over the Irish Universities Bill in March 1873. At Christmas 1866 during their last period together at Trinity Hall, Stephen wrote to his fiancée and described 'old Fawcett' as 'that attached member of the Church of England . . . who doesn't believe one of the Thirty-nine Articles, except perhaps that which says that a Christian may swear'.[93] We can only guess at Fawcett's reaction, therefore, when he met Gladstone in late October 1878 during the latter's visit to Cambridge as the guest of the Sidgwicks. After dinner, Gladstone apparently asked Fawcett for his

[86] [Stephen], *Sketches from Cambridge*, p. 139.   [87] Stephen, *Life of Fawcett*, p. 23.
[88] *Hansard*, ccxvii, 17 July 1873, 581.   [89] Strachey, *Millicent Garrett Fawcett*, p. 88.
[90] Parry, *Democracy and Religion*, pp. 199, 253. See Fawcett's speech to his prospective constituents at Hackney, *Daily News*, 19 March 1874, p. 3.
[91] *Daily News*, 25 Jan. 1871, p. 2.   [92] M. G. Fawcett, *What I Remember*, p. 92.
[93] Maitland, *Life of Leslie Stephen*, p. 190.

views on the situation in Afghanistan: 'I have not read the papers and I
have a speech to make on the subject. I have been at Corpus Christi
Library, looking at the Parker manuscripts, comparing the 39 Articles, so
that I have had no time.'[94]

Differences in personal outlook, persuasion and temperament were
only part of the problem, however. There were telling political differences
that divided Gladstone and the academic radicals like Fawcett. Not the
least of these was the difference between the Gladstone of the early 1860s
who was regarded as a radical himself and so invested with all the radicals'
hopes for the future, and Gladstone as Prime Minister after 1868 who
seemed opposed to all the social demands of the intellectuals and
noticeably more cautious in word and deed.[95] To Fawcett, the election of
1868, though disappointing because of the meagre representation in the
new House of Commons of university radicals, was a new beginning. The
Liberal Party with a majority of 112 now had a mandate for sweeping
reform in church and state. But, as Dr Matthew has pointed out, in
Gladstone's eyes his first term as Prime Minister was likely to be his last
and was to mark an end rather than a beginning: 'the setting of the sun at
the end of the day of building the mid-century edifice'.[96] In consequence,
his style of leadership appeared timid, unassertive and temporising to
Fawcett, who arrogated to himself the duty of forcing Gladstone onwards.
Ray Strachey recounted an anecdote in her biography of Mrs Fawcett.
Apparently,

Baby Philippa possessed a wooden horse which ran on wheels and was pulled
along by a string. She had discovered that if you pulled the string gently the horse
would not move at all, but if you pulled hard, it would come with a great rush; and
her father, on hearing this peculiarity, had named the horse Gladstone.[97]

The desire to pull Gladstone forward explains Fawcett's otherwise
astonishing behaviour.

There can be few more inflammatory resumés in the history of
Victorian politics of a government's inadequacies written by a member of
the party in power than Fawcett's article on 'The present position of the

[94] The original form of this anecdote as related by Winifred Holt is undoubtedly inaccurate.
According to her account, the meeting took place 'at a weekend house-party in the
country'. If the exchange as recorded did occur, however, it is more likely to have been on
28 October 1878 at the Sidgwicks' house in Cambridge. According to Gladstone's diary
entry for the day, he had indeed visited Corpus Christi to see 'the valuable MSS of the
Library'; he then met Fawcett at dinner; and three days later he did indeed give a speech
on Afghanistan to an audience of 5,000 people at Rhyl. See Holt, A Beacon for the Blind,
p. 244; H. C. G. Matthew (ed.), The Gladstone Diaries, vol. 9, 1875–80 (Oxford, 1986),
pp. 357–8. I am grateful to Dr Matthew for his help in this matter.
[95] H. C. G. Matthew, Gladstone, 1809–1874 (Oxford, 1986), pp. 172–3.
[96] ibid., p. 170.
[97] Strachey, Millicent Garrett Fawcett, p. 49.

government' of November 1871. Here he laid out the grounds of his opposition. The article runs through those areas, great and small, where Liberal policy and Liberal measures had failed. H. A. Bruce's administration of the Home Office had been 'a lamentable failure', his Licensing Bill pleasing no one, neither teetotallers nor brewers. The government had promised retrenchment but 'we have estimates far exceeding those which the Prime Minister, night after night when in opposition, used to characterise as excessive'. The government had promised 'greater political purity' but set to bestowing 'peerages, baronetcies and knighthoods, as rewards for party subserviency' as soon as elected. Robert Lowe's bungled budget of 1871 came under the lash, and Fawcett pointed the contrast between the radical principles of the 1870 Irish Land Act and the government's willingness to see the remaining English commons enclosed – an issue of growing interest to him. Fawcett, a relatively poor man in politics, was always exercised by the issue of electoral expenses and procedures and had looked for 'a great measure for the reform of parliamentary and municipal elections'. Instead they were being offered 'simply a Bill to secure secret voting', one that was 'mangled and incomplete'. But most important of all were the great questions of education. Fawcett had a clear position on elementary education: he would tolerate the existing denominational schools (which had the advantage of not burdening the ratepayers) but he insisted that the new board schools should provide a wholly secular education with compulsory attendance. Yet Forster's Act enshrined 'permissive compulsion' under which school boards were empowered but not compelled to frame bye-laws to enforce attendance. This compromise, and the failure to achieve a settlement of denominational grievances, drew his condemnation. In turn, his own attempts to secure the abolition of clerical Fellowships in the English universities and his repeated attempts to abolish university tests in Ireland – two issues that must be dealt with separately and in detail – drew allegations of betrayal: the Liberal leaders were acting like 'the strongest Tories' in these matters.[98] Throw in Fawcett's opposition to the compensation paid to Irish landowners under the terms of the Irish disestablishment settlement in 1869 and his opposition to the abolition of the purchase of commissions in the army in 1871 by royal warrant rather than Act of Parliament – issues not dealt with in the article but which exercised him nonetheless – and it amounts to a long and significant set of grievances made public in the journals, in letters to the press, from the platform and, above all, on the floor of the House.[99]

[98] Henry Fawcett, 'The present position of the government', *Fortnightly Review*, vol. 16 (o.s.) (Nov. 1871), pp. 544–58.
[99] Stephen, *Life of Fawcett*, pp. 272, 276–7.

Yet it was not the specific policies so much as the strategy of government that appalled Fawcett most: there was an absence of strong leadership and confidence in Liberal principles. Fawcett made his point referring to the number of permissive clauses in the Elementary Education Bill: 'it might be fairly inferred', he argued, 'that instead of emanating from a powerful Liberal Government, it was brought forward by a Government which was compelled to buy indulgence from their opponents, and which was hoisting signals of distress for Tory support'.[100] Forster had contended that compulsion would be in advance of public opinion: Fawcett's reply in a letter to *The Times* was simple: 'If Mr Gladstone and his colleagues boldly declared that any proposal were right and just, would they not thus do much to make the country accept it?'[101] Great statesmen had to 'instruct public opinion', to lead from the front and by example rather than lag behind it: 'nothing in political life is so discouraging as to find that our statesmen will never do anything which is worth doing unless they are forced into it by popular pressure'.[102] A similar critique of Gladstone's leadership – or the lack of it – was to be made by whig-liberals on the centre-right of the party who were opposed to Home Rule in 1886. They also came to believe that Gladstone was evading a leader's duty of winning support for difficult policies and guiding the electorate: Home Rule was a renunciation of the responsibilities of a leader, palpably a way out of, rather than a solution to, perennial Irish problems.[103]

It is customary to view Gladstone's first administration as his most successful; to depict a government legislating across the whole range of social, religious and political issues and amassing a collection of important reforms unsurpassed in the nineteenth century. But this was not how Fawcett construed the Liberal government between 1868 and 1874. To him, adopting a position that has become customary on the left of British politics in subsequent decades, government by his own party was a catalogue of missed opportunities, half-measures and errors which often defied true Liberal principles. He called on Gladstone to show 'that he can again be faithful to those political principles the advocacy of which made him the most popular man in England at the last election'.[104] But, like another academic radical, G. C. Brodrick, he probably concluded that Gladstone, with his Tory background, aristocratic connections and religiosity, was not 'a sound liberal', paradoxical as that may seem.[105] The result was disillusion with the Liberal Party as the historic vehicle of

[100] *Hansard*, cc, 28 March 1870, 279.   [101] *The Times*, 21 Feb. 1870, p. 12.
[102] 'The present position of the government', p. 557.
[103] Parry, *Democracy and Religion*, pp. 443–4.
[104] 'The present position of the government', p. 556.
[105] Brodrick, *Memories and Impressions*, p. 238.

progress in Britain. Writing to Harcourt in January 1873 to comment on two of the latter's recent speeches, Fawcett admitted that he

> could not go with you in your glowing panegyric of the Liberal Party. It seems to me that the history of every great political movement, such as free trade, household suffrage, university tests etc., shows that these changes have been opposed almost as much by the Liberals as by the Tory Party. They were only accepted when resistance was no longer possible. Pitt was a much better free trader in 1784 than Lord John Russell, the leader of the Liberal Party, was in 1844. Political progress has not been secured by the Liberal Party, but it has been forced upon the Liberal Party by Radicalism out of the House, and by advanced political thinkers.[106]

This was his excuse for making trouble – without it, progress was impossible – and in early 1873 Fawcett's opposition was about to reach a spectacular crescendo which brought the Liberal Party down over the issue of Irish university reform and marked the apogee of his political career.

VI

It was only to be expected that Fawcett should have shown special interest in questions affecting universities, and his attitude to Irish university reform came out of his pre-existing commitments on the question of English university reform. Long before his opposition to Gladstone's Irish proposals in 1873, Fawcett had made his hostility to sectarian higher education abundantly clear. His second speech in the House was on university tests in England and his view 'was perfectly clear and straight-forward. Every religious test which excluded any sect from the University should be abolished.'[107] Moving the second reading of his bill to abolish the tests and throw Fellowships open at Oxford and Cambridge in the following year, 'he could conceive nothing more mischievous than the establishment of a sectarian university'.[108] And speaking in Cambridge in 1870, a year before the tests were finally abolished, he welcomed a measure which would, in the English universities, 'neutralise the narrowing and benumbing influence of sectarian differences'.[109] Fawcett's Liberalism was predicated on undenominational education, on equalising opportunities as between all sects and creeds, and he would not compromise this principle above all. Yet legislation to abolish the tests in Oxford and Cambridge – the favourite cause of academic radicals in the 1860s – seemed to take an unacceptably long time, and Fawcett rightly detected a marked ambivalence in Gladstone and sections of the Liberal Party

[106] Fawcett to Harcourt, 7 Jan. 1873, Harcourt Papers, 204, fos. 13–15.
[107] *Hansard*, clxxxii, 26 April 1866, 2031–7.
[108] ibid., clxxxvii, 29 May 1867, 1250.   [109] *The Times*, 8 Jan. 1870, p. 4.

generally over the issue. In addition, Fawcett's amendments to the two
tests bills of 1870 and 1871 to abolish clerical Fellowships were only
defeated by concerted government action and Gladstone's over-zealous
deference to the supposed views of the House of Lords on the question –
the sort of consideration that cut little ice with Fawcett.[110] Once more
Gladstone seemed to be evading unambiguous commitment to principles
Fawcett interpreted as fundamental to the historic mission of Liberalism.

In tandem with this unsatisfactory progress on the tests in England,
Fawcett began a campaign in 1867 to have the tests abolished at Trinity
College, Dublin, which restricted Fellowships and foundation scholar-
ships to Anglicans. He may well have calculated that a wider campaign
pointing to the anomalies in Irish higher education would add impetus to
his existing agitation to abolish the tests in England. But there is no
doubting his genuine interest in Irish university reform – nor his contempt
for the meddling of the Irish Catholic hierarchy in the question. His
campaign in Ireland began from the same principles that inspired the
struggle against the tests in England but added the contention that a
solution to wider Irish problems had to involve 'national education'.
'What was so likely to stereotype sectarian rancour as separating men in
early youth according to their religious creeds?'[111] he asked. Designed to
emancipate men from the prejudices and suspicions that caused civil strife,
it was the classic Liberal analysis of the Irish situation. Thus, on 18 June
1867, he presented a motion to turn Trinity College into 'the nucleus of a
great university, where men of different religious opinions might live
together, and from it extend over the entire country a religious harmony
which could not fail to produce effects of the most tranquilizing and
beneficent character'.[112] Annual resolutions followed from Fawcett in
1868 and 1869, and in April 1870 when he introduced a bill to abolish the
tests at Trinity, Gladstone declared it an issue of confidence in the
government and Fawcett was beaten 296 to 232 votes on a motion of
adjournment; it was an ominous foretaste of the clashes to come.[113] In
1871 Fawcett's bill was talked out. The evident disinclination of the
government either to deal with the issue or support Fawcett's measure
once more brought Gladstone's commitment to Liberal principles into
question and succeeded in turning a small issue into one that might
conceivably unhinge the administration. Fawcett was not put off,
however: he pressed on with another bill in 1872 which not only sought to
abolish the tests (and so bring Trinity College, Dublin, into line with the
now reformed English universities) but which included certain consti-

[110] Stephen, *Life of Fawcett*, pp. 245–9.   [111] *Hansard*, cc, 1 April 1870, 1096.
[112] ibid., clxxxviii, 18 June 1867, 58.
[113] ibid., cc, 1 April 1870, 1146.

tutional provisions for the college.[114] Gladstone criticised the constitutional clauses for conceding too much power to Protestants who would continue to hold most of the senior positions for many years into the future. And after the second reading was carried on 26 March 1872 he insisted on dividing the bill, ignoring the constitutional clauses, and threatened resignation if defeated.[115] Fawcett was livid: 'For five years I have been trying to obtain a decision upon this question. Twice my proposals have been talked out. Twice they have been counted out. Twice they have been got rid of by threats of ministerial resignation.' Meanwhile, it was impossible to extract 'anything like a clear declaration as to the meaning of Ministers upon this subject'.[116] The government was not prepared to declare a policy or legislate, but was quite content to use threats and menaces to defeat the one constructive suggestion before Parliament. But Fawcett was not prepared to precipitate a crisis himself and so he withdrew his bill, moving the adjournment of the House on 25 April.[117]

What, then, was the government's position? Gladstone's excuse in 1872 was pressure of business – there was no sinister conspiracy against legislating on Irish higher education.[118] But the government faced some serious difficulties: it had to ensure that it did not alienate Irish Catholic M.P.s with any of its proposals while simultaneously exciting some enthusiasm in the Liberal Party as a whole. The problems of Irish education were extremely complex, lacked electoral appeal and led inevitably to uncomfortable questions concerning the relations of the state to the Catholic church. As for Gladstone, he was opposed to any reform of Irish higher education which went no further than the abolition of the tests: if the universities were to be reformed then that reform should be comprehensive and concern itself with defective institutional structures and the problem of improving educational standards in Catholic colleges. In addition, he was in general opposed to 'godless colleges' – undenominationalism – which offered an obvious solution to the problem of Irish higher education as Fawcett diagnosed it. With reference to Oxford and Cambridge, Gladstone always favoured the establishment of denominational colleges, Roman Catholic and nonconformist, which would be affiliated to the universities in the usual manner, as a solution to the religious difficulty.[119] In this way the Anglican foundations at the two universities would be able to retain their religious identity intact. As regards Ireland, he was deeply conscious of Catholic grievances – that they had no institution of higher learning comparable with Trinity

[114] ibid., ccx, 20 March 1872, 327.   [115] Parry, *Democracy and Religion*, pp. 344–8.
[116] *Hansard*, ccx, 25 April 1872, 1818–19.   [117] ibid., 1814–22.
[118] ibid., 1831.
[119] Parry, *Democracy and Religion*, pp. 165–6.

College, Dublin – and was strongly in favour of widening their opportunities. But not in undenominational and secular institutions which he and
the Catholic hierarchy disapproved of in principle. It was, said Gladstone,
'an extreme hardship on that portion of the Irish population who do not
choose to accept education apart from religion that they should have no
University open to them in Ireland at which they may obtain degrees'.[120]
And he therefore favoured giving Irish Catholics their own denominational colleges alongside Protestant and undenominational colleges
within one national university. The affiliated Catholic colleges would thus
be able to provide an education leading to a recognised degree, and the
competition of examinations taken in common with the other colleges
would, he hoped, have the effect of raising the standards of Catholic
higher education.

The 1873 session began with Fawcett introducing his bill to reform
Trinity College. Although a bill from the government was expected,
Fawcett explained that if it should fail, then, with his bill in place, the
House would still have an opportunity of legislating on the matter.[121]
Gladstone's bill soon followed. It dealt with much more then Trinity
College's affairs. It amounted to an attempt to overcome the religious
difficulties in Irish higher education and to reorganise the university
system there in one grand measure. It would have created a new University
of Dublin made up of various component colleges: Trinity itself (with the
tests abolished); the Belfast and Cork Colleges of the old Queen's
University which was to be wound up along with its third college at
Galway; and those voluntary colleges that would affiliate as denominational institutions such as the Roman Catholic College in Dublin and
the presbyterian Magee College. Initially, Parliament would nominate the
members of the university's governing council: in time, as the ratio of
Catholics and Protestants passing through the university evened out, it
could be chosen by the graduates. But the really controversial elements of
the plan, so far as Fawcett was concerned, were the so-called 'gagging
clauses'. To minimise friction between the sects, the university would have
no Chairs and examinations in theology, philosophy and modern history,
leaving these subjects to be taught by the separate colleges in the light of
the theological assumptions of the various denominations. And a university teacher might be suspended or removed 'who should in speaking or
writing be held to have wilfully given offence to the religious convictions
of any member'.[122]

---

[120] Hansard, ccx, 20 March 1872, 348–9.   [121] ibid., ccxiv, 7 Feb. 1873, 177–8.
[122] Matthew, *Gladstone*, p. 199; Parry, *Democracy and Religion*, p. 180; Stephen, *Life of
Fawcett*, p. 283; John Morley, *The Life of William Ewart Gladstone* (3 vols., London,
1903), vol. 2, pp. 438–9.

The bill was opposed staunchly on all sides. Irish Catholics wanted endowment by the state of their own separate college, equivalent and counterposed to Trinity College, Dublin – concurrent endowment as it was known. But Protestants in Britain, especially the nonconformists, would not tolerate such a subsidy to papism. Meanwhile, in the Liberal Party itself there was strong opposition from whig-liberals to the concessions being promised to Catholics. Gladstone was evidently proud of his scheme: at the end of his life he described it as an 'excellent measure' and dismissed the opposition to it as 'the merest matter of detail'.[123] Somewhat surprisingly, historians recently reviewing the history of the bill have sympathised with this view. According to one, it was 'in theory ... a brilliant scheme'; according to another, it 'offered a bold means of solving this vexed question' and constituted an 'appeal to reason'.[124] But it did not seem reasonable to Fawcett and many of his contemporaries (and probably does not seem at all rational to modern readers) to establish a central university (as opposed to its affiliated colleges) that deliberately limited freedom of expression and ignored vital components of the curriculum for fear of offending denominational scruples. And so, in the most successful speech of Fawcett's career, relatively short but to the point, he pulled the bill to pieces at the climax of his six-year campaign to reform the Irish universities.[125]

He protested against the abolition of the Queen's University and Galway College, viable institutions both. He protested against establishing the proposed university council as 'the creature of political nominations'. He contended that the bill lacked a mechanism for regulating the affiliation of colleges and the university could thus, in theory, 'affiliate 20 Roman Catholic seminaries in Ireland'. But the 'gagging clauses' exercised him most: 'If modern history and moral philosophy were excluded, what is the University going to teach? Why, even the teaching of the favourite language of the Prime Minister would be rendered a farce, as a Professor would not be able to lecture on the most distinguished classical authors.' No Greek, and no political economy either, contended Fawcett, since his own discipline depended on the study of history. In 1872 Fawcett had described his object in reforming the Irish universities: 'to secure the great cause of intellectual freedom, of liberal learning, and of high culture'.[126] Gladstone's proposals were anathema – 'almost a sin against the Holy Ghost' as Mrs Fawcett later put it.[127] The bill was at one with all of Gladstone's previous conduct as interpreted by Fawcett: 'it was just

[123] B.L., Add. MS 44791, fos. 131–66, 23 Sept. 1897. See J. Brooke and M. Sorenson, *The Prime Minister's Papers: W. E. Gladstone*, vol. 1, (H.M.S.O., 1971), p. 98.
[124] Parry, *Democracy and Religion*, p. 181; Matthew, *Gladstone*, pp. 199–200.
[125] *Hansard*, ccxiv, 3 March 1873, 1240–51.
[126] ibid., ccx, 25 April 1872, 1819.   [127] M. G. Fawcett, *What I Remember*, pp. 92–3.

one of those compromises on the give-and-take principle, which, intended
to please everybody, ended by pleasing nobody'.[128] Faced once again with
a clear issue of principle, Gladstone had backed away from the historic
tenets of Liberalism (as Fawcett understood them) and in a show of
ideological defeatism had set about appeasing obscurantists, fanatics and
reactionaries.

The subsequent vote was lost by the government by 287 to 284. The
majority of the forty-three Liberal M.P.s who voted against the bill (in
addition to the many Liberals who abstained) were Irish. But Fawcett's
role in criticising the bill and marshalling the votes of his radical followers
was very important. His criticisms were more intense than those of most
Liberals with reservations about the bill and few shared his particular
educational views, but he was able to stir the party on several emotional
issues – the role of priests in educational administration, the place of
denominational colleges, the gagging clauses and the like. It must have
seemed like justification to Fawcett after years of opposition and
undoubtedly provided a type of bitter satisfaction. He had precipitated the
Liberal defeat, though he was confident that the blame lay elsewhere. To
have helped to bring down a government is a strange claim to fame, but it
was this which marked the pinnacle of his career. For the government,
insult was added to injury, when, after this defeat, Fawcett (with
Gladstone's reluctant consent) then introduced those clauses of his bill
concerned with the abolition of the tests at Trinity which subsequently
passed the Commons on 26 May 1873.[129] According to Mrs Fawcett,
whose attitude to the Prime Minister was, if anything, more hostile than
her husband's, 'I do not think Mr Gladstone ever forgave my husband for
this defeat of his own measure and the passing into law of its rival.'[130] But
this was an exaggeration, perhaps coloured by later disillusion, when, in
the 1880s, Gladstone stood out against women's suffrage. It is clear,
however, that Fawcett and his radical allies severely tried the Prime
Minister's patience. When Gladstone's neice, Lady Frederick Cavendish,
dined in Downing Street in February 1871 she 'found Uncle W. agog
about another piece of Fawcettism' – on this occasion the abolition of
clerical Fellowships which had been 'pulled neck and crop across the Tests
measure'.[131] Lord Granville, Gladstone's former Foreign Secretary,
writing to Bright in early 1875 considered that Gladstone had been

[128] *Hansard*, ccxiv, 3 March 1873, 1241–2.
[129] ibid., ccxv, 28 March 1873, 302–4, 21 April 1873, 727–32; Parry, *Democracy and Religion*, pp. 369–70.
[130] M. G. Fawcett, *What I Remember*, p. 93.
[131] J. Bailey (ed.), *The Diary of Lady Frederick Cavendish* (2 vols., London, 1927), vol. 2, p. 95 (21 Feb. 1871).

'scandalously treated' by Fawcett among others.[132] And Gladstone himself, writing to his brother in the wake of defeat at the polls in February 1874, complained about a 'class of independent liberals who have been represented by the *Daily News,* and who have been one main cause of the weakness of the government … We have never recovered from the blow which they helped to strike on the Irish Education bill.' He also complained, a month later, about 'the habit of making a career by & upon constant active opposition to the bulk of the party & its leaders'.[133] How much this could be applied to Fawcett is open to debate; his stance since 1868 had certainly brought him influence and notoriety, but, equally, it had its foundations in adherence to unambiguous principles.

Indeed, 'principled opposition' and 'independence' were the terms used most frequently to describe Fawcett's position in politics. They brought him little joy in his dealings with the party. The whip was withdrawn from him; he was snubbed and ignored by ministers; his constituents grew restive.[134] But he was not a 'crotcheteer' – he took his stand on central issues. And he was not eccentric – there was a coherence and consistency to the positions he took up. As *The Times* put it, his 'distinguishing excellence' was that 'he never temporizes or conceals his opinions. He forms his conclusions for himself and when once formed he holds them with the utmost confidence, and no deference to authority can induce him to abstain from expressing them … These are characteristics precious because they are rare.'[135] And so he had influence. An article in *The Economist,* probably by Walter Bagehot, concluded that there was not 'a more useful member in the House of Commons'. His speeches told 'distinctly on divisions' because of 'the hard common sense and adherence to scientific principles by which his radicalism is modified'. He also talked 'a language Whigs can understand'.[136] In consequence, he was not isolated on the back benches, but could on occasion sway the massed ranks of the whig-liberals. One such was his amendment to abolish clerical Fellowships in February 1871. This 'Fawcettism' was only defeated by 182 votes to 160, and all of the 160 were Liberals. As Fawcett told the House, 'probably a Liberal Government, on a question involving Liberal principles, had never found so few of their supporters voting with them, and been opposed by so many of their strongest and best support-

[132] Granville to Bright, 15 Jan. 1875, in Lord Edmond Fitzmaurice, *The Life of Lord Granville, 1815–1891* (2 vols., London, 1905 edn), vol. 2, p. 143.

[133] Morley, *Life of Gladstone,* vol. 2, pp. 495–6; B.L., Add. MS 44762, fo. 37. This is a holograph dated 7 March [1874]. It is reproduced in H. C. G. Matthew (ed.), *The Gladstone Diaries,* vol. 8, 1871–4 (Oxford, 1982), p. 472.

[134] Stephen, *Life of Fawcett,* pp. 275, 289–90. *Daily News,* 25 Jan. 1871, p. 2.

[135] *The Times,* 27 April 1874, p. 11.

[136] *The Economist,* 8 Feb. 1873, pp. 154–5.

ers'.[137] On such issues of Liberal conscience Fawcett was a considerable force in politics.

It is difficult to assess the effect of this outspoken opposition as a factor in his defeat at Brighton in the general election of 1874. Gladstone blamed overall defeat on 'the torrent of gin and beer'; Fawcett blamed his local defeat on 'beer and money'.[138] The nature of the two Tories elected – a well-known yachtsman and a cavalry officer – suggests that his constituents had grown tired of 'advanced Liberalism', preferring free-spending gentlemen to incorruptible economists. But luck was on Fawcett's side. The result in the large London borough of Hackney, a safe Liberal seat, was declared invalid, and the incumbent declined to stand again. Dilke, M.P. for Chelsea, acted quickly 'to bring back Fawcett', and set up a committee, of which he was treasurer and Fitzmaurice the chairman, to raise funds to pay Fawcett's election expenses. Following Dilke's exertions, Fawcett received a requisition signed by over 5,000 calling on him to stand in the forthcoming by-election. He addressed the electors of Hackney for the first time on 18 March 1874 and was duly elected six weeks later to the amazement of a *Times* leader-writer who could not fathom the success of a man whose 'independence' had offended the local publicans, teetotallers, shopkeepers and working men, among others, in the course of his campaign.[139]

VII

Fawcett's tone softened appreciably in the later seventies and he was able to repair his relations with the rest of the Liberal Party. A Conservative administration pursuing an opportunistic foreign policy gave plenty of scope for united action against 'Beaconsfieldism'. And Fawcett could fall in behind Gladstone's revived leadership on issues like the Bulgarian atrocities campaign and the Afghan war. He was part of the radical group who brought the Bulgarian atrocities to the attention of the public in 1876.[140] He chaired a meeting of 5,000 working men at the Exeter Hall in September; he spoke at the great 'National Conference on the Eastern Question' at St James's Hall at the end of the year.[141] And on both occasions he produced a pugnacious, populistic rhetoric aimed in equal

---

137 *Hansard*, cciv, 20 Feb. 1871, 521.
138 Fawcett to A. J. Mundella, 10 Feb. 1874, Mundella Papers, GP/7/6/i. See also Fawcett to Harcourt, 8 Feb. 1874, Harcourt Papers, 205, fos. 33–4.
139 S. Gwynn and G. M. Tuckwell, *Life of the Rt. Hon. Sir Charles W. Dilke, Bart., M.P.* (2 vols., London, 1918), vol. 1, p. 173. *Daily News*, 19 March 1874, p. 3; *The Times*, 27 April 1874, p. 11.
140 R. T. Shannon, *Gladstone and the Bulgarian Agitation* (London, 1963), pp. 48, 58, 212.
141 *Daily News*, 19 Sept. 1876, p. 2; *The Times*, 9 Dec. 1876. p. 7.

measure at Disraeli's government and 'Turkish corruption ... Turkish savagery and Turkish lust'. His differences with the Liberal Party could be forgotten in a common cause. In addition, Fawcett turned his attention in the 1870s to two questions that only obliquely affected his relations with his own party – the preservation of commons and the administration of British India. His stance on both issues won him respect and allowed him to launch attacks on more traditional objects of liberal scorn, rapacious landlords and inefficient government.

Fawcett's interest in the preservation of common land dates from the spring of 1869 and his opposition to the annual enclosure bill of that year. Until 1845, enclosures had been legalised in the traditional way by private Act of Parliament. After that, global bills scheduling a number of commons to be enclosed, and drawn up by Enclosure Commissioners, were presented annually and usually seen through on the nod at late-night sittings. But the foundation in 1865 of the Commons Preservation Society had alerted Fawcett to the steady transfer of common land into private ownership, and his stubborn opposition to the 1869 bill marked the first stage in his campaign. There was certainly ammunition here to fire off at his own party: Fawcett was amazed that 'so many ardent friends of the poor and so many persistent asserters of popular rights' could acquiesce to schemes that were fundamentally opposed to communal rights and traditions.[142] But he was drawn to the question from more generous impulses as well – from a concern for the rights of agricultural workers who stood to lose their grazing land and urban workers who might lose recreational facilities in and around the cities. And the issue allowed an 'advanced Liberal' in the Cobdenite mould to lambast the landowning classes, 'people who spend a great part of their lives in slaughtering half-tamed pheasants' and who were 'willing that the enjoyment of the public should be sacrificed' in order that they 'may kill a few more'.[143] Fawcett did not begin the campaign and did not fight alone: Shaw-Lefevre, the first chairman of the Commons Preservation Society, probably did more, and Harcourt, Dilke, Fitzmaurice and William Cowper-Temple M.P. played their part. Their success can certainly be measured in those areas saved as common land: Epping Forest (saved for the Sunday recreation of East-Enders), the New Forest and the commons at Mitcham, Barnes and Wimbledon, were, among others, the subject of successful campaigns against enclosure by private landlords. More to the point, by arguing their case on the floor of the House and in committee, they reversed the presumption that the burden of proof should fall on those

---

[142] Henry Fawcett, 'The enclosure of commons', *Fraser's Magazine*, vol. 1, (n.s.) (Feb. 1870), p. 185. See also *Daily News*, 25 Jan. 1871, p. 2.
[143] Fawcett, 'The enclosure of commons', p. 191.

who opposed the enclosure. Under the terms of the 1876 Enclosure Act (though it possessed many drawbacks in Fawcett's estimation) it was the enclosers themselves who had to prove that their schemes would not injure the public interest.[144]

The campaign to preserve the commons thus began as an attempt to save actual tracts of threatened land and broadened into an agitation to secure certain principles regulating public and private interests. Fawcett's involvement in Indian affairs was a similar mixture: a concern with the specific details of Indian finance and administration on which he felt competent to give an opinion even though he never visited the sub-continent or knew much about its cultures, and a more general interest in establishing certain attitudes and principles that might regulate the conduct of British imperialism there.[145] Fawcett was no anti-imperialist (as his later attitudes towards Ireland reinforce) but he was passionately concerned that British rule in India should be competent, cheap and fair to the native population. That it was none of these things concerned him deeply and explains his campaign to engage Parliament and opinion more generally in close consideration of Indian affairs: only then could the required sense of responsibility be assured. Just as he had been amazed that the annual enclosure bills passed almost without comment, so he was similarly concerned that 'Indian questions do not excite so much interest in the House of Commons as a squabble about the cost of a road through St James's Park'.[146] As he wrote to Harcourt in 1876, 'The Indian people would be a great deal more grateful for a little attention from Parliament than they will be for having the Queen called "Empress of India".'[147] He thus became known, in Britain and in India, as 'The Member for India', scrutinising policy and suggesting improvements not just because he opposed aspects of the administration of India (though he invariably did) but because it was in this way that the duties of Empire would begin to be taken seriously. Twenty years later in an age of self-conscious 'imperialism', such attitudes would be commonplace. But in the early 1870s Fawcett was almost a lone voice, independent once again.

As might be expected from a professor of political economy who so admired Gladstone's earlier financial statesmanship, for Fawcett the key to the moral regeneration of British administration lay in careful financial management. In his most important speech on Indian finance during the Indian budget debate in 1872, he painted a grim but accurate picture of 'a slowly increasing revenue, a rapidly increasing expenditure, administra-

---

144 Stephen, *Life of Fawcett*, pp. 330–2.   145 ibid., pp. 348–9.
146 Henry and Millicent Garrett Fawcett, *Essays and Lectures on Social and Political Subjects*, (Cambridge and London, 1872), 'The House of Lords', pp. 312–13.
147 Fawcett to Harcourt, 20 Feb. 1876, Harcourt Papers, 207, fos. 16–18.

tion each year becoming more costly, [and] a determination to embark on a vast and indefinite expenditure on public works'.[148] It was impossible to extract more revenue from the Indian population who were already taxed as heavily as they could be without provoking further hardship and civil unrest. Consequently, the only solution was for the British administration – military as well as civil – to live within its straitened means. Fawcett could not resist denunciations of profligacy with other people's money at home or abroad: when the expenses of the Prince of Wales's visit to the sub-continent in 1875 were charged to the Indian revenue; when £175,000 was spent building a country house for the Governor of Bombay; when the Indian government bought up the shares of bankrupt land schemes which were unsaleable in the open market at par, Fawcett was swift in condemnation.[149] As he wrote to Gladstone in 1879, knowing that on this issue he could win his leader's support, 'The chief object I have had in view since I have given any attention to the subject is to make English public opinion lean on the side of Economy and not on the side of Extravagance.'[150] As this suggests, Fawcett's engagement in Indian affairs was less the product of an interest in India *per se* than an outgrowth of his domestic political and economic faith. Despite improvements in colonial administration, he seems to have been genuinely appalled that the historic achievement of Liberalism in nineteenth-century Britain – the systematisation and improvement of government and bureaucracy – had not yet been achieved in the administration of India and the Empire more generally.

VIII

Fawcett's temperament, like that of many mavericks on the left of British politics, was suited to opposition and the vigorous pursuit of unfashionable causes. And yet he accepted office, and comparatively lowly office at that, when Gladstone formed his second administration. After the sound and fury of the early 1870s, the final phase of Fawcett's life as Postmaster General was thus a quiet, almost uncharacteristic coda. It is not clear why he wanted to leave the back benches, though Leslie Stephen's picture of 'the young gentlemen, Trevelyan and Fawcett and so forth, waiting for some crumbs to fall from the table of the Liberals' as they sat in the Athenaeum after the 1880 election, suggests that plain ambition was part

---

148 Henry Fawcett, speech on Indian finance. Delivered in the House of Commons in the debate on the Indian budget, 6 Aug. 1872. Reprinted with a few explanatory notes (London, 1872), p. 10.

149 Fawcett to Harcourt, 31 March 1875, Harcourt Papers, 206, fos. 74–6. *Daily News*, 19 March 1874, p. 3.

150 Fawcett to Gladstone, 10 May 1879, B.L., Add. MS 44156, fo. 36.

of the answer.[151] Fawcett began in government with high hopes: as he wrote to John Neville Keynes, his former pupil whom he had helped secure a Fellowship at Pembroke College, Cambridge, 'The office they have given me is one I think I shall like, as there are many interesting questions connected with it, & I shall have time to devote to other subjects.'[152] But three years later he was less sanguine: 'the chief drawback to being in Government is the extent to which one is withdrawn from general politics'.[153] It would seem that Fawcett had been outmanoeuvred by Gladstone, though the tactic of promoting and therefore muzzling an opponent while keeping him out of the inner circles of power should have been as obvious to Fawcett as it was to others. As Lord Aberdare (the former Home Secretary, Bruce) observed, 'The inclusion of their three ablest men in the Government (Chamberlain, Dilke and Fawcett) will greatly weaken the advanced Liberal party in the House, without affecting the general policy of the Cabinet, the composition of which ought to reassure the most timid.'[154] Gladstone had learnt his lesson.

There is something odd in the image of Fawcett – all moral fervour and righteous indignation – shackled to a desk in the Post Office. There was no doubting his administrative ability, diligence or the popular enthusiasm for a blind Postmaster General. And Fawcett certainly regarded the Post Office as an important vehicle for promoting thrift and prosperity: it had its place in the Professor's scheme of things, no doubt. Yet his achievements there – the introduction of the parcel post, of course, as well as cheaper postal orders and telegrams and improved facilities for small savers and investors – though creditable in themselves do not seem to match the assertive Liberalism and the great principles he had espoused. But if Gladstone had hoped to silence him completely in this way, he was mistaken. Fawcett strongly opposed that poorly kept secret of the early 1880s – that the letters of Irish M.P.s were being opened as they passed through the Post Office.[155] He abstained in July 1883 when the government proposed charging the cost of Indian soldiers garrisoned in Egypt on Indian funds.[156] And though Gladstone threatened to remove him from the administration if he openly defied policy again, he abstained again in the following year when instructed to vote down Woodall's amendment

---

151 Leslie Stephen to C. E. Norton, 28 April 1880, quoted in Maitland, *Life of Leslie Stephen*, p. 340.
152 Fawcett to J. N. Keynes, 3 May 1880, Cambridge University Library, Add. MS 7562/14.
153 Fawcett to C. H. Pearson, 16 March 1883, Bodleian Library, Oxford, MS Eng. lett. d. 187 fo. 158.
154 *Letters of the Rt. Hon. Henry Austin Bruce, Lord Aberdare of Duffryn* (2 vols., Oxford, 1902), vol. 2, p. 90.
155 M. G. Fawcett, *What I Remember*, p. 113.
156 Gladstone to Fawcett, 28 July 1883, B.L., Add. MS 44546, fo. 141; Fawcett to Gladstone, 30 July 1883, ibid., 44156, fos. 173–4.

to the third Reform Bill which would have enfranchised women. He was joined by Dilke, President of the Local Government Board, and Leonard Courtney, Secretary to the Treasury, though over a hundred Liberal M.P.s who had previously pledged support to the women's movement reneged when Gladstone threatened to withdraw the bill if the motion was upheld. The insubordination of the three errant ministers 'caused a miniature storm in the Cabinet'. But it was decided that they should retain their posts, and Gladstone sent them a stiff memorandum in lieu of a request for their resignations: it was no comfort at all to Mrs Fawcett who never 'forgave or forgot' this volte-face by a Prime Minister who had previously seemed sympathetic to 'the cause'.[157]

It is difficult to gauge just how disillusioned Fawcett had become by 1884. But there is plenty of evidence to suggest that he would have resigned from the government at the end of the year with Leonard Courtney over the issue of proportional representation. Both men hoped that the Franchise Bill – the third Reform Act – would include provisions to ensure the 'representation of minorities'. But when it did not, and Courtney came to justify his resignation on the floor of the House on 4 December 1884, he could assert that if the debate had taken place just a month earlier, 'I should not have been alone in standing here; I should not have been alone in deserting that Bench.'[158] Certainly Fawcett's last public address at Shoreditch Town Hall in October 1884 restated his lifelong devotion to Hare's scheme of electoral reform at some length.[159] But whether he was genuinely opposed to any extension of the franchise and redistribution of parliamentary seats that ignored proportional representation, or whether the issue provided him with a convenient pretext for a resignation that owed far more to his general loss of confidence in the government, is unclear. Fawcett was temperamentally unsuited to official life and the restraints it imposed. However ambitious he may have been, it seems plausible that he had come to recognise that his true place in politics would always be on the back benches. He was undoubtedly frustrated by the silence that a position in the administration enforced and antagonised by some of Gladstone's more high-handed methods and it may be conjectured that he chose to leave the ministry on a point of relatively obscure principle – though one that he had always upheld – that would not create controversy and discomfiture for his former colleagues. Yet whatever the plan and Fawcett's motives, it was

---

[157] Gooch, *Life of Lord Courtney*, p. 196; Gladstone to Fawcett, 16 June 1884, B.L., Add. MS 44547, fo. 73; Fawcett to Gladstone, 17 June 1884, ibid., 44156, fo. 188; M. G. Fawcett, *What I Remember*, pp. 111–12; Strachey, *Millicent Garrett Fawcett*, pp. 97–9.

[158] Gooch, *Life of Lord Courtney*, pp. 200, 209–12; Stephen, *Life of Fawcett*, pp. 450–1; *Hansard*, ccxciv, 4 Dec. 1884, 679–80.   [159] *The Times*, 14 Oct. 1884, p. 8.

cut short by untimely death. Fawcett had been dangerously ill at the end of
1882 when he contracted diphtheria and pneumonia.[160] 'It was a very
serious attack and I suppose I had a narrow escape' was how he later put
it.[161] He partially resumed his duties in March 1883 and was fully
recovered by the summer. A year later, at the end of the 1884 session, he
seemed in good health even though most of the summer months were
spent in London on negotiations with the new private telephone com-
panies.[162] But in late October, in Cambridge, a cold became pneumonia
with coronary complications, and, after a short illness, Fawcett died on 6
November 1884 in the presence of his wife and daughter. His early love,
Elizabeth Garrett Anderson, attended him during his final illness: as she
wrote to her husband on the day he died, 'It is a terrible calamity, a fine
loving heart and a face set towards good in everything.'[163]

Something approaching national mourning followed with tributes in
Parliament and the press, from the Queen and from many of her more
humble subjects. Gladstone's letter to Fawcett's father, still alive in 1884,
set the tone for these: 'he has left a record of some qualities which are
given to few; but of others, perhaps yet more remarkable, which all of his
fellow countrymen may in their degree emulate and follow'.[164] Emulation
was the key: his life could not fail to be 'read', didactically, as an
exemplification of certain obvious virtues like fortitude, courage and
optimism, and held up as a model and inspiration to others. Even Leslie
Stephen's inscription in brass on the national memorial to Fawcett in
Westminster Abbey paid tribute to 'a memorable example of the power of
a brave man to transmute evil into good and to wrest victory from
misfortune'.[165] Fawcett had originally set out, as contributions to this
volume make clear, to instruct the working class in the economic ways of
the world. Ironically, perhaps, in this role as teacher, the greatest lesson of
all became the legend of his life. It was taught by Fawcett in and through
his life and perpetuated by others – Leslie Stephen, Archbishop Benson
unveiling a memorial to the blind M.P. in 1893, and even the members of
the Rectory Road Literary Society in Hackney – after his death.[166] And

---

[160] Leslie Stephen reports his illnesses as diphtheria and typhoid. But this does not square
with Fawcett's description of 'diphtheria and congestion of the lungs from which I
suffered'. See Stephen, *Life of Fawcett*, p. 458; Fawcett to Gladstone, 12 June 1883,
B.L., Add. MS 44156, fos. 166–7.
[161] Fawcett to C. H. Pearson, 16 March 1883, Bodleian Library, MS Eng. lett. d. 187, fo.
158.
[162] Strachey, *Millicent Garrett Fawcett*, p. 100.
[163] Manton, *Elizabeth Garrett Anderson*, p. 271.
[164] Gladstone to William Fawcett, 25 Nov. 1884, B.L., Add. MS 44547, fo. 140.
[165] The memorial is in the St George Chapel in Westminster Abbey.
[166] *The Times*, 8 June 1893, p. 5; *The Late Professor Fawcett M.P., or Lessons Gleaned
from a Noble Life. Being a Paper Read at a Meeting of the Rectory Road Literary
Society, West Hackney, Dec. 1st 1884, by a Member of that Society* (London, 1884).

the legend of the blind M.P., softening Fawcett's rough edges, downplaying his radicalism and cussedness, and understating his differences with Gladstone and their significance for an understanding of the politics of the period, has made it that much more difficult to appreciate his career.

Fawcett's death was untimely, but it did at least spare him from the painful decisions that divided the academic radicals as a group and marked the end of their influence in national politics within eighteen months. The Home Rule crisis in 1886 forced many of them to question convictions and affiliations of a lifetime. Some stayed faithful to Gladstone; more went into opposition though many of them lived to regret the decision.[167] Christopher Harvie's contribution to this volume considers briefly how Fawcett might have reacted had he been alive. Mrs Fawcett was in no doubt, certainly. An active Liberal Unionist herself, who had needed little excuse to take up formal opposition to Gladstone, she could guarantee in June 1886 'that had Mr Fawcett's life been spared, he would now have been found acting with Lord Hartington and other leading Liberals in opposition to the Irish bills of the present Government'. The quotation is from a letter to *The Times* in which she presented several extracts from his later speeches to prove his opposition to Home Rule.[168] But opposition in principle was one thing: it was not the same as following Joseph Chamberlain – a radical of a different generation from a different background with whom Fawcett had relatively little contact – into even temporary alliance with the Conservatives, let alone eventual fusion.[169] To Fawcett, as to Mill, the Tories were always 'the stupid party'. Whether or not Fawcett would have become a Liberal Unionist; whether he would have decided to take the easier course and stay in the Liberal Party or whether he would have reverted to splendid isolation and angry independence of his party on the back benches, there can be little argument that the actual political future (as opposed to any future he might have envisaged then) would have been barren for him. The combination of an almost unbroken generation of Conservative governments up to 1906, of a Liberal Party dedicated to Home Rule while tending increasingly towards a style of programmatic collectivism, and the beginnings of a Labour politics independent of the Liberal Party, would have dashed any

[167] Christopher Harvie, *The Lights of Liberalism. University Liberals and the Challenge of Democracy, 1860–1886* (London, 1976), pp. 218–43.

[168] *The Times*, 4 June 1886, p. 10. To give one example from a speech Fawcett delivered in Hackney in October 1879, 'He had said in the House of Commons, and he repeated there, and he believed he expressed the opinion of the vast majority of Liberals throughout the country, that it would be better for the Liberal party to remain out of office till its youngest member was grey with age, rather than come into power by any compromise with Home Rule.'

[169] See Chamberlain to Dilke, 19 April 1880, in Roy Jenkins, *Sir Charles Dilke. A Victorian Tragedy* (London, 1958), p. 128.

further ministerial ambitions and left Fawcett high and dry, the relic of a former political configuration in a changed world. And it is this configuration that makes him distinctive: despite his independence and the purity of his principles, he was also a representative figure. His political career, from the late 1850s until the mid-1880s is coextensive with Liberalism in its heyday. The range of his interests and the complex of attitudes he developed, though spiced with his own individual ingredients (more Mill and more political economy than usual) were common to a group of Liberals who entered politics in the late 1850s and 1860s from a base in the reformed universities. For three decades the drift of affairs and the spirit of Liberal measures, though never as swift and as radical as Fawcett wished, were in their favour. But by the mid-'eighties, the issues and generations were changing. When Fawcett made his last speech in October 1884 he could not 'recall the time when political issues before the country were graver and when consequently a public man speaks with greater responsibility'.[170] He could sense the altered nature of the political future, and, as the product of a discrete political culture then drawing to its close, he was fortunate, in a sense, in not having to face it.

[170] *The Times*, 14 Oct. 1884, p. 8.

PART I

PERSONAL LIFE AND SENSIBILITY

'Manly Fellows': Fawcett, Stephen and the Liberal temper*

STEFAN COLLINI

Since we are to have later today papers by people who are much more expert than I about, respectively, Fawcett's economics and his politics, I have taken the opportunity in this paper to explore a wider theme, namely the temper, the values, the moral and aesthetic sensibilities which informed Fawcett's social and political thought, and, more ambitiously and more sketchily, their place in mid-Victorian public debate. I hope this may go some way towards providing a suggestive context into which to set the more detailed analyses which are to follow. Speaking purely selfishly, one great advantage of this strategy has been that it enabled me to persuade myself that the best way to prepare for writing a paper about Henry Fawcett was to spend a lot of time reading Leslie Stephen. Any shame that I might otherwise have felt about this transparently self-indulgent strategy has been dissipated by the thought that if part of the rationale for this conference is the urge to honour one of the distinguished sons of Trinity Hall, then I have placed myself beyond reproach by honouring two of them simultaneously.

'There has been no more striking example in our time of how self-reliance and strength of purpose can triumph over adverse fortune than that presented by the career of Henry Fawcett.'[1] Even discounting for memorialist's piety, we are properly reminded by James Bryce's words that in dealing with Fawcett we are dealing with a figure who commanded his contemporaries' attention as much for his exemplary value as for the

---

* As this paper was written in the summer of 1984, it does not take into account work, particularly on the theme of 'manliness,' published since then.

[1] Viscount Bryce, 'Preface' to Winifred Holt, *A Beacon for the Blind. Being a Life of Henry Fawcett, the Blind Postmaster General* (London, 1915), p. vii. See his similar remark in his obituary notice, 'The late Mr. Fawcett', *Nation* (N.Y.), vol. 39 (1884), p. 457: 'Mr Fawcett's career is an admirable illustration of the truth that in life – literary and scientific life almost as much as practical life – force of character counts for more than pure intellectual capacity.'

substance of his achievements, and we may do well to follow this lead. It would be foolish to pretend that as an economist and political theorist Fawcett can be credited with any significant originality, or that as a writer he displayed any qualities more noteworthy than vigour and a high tolerance for repetition. And even his career, remarkable though it was given his blindness, would not in itself have required extensive consideration by historians: after all, parliamentary politics was his chosen métier yet he never attained cabinet rank. But during his lifetime Fawcett represented a particularly important set of political attitudes with a revealing purity, and I think he provides a rewarding route to a historical understanding of the intellectual and emotional dynamic underlying those attitudes.

First, however, we must acknowledge a special difficulty about the nature of the evidence available for this particular enquiry. We cannot but approach Fawcett through the medium of the *Life* written by his old friend Leslie Stephen.[2] Indeed, one may be forgiven for thinking that it was Fawcett's greatest achievement, or at least stroke of good fortune, as far as posthumous celebrity was concerned, to have obtained the affectionate attention of the acknowledged master among Victorian biographers. Certainly the *Life* enjoyed considerable contemporary success, going into its fifth edition within a year, thereby firmly establishing its subject's exemplary status. Maitland recorded that it was 'often thought of as the most attractive of [Stephen's] books', and recent historians have treated it as one of the best guides to the economic and political thought of the whole generation of the young intellectuals to which Fawcett and Stephen belonged.[3] The book effectively falls into two halves – a fact which Stephen himself seems to have recognised[4] – and these judgements must both apply only to the first half, that perceptive, evocative, sympathetic portrait of the young Fawcett, and especially of his circle at Cambridge, which displayed Stephen's special talent for capturing the interplay between temperament and belief. The second half, the somewhat dry narrative of Fawcett's parliamentary career, is not without interest, but Stephen was, as he acknowledged, too remote from that

[2] Leslie Stephen, *Life of Henry Fawcett* (London, 1885); no changes were introduced in subsequent editions. Hereafter cited as *Life*.

[3] F. W. Maitland, *The Life and Letters of Leslie Stephen* (London, 1906), p. 374; Christopher Harvie, *The Lights of Liberalism. University Liberals and the Challenge of Democracy, 1860–1886* (London, 1976), p. 305, where Stephen's chapter on Fawcett's political economy is described as the 'best account of the economic beliefs held by Fawcett's generation'. Stephen himself was characteristically dissatisfied. As his friend Henry Sidgwick reported in his diary after a conversation with Stephen's wife: 'She tells me that Stephen is depressed because his life of Fawcett has only reached a 4th edition.' Sidgwick Journal, 25 March 1886, Henry Sidgwick MSS, Trinity College, Cambridge.

[4] Maitland, *Life of Leslie Stephen*, pp. 387–8.

world to bring it to life with anything like the same sureness of touch, and
it does not offer that kind of insider's view of the machinations of high
politics contained in the biographies of some of the more eminent
politicians of the time.

What may not be so obvious is that through Stephen's biography we are
encountering Fawcett at a double remove. To begin with, it is an account
of a set of political attitudes which were already coming to be regarded as
distinctly old-fashioned. There are frequent reminders in the book that it
is being written with the controversies of the 1880s in full swing,[5] and
Stephen is constantly having to defend – and where he cannot defend, at
least make intelligible – a claim about the essential principles of Liberalism which he knew many of his readers would regard as either archaic or
tendentious. In several areas, notably on the question of the grounds of
state intervention, Stephen could do this with conviction because he was
presenting a view which, as I shall bring out later, he still shared, and to
this extent the book constituted something of an appeal from the old to
the new Liberals. But, secondly, we have also to recognise that intellectually and, in some ways, politically Stephen and Fawcett had moved
far apart since the days of their radical comradeship of the 1850s and early
1860s. Partly this involved a growing distaste on Stephen's part for active
politics generally, and in particular for what he, like so many others of his
type, saw as the disappointment of the reforming hopes of the mid-1860s
and the decline into Gladstonian demagoguery. It also involved Stephen's
increased absorption in literature, scholarship and family life; it involved
an intellectual development which led him to emphasise more strongly
than before the power of history and the forces of social change at the
expense of mere political 'machinery'; and it involved what might be
called an emotional development as a result of which the confident
no-nonsense relation to life which they had shared in their twenties, and
which stayed with Fawcett to the end, came to Stephen to seem thin and
unsatisfying.

Indeed, on reflection one is bound to wonder, as some of Stephen's later
friends like Maitland clearly did,[6] how the ironical, sceptical, moody
Stephen could ever have been so close to the straightforward, emphatic,
insufferably cheerful Fawcett. In part it was the usual story of a friendship
made in youth becoming itself the chief bond of attraction between two
men who have become very different; the loyalty is now to the friendship
as much as to the friend, a nostalgic and slightly contrived celebration of

[5] See, for example, his remarks about Spencer's 'New Toryism', in *Life*, p. 265, a reference
to a series of articles on 'The man versus the state' that Spencer published in 1884, and
which caused a considerable controversy about the changing nature of Liberalism.
[6] See Noel Annan, *Leslie Stephen. The Godless Victorian* (London, 1984), p. 40.

an intimacy that was once spontaneous. But when a later biographer, pondering this puzzle, observed that the two men 'seem to have shared little but their earlier politics and their love of walking',[7] she was pointing, unknowingly, to a cluster of associations which lay at the heart of the affinity between Stephen and Fawcett, associations which pervade Stephen's biography, and which, I want to argue, were a crucial source of the political attitudes of which Fawcett was such an undeviating representative. But first I want to look very briefly at the alleged theoretical basis of those attitudes, and to examine more closely the nature of the political identity they expressed.

As I have already implied, part of Fawcett's interest for the intellectual historian of the period lies in the fact that whatever position he took up he could be relied upon to take it up in its purest and most uncomplicated form.[8] Politically, he stood, proudly conscious of his unswerving rectitude, for a severe form of Individualism, and economically for a dogmatic attachment to the principles of classical political economy, though he considered himself a pragmatist in their application. Insofar as Fawcett is credited with any systematic theoretical basis for his political convictions, he is normally described as a Utilitarian. Since my way of stating these received views may hint at revisionist intentions, let me say at once that I am not about to make the improbable suggestion that Fawcett was in fact a proto-socialist, an unrecognised forerunner of historical economics, or, more unimaginable still, an adept of the mysteries of philosophical idealism. But in trying to understand Fawcett's political thinking and political identity, and to place it on the map of Victorian public debate, I do want to suggest that we need to operate with slightly more probing categories than those provided by the conveniently prefabricated label 'Utilitarian Liberal'.

Let me start with the question of Utilitarianism. Whatever its importance at the level of systematic moral and political philosophy, I would argue (though the case cannot be substantiated here)[9] that historians have tended to speak in exaggerated terms of its impact on political discourse and political action in mid-nineteenth-century England. Certainly, a number of originally Utilitarian formulae found their way into the language, or, less generously, perhaps just the rhetoric, of political debate;

---

[7] Holt, *A Beacon for the Blind*, p. 78.

[8] There is no secondary literature on Fawcett to speak of; for a brief discussion, with a few further references, see J. C. Wood, *British Economists and the Empire* (London, 1983), pp. 77–93.

[9] For further elaboration of this point, see Stefan Collini, *Liberalism and Sociology. L. T. Hobhouse and Political Argument in England 1880–1914* (Cambridge, 1979), pp. 43–6; and idem, 'Political theory and the "science of society" in Victorian Britain', *Historical Journal*, vol. 23 (1980), pp. 218–19.

it is also true that some of the views and policies historically associated with the Philosophic Radicals, though not necessarily derivable from strict Utilitarian theory, continued to command attention long after the demise of their sponsors as an active parliamentary force. But mid-Victorian political discourse, even among those of reforming inclinations, was effectively constituted by values and arguments drawn from other sources, largely of a more traditionally constitutional, historical, religious or, above all, moral kind. Certainly it could matter *which* vague formulae a writer chose to flourish, and at this level Fawcett undeniably relied upon broadly Utilitarian considerations. Thus, he explains his purpose in his book, *The Economic Position of the British Labourer*, as being to show 'what arrangements may be adopted so as to bring the greatest happiness to the community in general', and later he emphasises that no arguments in favour of the greater economic efficiency of enclosures ought to be allowed any weight 'if it could be shown that this augmented wealth has tended not to promote but to diminish the comfort and happiness of the people'.[10] But when such phrases are not part of any systematically deployed theoretical framework, as in Fawcett's writings they are not, they tell us very little about the really operative sources of the ideas to which they are juxtaposed.

What mattered far more was that Fawcett saw himself as, was seen by others as, and to a surprisingly consistent extent was, a disciple of John Stuart Mill. I say 'surprisingly' consistent extent because although his-torians refer expansively to the impact of Mill's teaching in the mid-century, in many cases this turns out on inspection to involve less than meets the eye. Fawcett's exceptional fidelity may be brought out by distinguishing three categories or stages of discipleship among the alleged teeming Millians. The first, both chronologically and in terms of its incidence, was to be a keen student of Mill's double-decker treatises on logic and political economy.[11] In general terms, basing oneself on Mill's work in these fields might well involve laying claim to a modern, scientific, often secular and 'advanced' identity, a process of self-definition par-ticularly common at the universities in the 1850s and 1860s, but even then it did not necessarily entail agreement with all of his later writings. The second stage involved enthusiastic endorsement of Mill as a public moralist, applauding his outspoken support for the North in the American Civil War, exulting in the symbolic value of his election to Parliament,

10 Henry Fawcett, *The Economic Position of the British Labourer* (Cambridge and London, 1865), pp. 7, 63.
11 For the impact of his *A System of Logic* (1843) see, in particular, Alexander Bain, *John Stuart Mill: A Criticism* (London, 1882), ch. 3; and for his *Principles of Political Economy* (1848) see N. B. de Marchi, 'The success of Mill's *Principles*', *History of Political Economy*, vol. 6 (1974), pp. 119–57.

admiring his campaign to have Governor Eyre brought to justice (though some who initially supported this campaign were eventually alienated by what came to seem the vindictiveness with which Mill pursued his quarry).[12] Again, by no means all the readers of his earlier treatises welcomed Mill's ardent partisanship on these issues, but for many of the radically inclined young intellectuals of the period his public career was an important embodiment of their ideal of the role to be played by 'the man of principle', and his courage and disinterestedness attracted a respect bordering on reverence. The third stage, the real inner sanctum of discipleship, was actually to advocate the same range of political and social measures as Mill. The number of true believers was considerably reduced at this stage, since on many practical matters Mill was thought to be the prisoner of certain theoretical 'crotchets', such as Hare's scheme for proportional representation, the enfranchisement of women, the extension of the cooperative principle, land tenure reform, and so on.[13]

Leslie Stephen himself provides a good example of these modulations of enthusiasm, in that as a young don he swore by the reasoning of Mill's treatises[14] (and as a young don swearing seems to have been his chief form of expression). In the 1860s he admired and shared Mill's moral protests against the selfishness and indifference of the governing classes, though he became increasingly uneasy with what he saw as the rather priggish dogmatism with which Mill pressed his case (a point to which I shall return later). But he never felt able to endorse the full range of Mill's crotchets, and the note of reservation one detects in his references to Mill in the early 1870s has swollen to a full-throated peal of distaste by the time he settled accounts in his study of the English Utilitarians in 1900.[15] Interesting variations on this theme could be played in the case of comparable figures such as Henry Sidgwick, A. V. Dicey and John Morley, in all of whose cases account would have to be taken of degrees of reservation or levels of ambivalence that fell some way short of uninhibited discipleship.[16] More generally, it is significant that the authors of the

12 For Mill's role as 'public moralist' see Stefan Collini, 'Introduction', John Stuart Mill, *Essays on Equality, Law, and Education*, in *Collected Works of John Stuart Mill* (25 vols., Toronto, 1963–   ), vol. 21, pp. vii–lvi.
13 For examples of those who had reservations about Mill's 'crotchets', see Harvie, *Lights of Liberalism*. chs. 2 and 7.
14 In addition to the biographies by Maitland and Annan, see Leslie Stephen, *Some Early Impressions* (London, 1924 (reprinted from the *National Review* for 1903)), pp. 71 et seq., on his early admiration for the 'pure, passionless reason' of Mill's treatises.
15 E.g. Leslie Stephen, 'The value of political machinery', *Fortnightly Review*, vol. 24 (1875), pp. 836–52; *The English Utilitarians* (3 vols., London, 1900), vol. 1, pp. 63–72.
16 For Sidgwick see Stefan Collini, Donald Winch and John Burrow, *That Noble Science of Politics. A Study in Nineteenth-Century Intellectual History* (Cambridge, 1983) ch. 9; for Dicey see Richard Cosgrove, *The Rule of Law: Albert Venn Dicey, Victorian Jurist*

Essays on Reform, a group of university men who formed part of Mill's natural constituency and most of whom had earlier enthusiastically embraced the first two stages of discipleship, conducted their analysis of the established political system with scant reference to the categories of Utilitarian philosophy, and endorsed a set of proposals that omitted most of Mill's distinctive constitutional recommendations.[17]

Fawcett by contrast, was among that much smaller band of followers who took up *Representative Government* and the *Subjection of Women* as ardently as they had subscribed to the *Logic* and the *Political Economy*, though since Fawcett had nothing like the range or subtlety of mind of his master, we should not be surprised to find the original ideas somewhat simplified in the process of transmission. Fawcett's enthusiasm for Mill's *Principles of Political Economy*, in particular, was legendary: he knew the book 'as a Puritan knew the Bible' commented Stephen later,[18] and given Stephen's known convictions, neither party was altogether being flattered by being compared, however flippantly, either to a Puritan or to the Author of the Bible. It possibly says something about the limits of all discipleship that even Fawcett could not be an utterly orthodox exponent of the holy book. Not only did he omit or minimise the role of Mill's speculations about the influence of social development on economic arrangements, but he was sceptical of the theory of the unearned increment and the proposed taxation of land-values, he did not share Mill's tenderness for certain forms of socialism, and, more technically, he adhered to a form of the 'wage-fund' doctrine after Mill had rejected it, and he denied the validity of Mill's 'infant industry' argument for protection.[19] On the whole, however, it was certainly true, as he himself insisted, that Fawcett's economic writings, the widely used *Manual* above all, were faithful expositions of Mill for a popular audience.

This was almost as true of his political writings as well. He was a

(London, 1980), ch. 1; for Morley see Christopher Kent, *Brains and Numbers: Elitism, Comtism, and Democracy in Mid-Victorian England* (Toronto, 1978), ch. 8.

17   Stephen and Dicey were both among the contributors to this volume, published in 1867; there is a good discussion of the group as a whole in Harvie, *Lights of Liberalism*.

18   Stephen, *Early Impressions*, p. 75. For Fawcett's extravagant praise of Mill's 'great work' as 'undoubtedly the most complete and the most perfect treatise that has ever been written on the science', see his 'Inaugural lecture on political economy', *Macmillan's Magazine*, vol. 9 (1864), pp. 495–503. See also his preface to *Manual of Political Economy* (Cambridge and London, 1863); this work went through six editions in Fawcett's lifetime.

19   Fawcett's *Manual* contains no real equivalent of Mill's Book Four on 'The influence of the progress of society on production and distribution'; for the 'unearned increment' and the taxation of land-values, see *Manual* (6th edn, 1883), pp. 286–7, and *Life*, pp. 165–6; on the wage-fund doctrine see Pedro Schwartz, *The New Political Economy of J. S. Mill* (London, 1972), pp. 91–100, and D. P. O'Brien, *The Classical Economists* (Oxford, 1975), pp. 111–18; for the 'infant industry' argument see Fawcett, *Free Trade and Protection* (London, 1878), p. 111.

persistent advocate of Thomas Hare's scheme, and was, with his wife, an active campaigner for women's rights. He closely followed Mill's lead in the 1865 Parliament, which confirmed his reputation as a doctrinaire, for, as Stephen observed, 'if the regular party-managers had an instinctive suspicion of Mill as a theorist and a crotchet-monger, they were not likely to be favourable to Mill's most ardent disciple'.[20] Indeed, Fawcett was to prove more intransigent and less adaptable even than Mill when faced with the demands of political compromise: thus, Mill conceded that in the short term a reformed Upper Chamber would have to contain a substantial number of hereditary peers, whereas Fawcett would allow no concession to 'the hereditary principle in legislation', and pressed for the immediate 'abolition of all political privileges enjoyed independently of merit'.[21] In other ways, too, he leaned towards a rather more conventional form of radicalism than his master: he continued, for example, to support the secret ballot despite Mill's well-publicised volte-face on the issue.

In considering what sort of political identity these views expressed in mid-Victorian England, it might seem natural to begin with some notion of Liberalism. But it is worth remembering – and may provide a more useful starting-point for the enquiry – that Fawcett's own preferred label was not 'Liberal' but 'Radical'. This was the identity he claimed, self-consciously invoking a Philosophic Radical pedigree, as a young Fellow in the 1850s; it was how he described himself when trying to enter Parliament in the 1860s; and it was the term by which he and a small group of M.P.s chose to be classified in *Dod's Parliamentary Companion* in the 1870s.[22] 'The most thorough Radical now in the House' was how he was described at the height of Gladstone's first Liberal government.[23] The relationship of the various types of Radicalism to what came to be known as Liberalism was complex and far from static. By the time of Fawcett's death in the mid-1880s it was common to regard Radicals as naturally forming a sub-section of the Liberal Party, though this was recognised as a recent development. A popular history of *The English Radicals* published in the 1890s, for example, traced the origins of Radical principles back to the early years of George III's reign and attributed a continuous existence to a distinctive Radical party from the 1820s to the

[20] *Life*, p. 182; see also Fawcett's early endorsement of Mill's *Considerations on Representative Government*, in 'Mr. Mill's Treatise On Representative Government', *Macmillan's Magazine*, vol. 4 (1861), pp. 97–103.

[21] Henry Fawcett, 'The House of Lords', *Fortnightly Review*, vol. 16 (o.s.), vol. 10 (n.s.) (1871), reprinted in Henry and Millicent Garrett Fawcett, *Essays and Lectures on Social and Political Subjects* (Cambridge and London, 1872), quotations at pp. 301, 317.

[22] Annan, *Leslie Stephen*, pp. 39–40; *Life*, pp. 189–95 and 203–14; John Vincent, *The Formation of the British Liberal Party 1857–1868* (London, 1966), pp. 65–8; Bryce, 'The late Mr. Fawcett', p. 457.

[23] Quoted in *Life*, p. 268.

1880s, by which point it had become indistinguishable from the Liberal Party itself.[24] It is important to remember that the notion of Liberal*ism* as a set of coherent political principles which found expression not only in the actions of the party formed at Willis's Rooms in 1859 but also in the reforming legislation of the 1830s and 1840s was itself essentially a retrospective creation, with its own polemical point, that only became current in the last three decades of the century. In the more fragmented political world of the 1850s, a world still very much dominated by Whig peers and Tory squires, Fawcett and his associates naturally and unhesitatingly classified themselves as 'Radicals'.

Fawcett's Radicalism was of a distinctively mid-nineteenth-century kind. It was not genuinely continuous with older and more popular notions of rights or of the protection, or restriction, of ancient liberties, nor did it embody any of those residues of the 'Country Party' ideology which lived on into early nineteenth-century Radicalism.[25] It was far more directly descended from the Philosophic Radicalism of the 1830s, though with a stronger emphasis upon self-help and with less tenderness for the centralising impulse in Benthamism; and it had much in common with the 'Manchester School's' fixation with what Cobden called 'the two plague-spots of aristocracy and landlordism'.[26] Crucially, it meant erecting hostility towards privilege to the status of a principle, and it was itself a mark of the Radical that his politics were explicitly based on principle, as opposed to the despised 'empiricism' – or, at best, the pious traditionalism – of the average county member. Fawcett's political career was shaped by his consistent antagonism to the aristocratic habits of privilege, patronage and corruption, an antagonism that always made his relations with the Whigs an uneasy one, and this alone ensured that he would be a fractious member of the Liberal party of the 1860s and 1870s. His relative indifference to religious sentiment further distanced him from large portions of that party; he was exasperated, for example, by what he dismissed as the 'miserable religious squabbles' over the Education Act.[27] His own sense of political identity was evident in his remark of 1871, where he sounds very like the elder Mill forty years earlier; 'Each day it is becoming more clearly proved that there is a far greater difference between Radicals and Whigs than between Whigs and Conservatives.'[28] To such an extent had Fawcett acted on this conviction in criticising

[24] C. Roylance Kent, *The English Radicals* (London, 1899), esp. pp. 7, 397; see also Leslie Stephen, 'The Good Old Cause', *Nineteenth Century*, vol. 51 (1902), pp. 11–23.
[25] For a recent discussion, with full references to the literature on these forms of Radicalism, see Gareth Stedman Jones, *Language of Class: Studies in English Working-Class History 1832–1982* (Cambridge, 1983), ch. 3.
[26] Quoted in Kent, *English Radicals*, p. 388.   [27] *Life*, p. 263.
[28] Fawcett, 'House of Lords ', in *Essays and Lectures*, p. 297.

Gladstone's ministry that by 1872, as Stephen recorded, the Whips 'ceased to send him the usual notices'.[29]

The corollary of Fawcett's principled aversion to privilege was an almost wilfully serene faith in the virtues of free competition. He had a very attenuated notion, at best, of the actual obstacles to the ideal working of the market, and a quite exaggerated sense of the capacity of individuals to control their own lives. As he remarked in opposing further state regulation of the hours of labour, 'if grown-up persons overwork themselves they do it of their own free-will',[30] and he used much the same sort of reasoning whether opposing any restriction on the drink trade or resisting any interference with the old Cambridge system of awarding Fellowships on the basis of success in the Tripos. The ideal of 'a fair field and no favour' elicited a very deep response in Fawcett, to which I shall return. He acknowledged that there continued to be real obstacles to the operation of this competitive principle in English life, the chief of which he, in common with Mill – and, for that matter, with Herbert Spencer and T. H. Green and Radicals of various hues – identified as 'landlordism' and the distorting effect of hereditary landed wealth and power. This analysis provided Individualism with a standing alibi – it meant, as Mill pointed out, that the principle of free competition had yet to be given a fair trial[31] – and it was the nearest Fawcett came to underpinning his politics with anything like an interpretation of history.[32] At the other end of the scale, he also found the institution of the Poor Law a derogation from the principles of strict Individualism. Like several other Radicals of this type, he regarded the principle on which the Poor Law rested to be essentially 'Socialistic': after all, it provided non-contributory benefits to those in need at the community's expense, and thus could not be justified in the same way as the state action involved in maintaining law and order or even sanitation.[33] This being so, the 'less eligibility' test and associated conditions imposed by the 1834 Poor Law seemed, if stringently enforced, to be the best means of limiting the damage such an institution might do, where the damage was seen primarily in terms of the 'moral injury' done to the habits of the class to which those in receipt of doles belonged. It is important to remember that the pre-1834 system of outdoor relief was

[29] *Life*, p. 275.
[30] Fawcett, 'The general aspect of state intervention' (1872), in *Essays and Lectures*, p. 36.
[31] John Stuart Mill, *Principles of Political Economy with Some of Their Applications to Social Philosophy* (1848), in *Collected Works of John Stuart Mill*, vol. 2, p. 207.
[32] This, admittedly pretty exiguous, historical account is sketched in the opening chapter of *The Economic Position of the British Labourer*.
[33] Fawcett, 'Modern Socialism' (1872), in *Essays and Lectures*, p. 25. For a more analytical exposition of the 'Socialistic' principle of the Poor Law see Henry Sidgwick, *The Elements of Politics* (London, 1891), pp. 156–9; and the discussion in Collini, *Liberalism and Sociology*, pp. 21, 107–8.

still fresh in the memory, and also that political economy had provided an interpretation, well established by the time Fawcett was writing, of how that system had nearly brought the country to economic ruin. This interpretation of the effect of the so-called 'Speenhamland system', and the tendentious explanation of the economic troubles of post-Waterloo England which it embodied, formed what might be called one of the crucial 'foundation myths' of Victorian Individualism, just as the coincidence of free trade and prosperity enabled a similar moral to be drawn from a celebratory account of the repeal of the Corn Laws and other pieces of economically liberalising legislation.

That Fawcett's politics drew heavily on the theorems of classical political economy hardly requires emphasis: his credentials as a 'scientific radical' depended upon this fact. By the 1850s and 1860s this association no longer excited the almost axiomatic working-class hostility of earlier decades, and among the developments that made this, and hence Fawcett's career as representative for popular constituencies, possible was what might be called the 'moralising of political economy'. It is certainly true that the reproachful contrast between the amoral, 'heartless' and even 'selfish' teachings of political economy and the dictates of humanity and morality never altogether disappeared – presumably something of the sort we shall have always with us – but in the fifty years after Waterloo there was a subtle change both in the moral tone of political economy itself and in its cultural standing. The morally educative effect of the discipline imposed by economic activity, for instance, bulked larger in the work of Fawcett's generation of economists, and perhaps in the characteristic preoccupations of their readers, than it had in that of, say, Ricardo and his contemporaries. The widely remarked improvement in political economy's reputation after the success of Mill's morally sensitive and socially conciliatory *Principles* also marked a significant expansion of the subject's political acceptability.[34] It is true that we can find a not dissimilar tone in some earlier writers, notably the evangelical political economists of the 1810s and 1820s, but in the later period this tone is independent of any sectarian beliefs about the operation of the Divine sanction and the rewards of the after-life.[35] Where the evangelicals had been primarily concerned about the way economic disasters revealed the workings of Providence, mid-Victorian economists tended to concentrate on the human moral failings manifested in improvidence. Though some may see only the cloven hoof of that protean creature 'bourgeois ideology'

[34] On this, see de Marchi, 'Success of Mill's *Principles*'.
[35] For an account of evangelical political economy, see Boyd Hilton, *Corn, Cash and Commerce. The Economic Policies of the Tory Governments 1815–1830* (Oxford, 1977), esp. 'Conclusion'; and idem, 'Peel: a re-assessment', *Historical Journal*, vol. 22 (1979), pp. 585–614.

in Fawcett's concern with maintaining the 'moral standard' of the
labouring class and with the danger of 'moral injury' in indiscriminate
charity, there was a consistent and widely shared picture of life as the
unremitting exercise of will embodied in these considerations, and these
in turn were inextricably interwoven with the fabric of his economic
writings.[36] When Fawcett was summarising his view of the limits of
state action, he declared that 'any scheme, however well-intentioned it
may be, will indefinitely increase every evil it seeks to alleviate if it
lessens individual responsibility by encouraging the people to rely less
upon themselves and more upon the state':[37] it would be hard to
disentangle the purely economic arguments in the pages that led up to
this declaration from those more general, and arguably more influential,
moral assumptions which he shared with the kind of audience his
writings were intended to reach. Or again, when Stephen spoke, as he
did more than once in his chapter on Fawcett's political economy, of
the 'nobler' aspects of the policy of non-intervention, he was using a
term – a very important term in the Victorian literature of 'enthusiasm'
– which his readers would not have found incongruous in such a
context.[38]

Here, then, we are approaching that pre-or sub-political level of moral
and aesthetic sensibilities which informed the kind of political attitudes
Fawcett represented. Let me address this topic indirectly in the first
instance, by way of a contrast between two stereotypes. There is a familiar
dichotomy in Victorian thought and sensibility between, on the one hand,
the temper of rational science, leaning to Positivism, receptive to Utilitarianism and political economy, and most commonly issuing in some
kind of Liberal or reforming politics; and, on the other hand, the temper of
essentially Romantic cultural critique, uneasy with modernity, suspicious
of the reductive tendencies of science, hostile to the soulless reasonings of
political economy, a temper whose political expression, where not
straightforwardly Tory, veered, by an intelligible affinity, from a
Carlylean authoritarianism to a Ruskinian or Morrisian socialism. The
simplicity of this picture is not, at first sight, particularly threatened when
we move on to consider the cult of 'manliness'. This term denoted a widely
esteemed Victorian quality, of course, not one that was the exclusive
property of any single sect. But in general terms its cultural affinities
would seem to have been with the second of my contrasting tempers,
where one also finds several of its most influential original sources such as

---

[36] For these phrases, see *Life*, pp. 154, 161.   [37] Fawcett, *Manual*, p. 310.
[38] E.g. *Life*, pp. 162, 173; for 'enthusiasm' see Walter Houghton, *The Victorian Frame of Mind 1830–1870* (New Haven, Conn., and London, 1957), pp. 263–304.

Coleridge, Carlyle, and the elder Arnold.[39] The list of virtues given in the
O.E.D. definition of manliness indicates well enough its core meaning:
'courageous, independent in spirit, frank, upright'. Its opposite was held
to be, in an interesting progression, 'childlike', 'effeminate', 'sentimental'.
The pejorative sense of 'sentimental' ('addicted to indulgence in super-
ficial emotion; apt to be swayed by sentiment') is, in fact, a nineteenth-
century usage – the eighteenth century had known a more favourable
sense – and manliness expressed a deep, possibly in some cases a
revealingly pathological, aversion to this trait.

Appropriately, the illustrative quotation appended to this sense of the
word is Carlyle's inclusive denunciation of 'that rosepink vapour of
Sentimentalism, Philanthropy, and Feasts of Morals', and it was Carlyle
above all who put into circulation a particular conception of manliness as
part of a larger vision of the place of bracing conflict and stoically borne
suffering in a power-governed universe. As the reference to 'Philanthropy'
also suggests, the political bearing of this vision involved a stern antipathy
to well-meant schemes of social reform and other expressions of the
humanitarian impulse, which he pilloried in his satires on the 'Universal
Abolition of Pain Association'. This impatience with the delicate scruples
and tender consciences of the liberal humanitarians (led, in this instance,
by Mill) found classic expression in the confrontation over the Governor
Eyre case, where Carlyle and several others prominently associated with
the ethos of manliness, such as Charles Kingsley, lined up to support a
man who had bravely done his duty, and they implied that it was not
obviously to be regretted that the execution of that duty had involved the
spilling of blood and the assertion of a masterful white man's will over a
mob of riotous Negroes.[40]

The mention of Kingsley should alert us to the fact that manliness could
take many forms, and also that we are not so far from Leslie Stephen as my
concentration on Carlylean anti-liberalism might at first suggest. For, the
term 'muscular Christianity', which designated the variant of manliness
particularly associated with Kingsley, had in fact been freely applied to the
Reverend Leslie Stephen in his days as a long-striding and strong-mouthed
athlete and rowing coach; indeed, it is alleged that Stephen ought to be
recognised alongside Kingsley as the founder of muscular Christianity.[41]
Certainly, at this stage of his life he incarnated the tenets of the creed: 'the

---

[39] For brief discussions of manliness, see Houghton, *Victorian Frame of Mind*, ch. 9, and
   David Newsome, *Godliness and Good Learning. Four Studies on a Victorian Ideal*
   (London, 1961), ch. 4; and esp. pp. 196–7, for the, possibly surprising, inclusion of
   Coleridge in the list.
[40] See Bernard Semmel, *The Governor Eyre Controversy* (London, 1962).
[41] Annan, *Leslie Stephen*, p. 29; for a contemporary application of the term to Stephen, see
   Maitland, *Life of Leslie Stephen*, p. 77.

duty of patriotism; the moral and physical beauty of athleticism; the salutary effects of Spartan habits and discipline; the cultivation of all that is masculine and the expulsion of all that is effeminate, un-English, and excessively intellectual'.[42] Though Stephen outgrew his always partially assumed identity as a 'rowing rough', the underlying sensibility, and much of the language, of this form of manliness was characteristic of him for the rest of his life. He was being only half ironic when he wrote that he was 'much inclined to measure a man's moral excellence by his love of walking'.[43] He made this remark in speaking of Fawcett, and this recalls the slightly puzzled observation of a subsequent biographer, which I cited earlier, that 'they seem to have shared little but their earlier politics and their love of walking'. Not only were these, for both Stephen and Fawcett, no insignificant matters to share, but, I now want to suggest, there was a more than contingent connection between them.

If this is so, however, it generates a minor paradox, or at least calls for a modification of my earlier contrast of tempers. For, Stephen and Fawcett were not only undeniably Radicals and emphatically of the 'humanitarian' party on such test issues as the American Civil War or the Eyre case; but they were also keen devotees of political economy, sympathetic to Utilitarianism, eager to apply the methods of science. They seem, in other words, to be on the wrong side. This is, of course, partly an illusion created by the starkness of my initial dichotomy and by the too-exclusive association of manliness with the second of my stereotypes. Still, the recognition that in Stephen and Fawcett this sensibility was congruent with, or even partially explanatory of, their politics is in itself a worthwhile modification of the familiar contrast, and may point towards a conclusion of more general interest. For, insofar as Stephen and Fawcett are representative of one important strand in mid-Victorian Liberalism, it may indicate that the temper of that Liberalism had more in common with that of some of its best-known contemporary critics than the later Liberal myth would suggest, or even, perhaps, than it did with that of later Liberalism itself. If the cardinal values of the mid-Victorian Liberal intelligentsia turn out to have more to do with stoicism and strenuousness than with liberty or utility, it would then hardly be surprising if those of them who lived on into the rather different moral world of the early twentieth century were to find what then passed for Liberalism pretty alien, despite some much-touted theoretical continuities.

When we look more closely at Stephen's evocative description of the frame of mind that he and Fawcett and their Cambridge circle shared, we

---

[42] This list of the constitutive qualities of 'muscular Christianity' is given in Newsome, *Godliness*, p.216.
[43] *Life*, p. 57.

find running through it a constant stylistic contrast between the cluster of terms centred on 'manly' and 'masculine' and that centred on 'senti-mental'. There are fashions in these as in other matters, and Fawcett's set affected a stern contempt for 'gushing' or the expression of 'high-flown' feelings. Stephen recognised that they may have cultivated this to excess, but he was unwilling to disown their youthful tastes altogether:

> The kind of stoical severity which was our pet virtue at Cambridge, the intense dislike to any needless revelations of feeling, had certainly its good side. It was at worst an exaggeration of a creditable and masculine instinct. We preferred to mask our impulses under a guise of cynicism rather than to affect more sensibility than we really possessed.

'I for one', he added with appropriate gruffness, 'should be sorry to see the opposite practice come into fashion.'[44] In addition to the obvious contrast between sincerity and affectation, the superiority of 'downright straight-forwardness' over either aristocratic hauteur or intellectual finesse also came into play here (interestingly, imported French words are needed to designate the rejected qualities). One begins to wonder whether Stephen ever met anyone who was not a 'downright, straightforward, manly fellow', so frequent is this description in his recollections. Indeed, in his *Life of Fawcett* alone he uses the terms 'manly' and 'masculine' fifteen times before the narrative reaches 1865 (and my patience ran out). In several instances he is using the term in the expected way to characterise Fawcett, praising his spirit of 'manly independence' or his 'masculine courage'. But on other occasions he is referring to institutions or practices. For example, when explaining Fawcett's defence of the prize Fellowship system at Cambridge against proposals for the 'endowment of research', he commented: 'The "endowment of research" is a pretty phrase, but it may cover much that was condemned by the old narrow but masculine school to which Fawcett belonged.' He amplified the point by describing the danger that 'instead of the old strenuous competition, the students would be encouraged to listen to professors spinning fine phrases and creating sham sciences to justify the existence of their chairs'.[45] That the competition should be 'strenuous' is clearly the chief positive ingredient in this judgement, and is the clue to why an attitude to educational arrangements might be characterised in terms of the ostensibly incon-gruous male/female dichotomy. The same responses are at work when Stephen describes the dominant intellectual style of the place as favouring 'a masculine but limited type of understanding', and as providing 'a most

[44] ibid., p. 37; a similar account is given in *Some Early Impressions*, pp. 71–6.
[45] *Life*, pp. 114–15. And note the positive qualities associated with this: 'A prize openly offered and fairly won has certain definite and intelligible merits.'

strenuous and masculine training'.[46] The range is extended at later points
in the book when a particular course of political action is described as the
'plainer or more manly course', when a style of argument is referred to as
'manly and outspoken criticism', and so on.[47] In other words, terms that
are literally descriptive of human qualities are constantly being applied to
subjects apparently far removed from their literal sense. What is at work
here is surely something like what literary critics are identifying when they
investigate 'image-clusters', that is, the repetition signals the presence of a
set of responses which are activated by some, possibly only subliminal,
association between the human qualities and certain congenial properties
of the ideas or policies or whatever that are under discussion. In the strong
version of this kind of analysis, the very congeniality of the latter
properties may be dependent upon the prior work of association.

The In Stephen's case, the contexts in which the contrasting pejorative term
'sentimental' occurs reveal the same patterns of association. For example,
when he is seeking to explain the appeal of Mill's work to their circle, it is
not strictly the theoretical content of the treatises he cites, but something
more like a style of reasoning: the *Logic* and *Political Economy* 'possessed
the merits which we most admired – good downright hard logic, with a
minimum of sentimentalism'. Or again: 'We held . . . that Ruskin, when he
attacked Mill, was a sentimentalist, who could neither look facts in the
face nor reason coherently.'[48] The suggestion, of course, is that the 'facts'
might not be pleasant; all the more reason why the intellectual equivalent
of 'funk' has to be severely repudiated. By contrast, political economy
gratified this taste for uncluttered reasoning and unsentimental description. Science did not flinch. The same associations are evident in his and
Fawcett's political attitudes. Stephen described the 'kindly philanthropists' who advocated the relaxation of the conditions of the Poor Law as
'sentimentalists': they were indulging their immediate feelings of pity or
guilt at the expense of 'facing' the facts. Those whose hostility to the
concerns of political economy Fawcett anticipates in the Introduction to
his *Manual* he refers to as 'sentimental moralists', and so on.[49]

The ideal of 'fair competition' excited a similar set of associations for
both Stephen and Fawcett. When Stephen wrote of his friend that 'a
spontaneous and intense hatred of everything unfair showed itself in all
his most active impulses', his mind immediately associated this key value
of individualism with manliness: 'Fairness of this kind is a fine quality,
and is common to many virile athletes of Fawcett's stamp.'[50] When

---

46 ibid., p. 90.   47 ibid., pp. 172, 291.   48 *Some Early Impressions*, pp. 73, 84.
49 *Life*, p. 153; Fawcett, *Manual*, p. 7.
50 Leslie Stephen, 'Henry Fawcett. In Memoriam', *Macmillan's Magazine*, vol. 51 (1884),
   p. 131; see *Life*, p. 180.

Fawcett had attacked primogeniture, a traditional Radical target to be sure, it was its 'unfairness' that particularly roused him: 'Every feeling in our nature is opposed to it.'[51] In fact, the very notion of struggle and effort in itself had an invigorating suggestive power for Fawcett, and his zealous propagation of the gospel of self-help involved projecting an ideal charged with these associations onto the economic activity of the working classes. Energy was the prerequisite and the expression of the manly life, and the constant refrain of his political recommendations is the need to 'call out the energy of all classes'. As Stephen paraphrased Fawcett's non-intervention principle: 'It meant ... be exceedingly jealous of all restrictions upon the energies of any class, especially of the poorest class', and the test of all proposed measures was whether they were 'calculated to stimulate the energies of the persons affected'.[52] The association between the 'enervating' effect of dependence and the 'invigorating' impact of self-reliance is a constant feature of Fawcett's writing, as deep an expression of his temperament as Kingsley's refrain about 'healthiness' and 'sickliness' was of his. When Fawcett wrote that the aim should be to 'replace the depressing misery of dependence by the buoyant activity which comes from self-reliance and from the consciousness of the power to earn one's own living', he might well have been referring to policies to encourage working-class thrift; in fact he was speaking of the best way to help the blind.[53] After he was blinded, 'there was only one thing, he told his sister, which he dreaded – namely, a loss of energy'.[54]

The full dimensions of this sensibility and its political implications obviously cannot be explored here, but let me make just one further point that is particularly relevant given my earlier remarks about the ambivalence with which Mill was regarded even by many of his ostensible disciplines. I think it is arguable that this sensibility, though it initially led them to find the style of reasoning of Mill's treatises attractive, was not in fact something they shared with Mill himself, and in Stephen's case it surely contributed to his growing impatience with a figure whose personal qualities were in some respects so far from 'manly'. Looking back on the culture of athleticism which he had so enthusiastically fostered when a young don, Stephen conceded that it was not without its limitations, but even in 1903 he could not resist adding: 'Interest in such pursuits is, at any rate, antagonistic to the intel-

[51] Fawcett, *Economic Position of the British Labourer*, pp. 9–11.   [52] *Life*, pp. 162–3.
[53] Speech of 18 March 1884, quoted in *Life*, p. 171.
[54] *Life*, pp. 54–5. For an interesting contemporary discussion of energy as the essential foundation of 'character', see Alexander Bain, *The Study of Character* (London, 1861), esp. ch. 7.

lectual vice of priggishness.'[55] His aversion to priggishness was deep and
abiding, and it is clear that he increasingly associated Mill with this
quality, though at first he only suggested the identification indirectly. In
scorning Hare's scheme in the early 1870s, for example, he referred
directly to Mill's contention that it would lead to the selection of a better
class of representatives, and then noted: 'A cynic would say that the
scheme would probably result in selecting half a dozen prigs and twice as
many slaves of a crotchet.'[56] The 'cynic' was one of Stephen's favourite
defensive aliases: his own characteristic snort is plainly audible in this
judgement. By the time he wrote his study of Mill for his book on the
English Utilitarians, he could make the identification more openly.
Brooding on what he saw as a contrast between Mill's own character and
the ideal held up in On Liberty, he concluded: 'At the bottom of his heart
he seems to prefer a prig, a man of rigid formulae, to the vivid and
emotional character whose merits he recognises in theory.' Having
frequently remarked – he was far from alone in doing this – the
prominence in Mill of 'feminine qualities', he could now drive home the
negative charge: what, in the end, was wrong with the Saint of Rationalism was that he lacked 'masculine fibre'.[57]

That, at least, was one charge against which he did not have to defend
Fawcett. Rather to the contrary, he was aware that the style of his friend's
rigorous adherence to his Individualist principles invited the accusation
that such hard-headedness was indistinguishable from hard-heartedness,
and in the Life he is consequently at pains to bring out Fawcett's warmth
and generosity of feeling, and the strength and genuineness of his concern
for the welfare of the working classes. Though Stephen could no longer
muster the same enthusiasm as Fawcett for the full hand of their earlier
political convictions, he remained resistant to the new Collectivist fashions
of the 1880s and 1890s. For him they represented the old sentimentalism
in new guise. Even in the 1890s he was still upholding the merits of 'the
good old orthodox system of Political Economy', and insisting that

the essential condition of all social improvement is not that we should have this or
that system of regulations, but that the individual should be manly, self-respecting,
doing his duty as well as getting his pay, and deeply convinced that nothing will do
any permanent good which does not imply the elevation of the individual in his
standards of honesty, independence and good conduct.[58]

55 Some Early Impressions, p. 48; Stephen's definition of 'philistine' (another of his assumed
   identities) was 'a name … which a prig bestows on the rest of the species'; for Stephen's
   enduring hostility to priggishness see Annan, Leslie Stephen, pp. 39, 142.
56 Stephen, 'Value of political machinery', p. 850.
57 Stephen, English Utilitarians, vol. 3, pp. 70, 72.
58 Leslie Stephen, 'The sphere of political economy' and 'Social equality', both in Social
   Rights and Duties (2 vols., London, 1896), vol. 1, pp. 131–2, 219.

Modern Radicalism seemed devoid of the old 'masculine' virtues, and 'the contrast is painful to many who recall the ideals of their youth'.[59] Perhaps Stephen was not altogether displeased to have the opportunity offered in writing the life of Fawcett to display those ideals in an attractive light.

And here I return to my starting-point. Fawcett himself embodied the very virtues of character which his political creed had elevated as its ideal and which the measures he supported had always been designed to foster. One of the chief means of diffusing this ideal and rendering it with the vividness necessary to inspire emulation was, of course, the exemplary biography. Such biographies constituted the devotional literature of Individualism. Stephen was expressing a professional as well as a personal credo when he wrote in the *Life* of his brother Fitzjames: 'The impression made upon his contemporaries by a man of strong and noble character is something which cannot be precisely estimated, but which we often feel to be invaluable. The best justification of biography in general is that it may strengthen and diffuse that impression.'[60] And in the conclusion to the *Life of Fawcett* he made this educative purpose explicit when he referred to 'the living influence still exercised upon the hearts of his contemporaries by a character equally remarkable for masculine independence and generous sympathy', and he concluded with the suitably hortatory flourish: 'My sole aim has been to do something towards enabling my readers to bring that influence to bear upon themselves.'[61]

[59] Stephen, 'Good old cause', p. 11.
[60] Stephen, *The Life of Sir James Fitzjames Stephen* (London, 1895), p. 481.
[61] *Life*, p. 468.

🔲🔲🔲🔲🔲🔲🔲🔲🔲🔲🔲🔲🔲🔲🔲🔲🔲🔲🔲🔲🔲🔲🔲🔲🔲🔲🔲🔲🔲🔲🔲🔲🔲

2

Manliness, masculinity and the mid-Victorian temperament

BOYD HILTON

It may be as well to start by expressing complete agreement with Dr Collini's four main premises: (1) that Fawcett was an exemplar of a type or stage of nineteenth-century Liberalism; (2) that this type of Liberalism, which was peculiar to the 1850s and 1860s and thus distinguishable both from 'classical Liberalism' and 'new Liberalism', has to be defined not as a set of formal ideas but as a new temperament and a new range of moral and aesthetic sensibilities; (3) that in order to understand it, therefore, we need much more probing analytical categories than can be derived from a simple model counterposing utilitarianism and interventionist collectivism; and (4) that 'manliness' is a useful concept for investigating that mid-Victorian temper. It is the fourth proposition which this brief comment will attempt to elaborate.

Dr Collini points out that, although the conciliatory political economy of the mid-Victorians such as Mill and Fawcett contains much that is similar in tone to that of Thomas Chalmers, John Bird Sumner, and other evangelical economists of the 1810s and 1820s, their adoption of this tone no longer signified the possession of any beliefs about the operation of divine sanctions and the rewards of the after-life. It follows that, whereas evangelicals had mainly been concerned with the way in which economic disasters, both public and private, had revealed the workings of a transcendent providence, mid-Victorian economists tended to concentrate on the moral failings manifested in human *im*providence. This distinction is well made, but it may be worthwhile exploring the relationship between religious and economic ideas further if we are to understand fully the various shades of meaning that attached to the mid-Victorian notion of 'manliness'.

If the classical liberal economists of the earlier nineteenth century inhabited the same mental world as the evangelicals, with their retributive approach to the economy and belief that free trade and laissez-faire policies would reveal a providentially designed moral machinery,[1] then it may be thought that their political economy represented a secular version of the same ideals. For example, that thoroughly unevangelical free trader, Richard Cobden, imbibed a secularised version of the evangelical model from his friend George Combe, the celebrated phrenologist. Combe no more believed in original sin than Cobden did, but he did believe that mankind is mischievous and that one could identify particular types of mischief from the bumps on people's heads. For him the essence of free trade and laissez-faire was that by observing how certain actions turn out in the market place of human relationships – bad actions for the worst, good actions for the best – men would begin to discern their own failings without having to have their bumps examined. Then, by learning to moderate those failings, they would be gradually socialised, or, in the jargon of the day, would learn to live in harmony with the moral laws of the universe.[2] Again, Benthamite utilitarianism, which alongside evangelicalism is the obvious point of entry into the mind of the earlier nineteenth century's liberal individual or 'economic man', postulated not that men are born with original sin but that they are born dissocial, and the point of placing them down in the middle of a moral machinery under the sway of rewards and punishments was that men would be led, if not to grace, at least to the social graces, to some form of socialisation enabling them to live in harmony with others. In utilitarian thought the rewards and punishments were to be meted out by temporal governments whereas in evangelical thought they came from the governor of the universe, but in both cases society was conceived in static terms as a sort of judicial machine.

'Rewards and punishments': except that in the pessimistic first half of the nineteenth century, bedevilled by fears of war, class war, famine, and cholera, very much greater emphasis was placed on punishment than on reward. Gradually this emphasis began to change in the course of the more optimistic 1850s and 1860s. The governor of the universe was now thought to care about the material condition of his creation, and temporal governments became more concerned with preventing than with punishing social evils. In the same way, doing useful work in the world came to seem more important than merely agonising over lost souls. As a protagonist of the new attitudes, Benjamin Jowett, put it to Florence

---

[1] B. Hilton, 'Chalmers as political economist', in A. C. Cheyne (ed.), *The Practical and the Pious. Essays on Thomas Chalmers (1780–1847)*, (Edinburgh, 1985), pp. 141–56. Since the conference on Fawcett I have discussed these points further in B. Hilton, *The Age of Atonement. The Influence of Evangelicalism on Social and Economic Thought 1795–1865* (Oxford, 1988), pp. 73–162.

[2] R. Cooter, *The Cultural Meaning of Popular Science. Phrenology and the Organization of Consent in Nineteenth-Century Britain* (Cambridge, 1984), pp. 132–3.

Nightingale in 1862, 'it is a religious act to clean out a gutter and to
prevent cholera, and ... it is not a religious act to pray (in the sense of
asking)'.[3] A small but telling illustration of this shift from punishment to
prevention is the limited liability legislation of 1856, which ended the
retributive approach to capital investment by sheltering 'economic man'
to some extent from the danger of recurrent financial disaster, and thereby
dissociating bankruptcy from the stigma of supreme economic wickedness.[4] The doyen of limited liability legislation was the liberal-radical,
Robert Lowe. Dr Collini's remarks about Fawcett as a radical, particularly his belief in meritocracy and desire to make the world a fair field
of competition, could be applied with equal force to Lowe. Lowe certainly
admired Fawcett's *Manual of Political Economy* greatly, and the two
seem to have been fairly close until 1866. In that year Lowe offended the
radicals over reform, and henceforward he and Fawcett usually found
themselves on opposite sides of questions, as did Lowe and Mill, but until
then Lowe largely resembled the picture which Dr Collini had drawn of
Fawcett. Now, in the course of introducing limited liability, Lowe
remarked on the need for legislation to be based 'upon some presumption
of confidence ... Fraud and wickedness are not to be presumed in
individuals', and one should assume that people are good until they have
been proved bad.[5] This was a self-conscious declaration against the old
retributive system of political economy, which had indeed assumed the
worst about 'economic man' just as evangelical theologians had assumed
the worst about man in general, and it marks Lowe as belonging to that
optimistic, mid-Victorian type or stage of Liberalism which Dr Collini has
alluded to. It was a type of Liberalism which did not actually change the
rules very much (beyond allowing workers and capitalists to associate)
and so was not 'new Liberalism', but although it held to the wages fund it
nevertheless incorporated a vision of social advancement, amelioration
and progress. It was above all a new tone for the more optimistic times, a
shift from a 'dismal science' that was dissocial to a 'social science' that
was uplifting. Dr Collini cites a penetrating piece of analysis in
W. E. Houghton's *The Victorian Frame of Mind* where the ethos of
enthusiasm is contrasted with that of earnestness, these being alternative
modes for encouraging citizens to behave altruistically. Earnest fellows
stressed the duty to subdue one's baser self; enthusiasts sought to give men
nobler causes outside themselves to be excited about, so that selfish
passions might be swept aside in a flurry of philanthropic devotion.

[3] B. Jowett to F. Nightingale, 16 July 1862, *Dear Miss Nightingale. A Selection of Benjamin Jowett's Letters to Florence Nightingale 1860–1893*, ed. Vincent Quinn and John Prest (Oxford, 1987), p. 18.
[4] Hilton, *Atonement*, pp. 255–70.
[5] Lowe in House of Commons, 1 Feb. 1856, *Parliamentary Debates*, 3rd ser. 111, col. 124.

Though the two modes were not mutually exclusive (unless pushed to extremes), it is usually possible to place the Victorian sages in one camp or the other, and Houghton places Mill firmly among the enthusiasts.[6] Clearly that is where Stephen belongs, and Fawcett too. And though Stephen and Fawcett were not religious men, it might be possible to illuminate the moral and philosophical basis of their particular type of Liberalism, and to understand better what 'manliness' signified for them, by looking at the religious equivalent of optimistic enthusiasm, that is the liberal theology of Benjamin Jowett, that maker of manly Oxonians, and F. D. Maurice. Here there will only be time to look briefly at two exponents of this liberal theology: Fawcett's near contemporary at Cambridge, Frederic William Farrar, and an Oxonian celebrant of 'muscularity' and 'manliness', Thomas Hughes. As authors of the two most celebrated public school stories of the nineteenth century, Farrar and Hughes are especially relevant to a discussion of the Victorian ideal of manliness.

Farrar was brought up in a narrow evangelical way, then 'liberated' by the teaching of F. D. Maurice and E. H. Plumptre at King's College, London (1847–50), before going up to Trinity College, Cambridge, where he became an Apostle. Both at school and university he had the reputation of being a likeable sort of swot, oozing 'purity and unselfish gentleness' of the sort that he paraded in *Eric; or, Little by Little*, his famous school story of 1858. (Its title reflects a mid-nineteenth-century belief in the necessary gradualness of moral and spiritual progress, which was quite different from the expectations of catastrophe and the reliance on sudden conversions so prevalent in the more 'evangelical' first half of the century.) A contemporary wrote that Farrar appealed to 'a pure and exalted personal morality for all, not of the mere negative kind, but a very active one, and the imaginative literature illustrating such aspirations, – the *literae humaniores* in short. He delighted in "the cloud of witnesses".'[7] As an assistant master at Marlborough and Harrow (1845–71), Farrar stunned his rough and idle lower fifth forms by his disinclination for the rule of law as 'the only incentive and the sole civiliser'. He introduced 'a new idea of life, and the conviction that we were made for something better and higher than to be caned and cuffed'. Jam and cake, a little pathos and much genial chaff were his weapons, a manly lachrymosity which some claimed touched, via *Eric* and *St Winifred's*, the 'deeper emotions' and 'inner chord ... of boy life' in a way that 'no other writer has ever equalled'.[8] It is entirely typical that he should have regarded the

[6] W. E. Houghton, *The Victorian Frame of Mind 1830–1870* (New Haven, Conn., and London, 1957), pp. 263–5.
[7] *The Life of Frederic William Farrar, Sometime Dean of Canterbury*, by Reginald Farrar (1904; new and revised edn, 1905), pp. 23–6, 46–51.
[8] ibid., pp. 56–9, 81–2, 178.

parable of the Prodigal Son, with its emphasis on forgiveness, as 'the Epitome of the Gospel'.[9] That alone was enough to mark him apart from the thought of the first half of the century, when the most popular parables had been 'capitalist' ones like the Talents and the Unjust Steward, and when those of the Prodigal Son and the Good Samaritan had not been much regarded. In this way Farrar represented a distinctly 'liberal' phase of pedagoguery between Thomas Arnold and the Edwardian imperialists, a headmaster who at Marlborough (1871–6) 'made up for want of firmness by excess of kindness'.

Farrar was also an important influence on popular religious attitudes. After about 1860 there was a vogue for biographies of Christ,[10] as emphasis came to be placed on his ethical message, his exhortation to lead not only holy but socially useful lives, rather than on his role in a scheme of salvation. Farrar's *The Life of Christ* (1874) was the most successful of all essays in this genre. It went through more than thirty editions and sold over 100,000 copies before 1914, and helped gain its author a Canonry of Westminster in 1876. But two years later his published sermons *Eternal Hope* (1878), though reaching an equally wide audience – it sold through the first edition in three weeks and the eighteenth appeared in 1901 – aroused a storm of controversy among more conservative churchmen because of its Mauricean message 'that the expressions which have been interpreted to mean physical and material agonies by worm and flame are metaphors for a state of remorse and alienation from God'.[11] *Eternal Hope* clearly played an important part in the Anglican retreat from a literal belief in Hell-fire and retributive justice and the adoption of a more optimistic and gentle version of Christianity. It may have cost its author further preferment in the church but, as his son pointed out, in taking liberal theology down to the populace, Farrar helped to release thousands of his contemporaries 'from the gloom and terrors of a fetich worship [*sic*]'.[12]

Farrar despised heartiness and was no athlete, but he *would* have laid claim to the epithet 'manly'. And this calls in question Dr Collini's interpretation of 'manly' as having the primary meaning of 'masculine', 'uneffeminate', 'non-feminine', 'unsentimental'. Clearly these meanings did attach to the word: Fawcett's addiction to riding and skating and Stephen's love of rowing and mountaineering certainly did reflect a masculine self-image. It was, moreover, Stephen who wrote that 'no man ought to be effeminate, i.e. to let his feelings get the better of his intellect

---

[9] F. W. Farrar in *The Atonement: A Clerical Symposium*, ed. F. Hastings (1883), p. 67.
[10] D. L. Pals, *The Victorian 'Lives' of Jesus* (San Antonio, Texas, 1982), p. 3 and *passim*.
[11] F. W. Farrar, *Eternal Hope: Five Sermons* (1878), pp. xl–lvi, 49–89.
[12] *Farrar*, pp. 274–8.

and produce a cowardly view of life and the world'.[13] However, 'manly' also has another core meaning, which is 'unbeastly', 'non-animal', 'mannish' in the sense of not being 'boyish' (hence the phrase 'precocious manliness' cited below), someone who performs her or his duty and who has learned to control the baser animal passions. In this way 'manly' could come to signify 'humane'. Now in his interesting and highly perceptive discussion Dr Collini tends at points to slide backwards and forwards between 'manly' and 'masculine' as though these were the obvious and only synonyms. But it may be worth pointing out that of the many citations he lists from Stephen's *Life of Fawcett*, 'manly' is always used as a term of unqualified praise whereas 'masculinity' is invariably qualified, as in 'the narrow but masculine school' and 'a masculine but limited type of understanding'. Perhaps there is more daylight between the two terms than Dr Collini allows.

Dr Collini cites the considerable authority of David Newsome in deriving the term 'manly' from a Romantic and anti-utilitarian tradition pioneered by Coleridge, Carlyle and Thomas Arnold, and comments that the inclusion of Coleridge in this tradition is 'possibly surprising'.[14] Coleridge was certainly not a masculine type, but if we approach the term 'manly' from the point of view of the humanity propounded by liberal theologians, then Coleridge's manful protests against the evangelical simplicities of his own day give him a better entitlement than either Carlyle or Arnold to the epithet. The latter, though they were at odds with the evangelicals, were very much children of an evangelical generation, and their thought was therefore steeped in notions of retributive justice and, in Arnold's case, of the natural beastliness of boys. For Arnold the term 'manly' would not have carried any humanistic overtones, and to regard him as a progenitor of 'manliness' is to mistake the real Arnold for the caricature in Thomas Hughes's *Tom Brown's Schooldays*. Dr Newsome is well aware that the real and the fictional Dr Arnolds are quite different, that the real Arnold belonged to the earlier 'evangelical' generation while the headmaster of Thomas Hughes's *Tom Brown's Schooldays* propounds mid-Victorian values, but in one respect Newsome's analysis is misleading. He claims (rightly) that 'by the 1870s the pursuit of manliness had become something of a cult', but (wrongly) that 'for schoolboys, Tom Brown had become the model of boyish excellence. Farrar's saintly heroes could not compete with him for popularity.' Farrar's Eric, it seems, is to be regarded as an earlier (almost evangelical!) archetype, a standard and didactic homily of repentance for the sins of the

---

[13] Noel Annan, *Leslie Stephen. The Godless Victorian* (London, 1984), p. 304.
[14] D. Newsome, *Godliness and Good Learning. Four Studies on a Victorian Ideal* (London, 1961), pp. 196–7.

flesh.[15] Yet most high-minded middle-class people in the 1850s and 1860s, if they had been asked to nominate a 'manly' schoolboy, would have cited not Tom Brown but Eric; or, if they had cited Tom Brown, it would not have been the plucky lad who was frequently getting into scrapes and frequently being flogged, but rather Tom Brown after he had been converted to 'manliness' and maturity by the saintly – and also weakly and effeminate – George Arthur. Farrar's squeamishness over corporal punishment is relevant here. He would have agreed with C. J. Vaughan, another schoolmaster from the same Cambridge generation, who opined that beating was 'inconsistent with modern notions of personal dignity and modern habits of precocious manliness'.[16] In this way liberal 'manliness' was sharply opposed to the animality that had previously been supposed to lie at the root of human nature. Thomas Arnold had certainly believed in natural beastliness and had therefore relished corporal punishment. There were many others of his generation (though not Arnold himself) who, remembering Eve, had been inclined to ascribe the source of beastliness to femininity. But the new religious outlook of the 1850s and 1860s brought quite a different attitude. Now it was possible to shed a 'manly' tear, a phrase which hardly makes sense if 'manly' is associated exclusively with 'masculine'. It became 'manly' to turn the other cheek, to apologise rather than call someone out to a duel. God was still pictured in a bearded masculine way, but he was no longer conceived of as a vengeful Old Testament despot. Jesus, meanwhile, came to be redefined, in the words of another Cambridge fellow and contemporary, J. R. Seeley, as a creature of 'almost feminine tenderness and humanity'.[17]

Lurking around in the historiography is a misunderstanding of the thought of Thomas Hughes, the man who (as Newsome points out) made Arnold out to be more 'modern' than he was, and the man who is often identified wrongly with Kingsley's brand of 'muscular Christianity'. And if Hughes is misunderstood, so too is his 'manly' creation, Tom Brown. Dr Newsome describes Tom as 'the sort of boy of whom any father might be proud – manly, honest, plucky, thoroughly sound at heart. He might prefer games to Latin verses, fisticuffs to preaching, but when it came to deciding between right and wrong he could be trusted to choose the proper path.' This description is not incorrect, but it conveys a false impression because it suggests that Tom had been born that way and omits what Hughes quite deliberately calls 'the turn of the tide', a

[15] Newsome, *Godliness*, p. 199.
[16] C. J. Vaughan, *A Letter to Viscount Palmerston on the Monitorial System of Harrow School* (1853), pp. 5–12.
[17] [J. R. Seeley], *Ecce Homo. A Survey of the Life and Work of Jesus Christ* (London and Cambridge, 1866), p. 177.

reference to the profound and 'gentling' effect which Arthur has on Tom. The misunderstanding is compounded when Newsome contrasts Arnold's view of the 'manly' boy as 'putting away childish things' with what he regards as Hughes's view, i.e. that masculine 'manliness' is innate and quite compatible with boyishness: 'when Hughes portrayed Tom Brown as the paragon of manliness, he was expressing his admiration for the sort of boy "who's got nothing odd about him, and answers straightforward, and holds his head up ... frank, hearty, and good-natured ... chock-full of life and spirits" '. But having said this, Newsome gives the game away in a footnote, which comments: 'This is East describing to Tom how he has to conduct himself if he is to make a good impression as a new boy; the last part of the quotation is Hughes's description of East himself.'[18] Precisely: Hughes is describing two youngsters who have not yet attained 'manliness' in his sense of the term, who have not yet undergone the necessary 'dilemmas and deliverances' – responsibility for little Arthur in Tom's case, the embarrassments associated with Confirmation in East's.

Tom comes from 'a fighting family' but this is not to be the secret of his acquired 'manliness'. His destiny is mapped out in the celebrated prayer of his 'backbench Tory' type of father: ' "If he'll only turn out a brave, helpful, truth-telling Englishman, and a gentleman, and a Christian, that's all I want," thought the Squire.' There are at least two soft-nosed attributes here: 'helpful' and 'gentleman'. And the novel makes it quite clear that what is 'manly' about Tom is not the fighting scaramouch of the lower forms but the senior who achieves through trials a mature lowliness and sense of responsibility. Thus at one point, before the 'turn of the tide', Dr Arnold remarks that he will expel the incorrigible Tom Brown and Harry East 'if I don't see them gaining character and manliness'. What helps to 'turn' Tom is the realisation that Arthur, 'the poor little weak boy, whom he had pitied and almost scorned for his weakness, had done that which he, braggart that he was, dared not do' – say his prayers in full view of the dormitory. (This was before Dr Arnold's 'manly piety' had begun to 'leaven the school', as a result of which public orisons, according to Hughes, became the norm.) The point of importance here is that Tom's attainment of 'manliness' is entirely due to the influence of the effeminate and sickly Arthur with his winsomely insipid understanding of the meek and mild Christ Jesus. While Arthur is lying on what turns out not to be his death-bed, Tom puts off for good the masculine bravado of his childhood: 'Never till that moment had he felt how his little chum had twined himself around his heart-strings.'[19]

Like Farrar, Thomas Hughes was a devotee of Maurice and can be

---

[18] Newsome, *Godliness*, p. 198.
[19] Thomas Hughes, *Tom Brown's Schooldays* (London, 1856), p. 80, 234, 250, 340.

taken to exemplify mid-Victorian liberal theology; it is quite wrong, therefore, to depict him as a simple muscular Christian in the Kingsley mode. At any rate, it was the exertion of mental rather than physical muscle which mattered to him. It is therefore misleading to argue, as Dr Newsome does, that 'whereas Coleridge had equated manliness [with] the fulfilment of one's potentialities in the living of a higher, better and more useful life', Hughes (like Kingsley) on the other hand 'stressed the masculine and muscular connotations of the word and found its converse in effeminacy'. The claim is supported by a reference to Hughes's *The Manliness of Christ* (1879) where Hughes's concept of 'manliness' is said to be quite different from Arnold's search for purity, and to be a series of tales of 'endurance in the face of death and torment,... amply illustrated by gruesome extracts from Napier's *The Peninsular War*'. Second only to warfare, Newsome seems to imply, 'Hughes passionately believed in the moral and physical value of games-playing.'[20] In fact, this is a serious misreading of *The Manliness of Christ*, which was written in protest *against* attempts to revive muscular Christianity, meaning (in Hughes's eyes) the reduction of Christianity to a matter of mere physical prowess and athleticism in a cheap attempt to attract the working classes. In his view the old evangelical Christianity had been weak because it had been no more than an opiate and sustained by the fear of Hell; Maurice's brand of liberal Christianity, on the other hand, was strong because it was prepared to assert itself in a climate in which mankind had no superstitious need of it, and when its proclamation could often make its champions appear to be soppy and escapist.

'Manliness and manfulness' ... embrace more than we ordinarily mean by the word 'courage'; for instance, tenderness, and thoughtfulness for others [Squire Brown's 'helpfulness']. They include that courage, which lies at the root of all manliness, but is, in fact, only its lowest or rudest form. Indeed, we must admit that it is not exclusively a human quality at all, but one which we share with other animals, and which some of them ... exhibit with a certainty and a thoroughness which is very rare amongst mankind ... Courage, in this ordinary sense of the word,... is a valuable, even a noble quality, but an animal quality rather than a human or manly one.[21]

In the same way, 'athleticism is a good thing if kept in its place, but it has come to be very much over-praised and over-valued amongst us', and certainly it had nothing to do with 'manliness' as far as Hughes was concerned: 'True manliness is as likely to be found in a weak as in a strong body.'[22] At this point Hughes states categorically that the heroic exploits which Napier describes in *The Peninsular War* (and to which Dr Newsome

[20] Newsome, *Godliness*, pp. 197–8, 212.
[21] T. Hughes, *The Manliness of Christ* (London, 1879), pp. 21–2.
[22] ibid., pp. 24–5.

refers) were examples of courage but *not* of manliness. The excitement and danger of warfare and the physical effort involved in it 'relieves the strain', and so 'the highest temper of physical courage is not to be found, or perfected, in action but in repose'. 'In the face of danger self-restraint is after all the highest form of self-assertion, and a characteristic of manliness as distinguished from courage.'[23]

> The daily life of every one of us teems with occasions which will try the temper of our courage as searchingly, though not as terribly, as battle-field, or fire, or wreck. For we are born into a state of war; with falsehood, and disease, and wrong, and misery in a thousand forms, lying all around us, and the voice within calling on us to take our stand as men in the eternal battle against these. And in this life-long fight ... the last proof and test of our courage and manliness, must be loyalty to truth – the most rare and difficult of all human qualities. For such loyalty, as it grows in perfection, asks ever more and more of us, and sets before us a standard of manliness always rising higher and higher.[24]

It is comparatively easy to stand out for the truth when doing so merely brings us into combat with our enemies, but to do the same thing 'against those we love, against those whose judgment and opinions we respect, in defence or furtherance of that which approves itself as true to our own inmost conscience, this is the last and abiding test of courage and of manliness'.

> And then comes one of the most searching of all trials of courage and manliness, when a man or woman is called to stand by what approves itself to their consciences as true, and to protest for it through evil report and good report, against all discouragement and opposition from those they love or respect.[25]

This is not only a code of ethics for the public schoolboy who publicly prays on his knees at bedtime. It is also a code for the sneak and the tell-tale. It makes quite clear that in Hughes's estimation it is Arthur, not the pre-regenerate Brown, who epitomises 'manliness'. It also echoes sentiments of Jowett's:

> No earthly trial can be greater than to pursue without friends the work that you began with them. And yet it is the more needed because it rests on one only. If there be anyway in this world to be like Christ it must be by pursuing in solitude and illness, without the support of sympathy or public opinion, works for the good of mankind.[26]

Fawcett was raised in a secular tradition, while Stephen turned from his evangelical upbringing into atheism. Neither had any time for the liberal theology of Maurice, Farrar and Hughes,[27] and it may therefore be that their conception of 'manliness' was quite different, and that in its secular

---

[23] ibid., p. 33.   [24] ibid., pp. 34–5.   [25] ibid., pp. 35–6.
[26] Jowett to Nightingale, 19 Nov. 1861. *Dear Miss Nightingale*, p. 14.
[27] Leslie Stephen, *Life of Henry Fawcett* (3rd edn, London, 1886), pp. 24, 116; Annan, *Leslie Stephen*, p. 39.

version 'manliness' is indeed to be understood as predominantly 'masculine'.[28] As Dr Collini wisely remarks, 'manliness could take many forms'. But it seems unlikely that, in a predominantly religious culture, when even professing atheists owed such a debt to religious modes of feeling and thinking, two quite separate conceptions of 'manliness' could have prevailed side by side. Stephen's obsessive concern with long walks and mountaineering may signify, not mid-Victorian liberal 'manliness', but the longing of the agnostic to resurrect the 'manly' old athletic ways of days when a paterfamilias Old Testament God sat on his transcendent throne. At least, emphasis on the feminine side of 'manliness' may help us to understand Dr Collini's paradox – namely, that Fawcett and Stephen should have opposed Governor Eyre. They seem, he says, 'to be on the wrong side'. His point is perfectly valid in the context he had depicted: if Fawcett and Stephen placed so much faith in 'manliness', why did they not agree with Carlyle and Kingsley that Eyre was to be congratulated for having masterfully done his duty? Carlyle, as Dr Collini points out, was not going to wax squeamish over the spilling of a little blood. The answer to this paradox may lie in the fact that 'manliness' meant different things to the Cambridge humanitarians than it did to Carlyle and Kingsley. Carlyle was steeped from boyhood in the old evangelical mentality, in the old corpuscular tradition based on the atoning blood of Christ, not the new liberal and muscular version. It was typical of corpuscular Christians to mock those humanitarians who blenched at the thought of a little blood-spilling. Dickens, too, may have derived his sympathy for Eyre from similar instincts. Mill and Hughes,[29] on the other hand, had a humane distaste for Eyre's antics, as they also did for the old-fashioned scheme of salvation, and this distaste was both 'feminine' and 'manly'. Perhaps only in the third quarter of the nineteenth century was such a conjunction of epithets possible, a period in which the upper classes felt little social guilt, when 'all serene' was the common catchphrase, when fears of war and revolution barely surfaced, and when there was a widespread belief in the likelihood of economic, moral, intellectual and social progress. Only in such a climate might one indulge a feminine ideal of peaceful improvement without being accused of unmanly sentimentality in the face of natural (including market) forces. This was the hallmark of that distinct type or stage of Liberalism which, as Dr Collini rightly says, existed in this period.

[28] A suggestion of this sort appears in N. Vance, *The Sinews of the Spirit. The Ideal of Christian Manliness in Victorian Literature and Religious Thought* (Cambridge, 1985), pp. 181–9, on 'manliness and secular culture'. This interesting study, which appeared after the Fawcett Centenary Conference, explores some of the themes discussed here.

[29] That Hughes and Kingsley took starkly opposing sides over Eyre is an indication of the danger involved in lumping the two men together as typical 'muscular Christians'.

🪬🪬🪬🪬🪬🪬🪬🪬🪬🪬🪬🪬🪬🪬🪬🪬🪬🪬🪬🪬🪬🪬🪬🪬🪬🪬🪬🪬🪬🪬🪬🪬🪬🪬🪬🪬🪬

3

Victorian feminists: Henry and Millicent Garrett Fawcett*

DAVID RUBINSTEIN

On 8 May 1865 the twenty-eight-year-old Elizabeth Garrett wrote to her parents to inform them 'of an experience I have had this morning. Mr Fawcett came up from Cambridge to ask me to be his wife.' It is unlikely that she could not immediately make up her mind,[1] for the letter continued:

Of course I could only tell him it was impossible, that I had put myself to a certain work that made marriage out of the question ... I have not the least doubt about having been right in decidedly refusing though at the same time I know of few lives I should have liked better than being eyes & hands to a Cambridge Professor & an M.P.[2]

She swore her parents to secrecy, so that it is unclear whether her sister Millicent was aware that she had not been Henry Fawcett's first choice among the Garrett sisters, or indeed, that he had previously proposed to Bessie Rayner Parkes, a feminist of an earlier generation, and to Miss Eden.[3]

---

* I wish to express warm thanks to Mrs C. G. Williams of St Brelade, Jersey, for her generosity in allowing me access to the papers of Elizabeth Garrett Anderson, her great-grandmother, and for her hospitality during my stay on Jersey.
[1] As Jo Manton, her principal biographer (who has apparently not seen this letter) claims: *Elizabeth Garrett Anderson* (London, 1965), pp. 156–7.
[2] Elizabeth Garrett to Louisa and Newson Garrett, 8 May [1865], Elizabeth Garrett Anderson Papers, uncatalogued; henceforward E.G.A. Papers. Fawcett was in fact not elected to the House of Commons until the following July.
[3] I am grateful to Margaret Gaskell and Kate Perry of Girton College, Cambridge, for copies of a letter from Henry Fawcett to Bessie Rayner Parkes, 23 Oct. 1859 (B.R. Parkes Papers, Girton College, Cambridge, IX 21; henceforward B.R.P. Papers), a typescript article on Fawcett by Parkes's granddaughter Elizabeth, Countess of Iddesleigh (n.d., but probably written in the 1960s, B.R.P. Papers A 41) and an incomplete letter from Parkes to Barbara Bodichon, presumably written in 1867, expressing satisfaction at Fawcett's marriage and adding 'I don't think *we* should ever have done together' (B.R.P. Papers V 132). For Miss Eden see above, p. 11.

Although Newson Garrett's writing ability was evidently limited[4] he appears to have replied to his daughter Elizabeth at once, for on 10 May she wrote to him again, stressing that it had been better to decide at once than to wait. Foreshadowing Millicent's own married life, Elizabeth reflected: 'I shd. be living in a political circle with chiefly political society either at Cambridge or – during the session – in London. Mr Fawcett's wife wd. also have to give up her time to his pursuits even more than most people's wives need do.'[5]

In the autumn of the next year Millicent, now aged nineteen, was asked by Henry Fawcett to marry him and accepted. Elizabeth at first opposed the wedding but was soon brought round, partly through the agency of the eldest sister, Louisa, who wrote to her mother in revealing terms about both Harry and Milly. Although Fawcett had been an M.P. for little over a year Louisa commented: 'I should not think there can be any question as to his being a rising man in Parliament.' As for her sister: 'I do think Milly is admirably fitted to be happy as the wife of a man who is intensely interested in public work – to enjoy the society which this state of things will bring his wife – and to make her husband very happy and proud too.'[6] Louisa was to die, still a young woman, shortly before the marriage, but all that we know of the seventeen years which followed suggests that her diagnosis was remarkably accurate.

The history of the Garrett family is well known.[7] Newson Garrett, a merchant and shipowner, was a fiercely independent-minded man. The principal preoccupation of his wife Louisa was strict evangelicalism, a commitment which her daughters did not share. They did share, however, her strong sense of family, which provided a stable background to their various challenges to male monopoly of medicine, local government, parliamentary suffrage, higher education and the business world. Millicent, born on 11 June 1847, had relatively little formal education and left school before she was sixteen. She was, however, a woman of striking force of character, a feature which she shared with other members of her family. Elizabeth reflected on this point in a letter to her friend Harriet Cook written in 1864: 'No! I am *not* uncommon ... My strength lies in the extra amount of daring wh. I have as a family endowment. All Garretts have it & I am a typical member of the race & so can't help it any more than I can help being like them in face & physique.'[8] In a later letter to the

---

4 Manton, *Elizabeth Garrett Anderson*, p. 18; Louisa Garrett Anderson, *Elizabeth Garrett Anderson 1836–1917* (London, 1939), p. 29.
5 Elizabeth Garrett to Newson Garrett, 10 May [1865], E.G.A. Papers.
6 Louisa Smith to Louisa Garrett [Oct. 1866?], E.G.A. Papers.
7 It can be traced in the Manton biography and in Ray Strachey, *Millicent Garrett Fawcett* (London, 1931).
8 Elizabeth Garrett to Harriet Cook, 12 April [1864], E.G.A. Papers.

same friend she observed, possibly a little forlornly, that Henry Fawcett had initially been drawn to Millicent because of her close similarity to Elizabeth herself, adding: 'As a matter of fact she & I are more alike in every way than any of the others.'[9] In a letter to Lady Amberley written the following day Fawcett confirmed this account: 'In her whole character, she bears a remarkable resemblance to Miss [Elizabeth] Garrett, and I quite acknowledge with you that this is paying her a very high compliment.'[10]

It was a marriage in which each partner had an unusual amount to give the other. Henry Fawcett gained a wife committed to Liberal principles, and prepared to act as his 'eyes & hands' as his disability required. She was also young and pretty, with 'masses of most beautiful hair, the colour of brown amber',[11] intelligent and eager to learn. Such a 'very nice attractive ladylike little person [with] no trace of the "strong-minded female" about her', as she was described by Gladstone's secretary Edward Hamilton in 1882,[12] could hardly help but be an asset to the blind politician's career. Soon after her marriage she became a familiar figure in the precincts of the House of Commons, as a well-intentioned description published early in 1875 attests.

The visitor to the House of Commons ... will no doubt have his eye particularly arrested by a tall, fair-haired young man, evidently blind, led up to the door by a youthful, *petite* lady with sparkling eyes and blooming cheeks ...
As she turns away many a friendly face will smile, and many a pleasant word attend her as she trips lightly up the stairway leading to the Ladies' Cage.[13]

Millicent Fawcett was more talented than her husband, but there is no doubt that she had more to gain intellectually as she entered marriage than he. She was not yet twenty when she married, though 'practically she is as old as many people 10 years older',[14] Elizabeth commented, and she was already deeply interested in political and social questions. Henry Fawcett first became aware of her when, shortly before her eighteenth birthday, he

[9] 6 Nov. [1866], E.G.A. Papers.
[10] Henry Fawcett to Lady Amberley, 7 Nov. 1866, Bertrand Russell Papers, McMaster University, Rec. Acq. 754.
[11] Margaret Heitland, obituary notice in *Newnham College Roll: Letter*, January 1930, p. 19.
[12] Dudley W. R. Bahlman (ed.), *The Diary of Sir Edward Walter Hamilton 1880–1885* (2 vols., London, 1972), vol. 1, p. 287. The importance of personal appearance in the Victorian feminist movement is stressed by Rosamund Billington, 'The women's education and suffrage movements, 1850–1914; innovation and institutionalisation' (unpublished doctoral thesis, University of Hull, 1976), passim, and 'Ideology and feminism: why the suffragettes were "wild women"', *Women's Studies International Forum*, vol. 5 (1982), p. 668. I gratefully acknowledge my debt to Dr Billington.
[13] Moncure Daniel Conway, 'Professor Fawcett', *Harper's New Monthly Magazine* (N.Y.), vol. 50 (1875), p. 352.
[14] Elizabeth Garrett to Harriet Cook, 6 Nov. [1866], E.G.A. Papers.

heard her lamenting the death of Lincoln.[15] Eighteen months later he told
Lady Amberley: 'she is very clever, is a thorough Liberal, and takes the
keenest interest in politics. Between us, there is such perfect intellectual
sympathy that I am convinced we shall enjoy the most complete happiness.'[16]

Millicent was, as she commented later, 'a woman suffragist ... from my
cradle', but the move from her quiet Suffolk home to prominent and
influential radical-Liberal circles in both London and Cambridge meant
that she was now ideally placed to put her convictions into action. When
she married, she wrote, her political education had hardly begun, and her
early activity as her husband's secretary and amanuensis forced her to
read and write for him, to grapple with parliamentary papers and
newspapers and summarise their contents orally.[17] Moreover, Henry
Fawcett, whose political and economic beliefs were notable for their
inflexibility, was not only a believer in women's emancipation, but willing
to change and develop his ideas in this field. He had manifested his
support for women's suffrage before his marriage, but his continued
commitment was now put beyond doubt. 'So we may now rely upon his
being kept in the path of duty', the pioneer feminist Emily Davies
remarked more realistically than charitably in commenting on the
engagement at the end of 1866.[18] Despite his disability and her youth it
was a marriage which from its outset seemed likely to be unusually
successful, as Emily Davies sensed.[19]

In personal terms it is not an exceptionally well-documented marriage,[20] though their mutual affection and the similarity of their tastes is
not open to question. There is a delightful picture of Millicent nearly two
years married being mistaken for a schoolgirl on a train, in one of
Elizabeth's letters. 'You can fancy how Harry roared over the joke when
Milly told it', she commented.[21] The letters of another sister, Alice
Cowell, reflect a picture of Millicent recovering slowly from the birth of
her only child Philippa in 1868 and being unable to nurse her, and of
Philippa herself being at least briefly unwell in infancy. She was also given
to prolonged screaming fits though on the whole she seems to have been a

15 Millicent Garrett Fawcett, *What I Remember* (London, 1924), p. 54.
16 Henry Fawcett to Lady Amberley, 7 Nov. 1866, Bertrand Russell Papers.
17 M. G. Fawcett, *What I Remember*, pp. 52, 55, 64.
18 Quoted in A.P.W. Robson, 'The founding of the National Society for Women's Suffrage
   1866–1867', *Canadian Journal of History*, vol. 8 (1973), p. 15 n. 38, and in Josephine
   Kamm, *John Stuart Mill in Love* (London, 1977), p. 151.
19 Emily Davies to Helen Taylor, 15 Dec. 1866, Mill–Taylor Collection, British Library of
   Political and Economic Science, London School of Economics, 13/190.
20 Anodyne but interesting accounts are contained in Strachey, *Millicent Garrett Fawcett*,
   chs. 2–5, and M. G. Fawcett, *What I Remember*, ch. 6.
21 Elizabeth Garrett to Harriet Cook, 24 Dec. 1868, E.G.A. Papers.

healthy baby.[22] The Fawcetts believed in Malthusian theories of population and it is reasonable to suppose that they practised some form of
birth control.[23] In any case freedom from regular pregnancies and
childbearing must have done much to enable Millicent to begin and
develop a novel and controversial role as a feminist speaker and writer.
On the other hand she was, as we have seen, ladylike, well-dressed and
conventional in important respects. She knitted Philippa's baby clothes
and was described in 1890 as 'a most expert needlewoman'.[24] On her fell
the responsibility of making a relatively small income cover the expenditure of homes in London and Cambridge.[25] In short, the marriage may be
described as feminist not because either partner held revolutionary ideas
about the subject, but because of their convictions, relationship and public
careers. One would not expect a blind man, who employed domestic
servants, to cook, shop, sew or clean; what mattered in the context of the
age was the intellectual equality which existed from the start between the
Cambridge professor and M.P., and his inexperienced, relatively dis-
advantaged wife.

A revealing picture of what Millicent Garrett Fawcett expected from
marriage, as well as many of her other likes and dislikes is contained in her
only surviving novel, *Janet Doncaster*, published in 1875. The book is
characterised not only by pronounced feminism but also by wit, puritan
morality and a marked dislike both of upper-class pretensions and
adherence to the outward forms of Christianity. Like the author, Janet
possesses an alarmingly rigid moral code, which causes her to leave her
husband at once and permanently at the first manifestation of his
hereditary drunkenness: 'Janet was immovable. Though the whole world
should tell her that she ought to go back to her husband, she would not go
back to him ... "if I went back to him I should be selling myself, body and
soul. I should be no better than those poor creatures in the streets. I should
be much worse." '

She earns her living as a translator, and remains celibate despite the
arrival of a potential lover, to whom she had previously been drawn,

[22] Alice Cowell to Louisa Garrett, 14 May [1868], 12 April, 16 May, 1 July, 23 July 1869, 7
March 1870, E.G.A. Papers; Strachey, *Millicent Garrett Fawcett*, p. 40.
[23] Selections from the writings of both Henry and Millicent Garrett Fawcett were quoted by
the defence in the Bradlaugh–Besant trial (*The Queen v. Charles Bradlaugh and Annie
Besant* (London, 1877), pp. 92–5, 113), but they adamantly refused to give supporting
evidence (Strachey, *Millicent Garrett Fawcett* pp. 88–9; Hypatia Bradlaugh Bonner,
Charles Bradlaugh (2nd edn, London, 1895), vol. 2, pp. 3–4. For Elizabeth Garrett
Anderson urging Mary Costelloe to adopt contraceptive methods in 1888 see Barbara
Strachey, *Remarkable Relations* (London, 1980), p. 103.
[24] Strachey, *Millicent Garrett Fawcett*, p. 39; 'Millicent Garrett Fawcett & her Daughter',
Review of Reviews, vol. 2 (1890), p. 20.
[25] M. G. Fawcett, *What I Remember*, p. 55.

partly because he had treated her as a human being and an equal: 'Our lives must be lived apart; my marriage is a perpetual barrier between us.' Only after her husband dies some years later do the lovers come together and subsequently marry.[26] To a modern reader the book may seem a kind of morality tale with a rather priggish heroine, but Janet's independence of thought, speech and action were strong medicine for some readers. The *Saturday Review* found the book disagreeable and Evelyn (soon to become Countess) Stanhope, who read it soon after publication, commented: 'the heroine is meant for a model of the strong-minded female type ... Heaven forbid such a type of my sex should ever become common!' Even the liberal *Examiner*, to which Mrs Fawcett was a contributor, noted that the marriage preceded the love-making, though 'with the least possible impropriety', and it anxiously insisted that Janet sought employment not from adherence to principle but 'with a practical good sense worthy of a robust Englishwoman'.[27]

It is difficult to feel that Mrs Fawcett's unique work for women could have been stifled by a hostile husband any more than the feminist-atheist-socialist career of her exact contemporary Annie Besant. But the encouragement of Henry Fawcett helped to ensure that her work was more stable and productive, and less subject to pain and loneliness than that of Mrs Besant. Her debt to his 'perpetual encouragement ... to write' from an early stage of their marriage is acknowledged in her autobiography.[28]

Her principal intellectual interest lay not in economics but in the movement for the emancipation of women. But her intensive reading in classical economics, undertaken initially as her husband's assistant, but within a short period as a knowledgeable participant in economic debate, helped her considerably to develop a rationale for the case for women's suffrage, education and employment. In 1870 she published *Political Economy for Beginners*, specifically intended for schoolchildren. It ran through successive editions, reaching its tenth publication in 1911, and was favourably received by competent critics to whom she sent copies.[29] *Tales in Political Economy* (1874), lucidly and persuasively expressed like all her publications, put the case for free trade beneath a light layer of fiction, the 'raspberry jam of a story', as she wrote in her preface. In the

26 Millicent Garrett Fawcett, *Janet Doncaster* (London, 1875). Quotations are from pp. 219–20, 228, 296. Another novel, written under a pseudonym, was soon lost without trace (Strachey, *Millicent Garrett Fawcett*, pp. 55–6).

27 *Saturday Review*, 12 June 1875, pp. 761–2; Evelyn Stanhope, 8 July 1875, quoted in Pat Jalland, *Women, Marriage and Politics 1860–1914* (Oxford, 1986), p. 212; *The Examiner*, 22 May 1875. *The Times*, however, began a long and sympathetic review by calling the book 'a real story, without a purpose and without a moral' (25 June 1875).

28 M. G. Fawcett, *What I Remember*, p. 85.

29 J. E. Cairnes and E. E. Bowen to Millicent Garrett Fawcett, 31 May and 1 Nov. 1871, Fawcett Library, City of London Polytechnic, Archive Letter Collection (F.L.A.L.C.).

same decade she wrote periodic articles on economic and other themes for *The Examiner*.[30] She had become well known as a competent guide to the arduous peaks of economic doctrine, and among her notable students were J. A. Hobson and Margaret Ethel MacDonald.[31]

Indeed, before she had turned twenty-five she had some claim to be regarded as the leading woman economist of her day. Sir Charles Dilke wrote to John Stuart Mill early in 1871 to recommend her election as the first woman member of the Political Economy Club, a prestigious group of Liberal economists and men of affairs. Dilke cited in her support her 'little book' (*Political Economy for Beginners*), many articles 'both signed and anonymous', and a long and distressingly insensible letter in *The Times* published at the end of 1870, in which she had argued against free education and the Poor Law System: 'The Poor Law teaches the poor that self-restraint is no benefit to them, and that self-indulgence entails no additional suffering on themselves or their children.'[32] Mill's reply was disappointingly and, one hopes, uncharacteristically pharisaical, but he acknowledged that she had 'far better claims to be a member of the Political Economy Club than many of its present members' and promised to support her if her name was proposed and seconded by other leading members.[33] The prominence which Mrs Fawcett had thus achieved in the early years of her marriage was the result of her own intelligence and application, but she was obviously stimulated by her husband's knowledge and encouragement. Indeed, the preface to *Political Economy for Beginners* stated that it was when she was helping him to prepare a third edition of his *Manual of Political Economy* that the idea of her book occurred to them both.

The evidence of Mrs Fawcett's influence on the content of that and subsequent editions of the *Manual* is circumstantial but strong. In the first two editions, published in 1863 and 1865, there was no discussion of women's labour. The third edition, published in 1869, expressed the author's gratitude to his wife's 'care and assiduity' in assisting him. This

---

[30] H. R. Fox Bourne, *English Newspapers; Chapters in the History of Journalism*, vol. 2 (London, 1887), p. 291, lists her among contributors to the paper. Her articles were mostly unsigned; those I have been able to find deal mainly with economic subjects.

[31] J. A. Hobson, *Confessions of an Economic Heretic* (London, 1938), p. 23; J. Ramsay MacDonald, *Margaret Ethel MacDonald* (London, 1912), p. 80. Mrs MacDonald studied economics with Mrs Fawcett at the Ladies' Department of King's College, London, probably in the early 1890s.

[32] *The Times*, 14 Dec. 1870, reprinted in Henry Fawcett and Millicent Garrett Fawcett, *Essays and Lectures on Social Political Subjects* (Cambridge and London, 1872), p. 59.

[33] Dilke to Mill, 16 Jan. 1871, J. S. Mill Papers, Yale University Library, box 2, folder 34; Mill to Dilke, 17 Jan. 1871, in *Collected Works of John Stuart Mill* (25 vols., Toronto, 1963–), vol. 17, p. 1797. She was not elected. Soon afterwards Dilke wrote to Mrs Fawcett, subjecting her *Times* letter to detailed criticism. She defended herself in a spirited and effective reply (24 and 27 Jan. 1871, British Library, Add. MS 43909, fos. 170–5).

was during a period, it should be remembered, of initial adjustment to marriage, the birth and infancy of a child who 'screamed incessantly for many months'.[34] Nobody who knows anything of her character will be surprised that she 'pointed out many defects and some inaccuracies'.[35] The book now included a passage on the employment of women in the context of the discussion of pauperism. Obviously sympathetic to such employment, Fawcett pointed out that it was discouraged in every social class by 'social customs and legal enactments'. Women of higher social classes were told that they would 'unsex themselves' by employment, while working-class women were hindered by trade unions and legislative prohibitions. 'Women', he declared, 'should have the same opportunity as men to follow any profession, trade, or employment to which they desire to devote their energies. There is scarcely any labour which is necessarily degrading. At any rate, a life of dependent pauperism must be far more pernicious than honest industry.'[36]

The fact that this passage reads like a hundred written in later years by Millicent Garrett Fawcett does not mean that it was written at her behest. Her own 'little book' published in 1870 does not deal with the employment of women, a subject to which Henry Fawcett was in any case known to be sympathetic.[37] But it now loomed larger in his thought, as a topic suitable for treatment in a textbook on political economy. It is difficult not to see the hand of the woman suffragist from the cradle in the passage, or, more plausibly, a process of discussion between husband and wife in which their ideas and convictions developed jointly.

Further evidence of Mrs Fawcett's likely influence on her husband's thinking on women's employment is available from the same period. In the 1870s Henry Fawcett was undoubtedly the most influential opponent of extending factory legislation to cover new groups of workers, mainly women. Yet he had not always taken this line. Three months after his marriage, speaking in Parliament on an important factory bill which was to bring many new industries into the protective net,[38] Fawcett put the prestige of the Cambridge Professor of Political Economy behind the assertion that 'it was easy to prove that there was no contravention of the principle of [political] economy in legislation such as was proposed in this Bill'. Those who had opposed previous factory legislation were the first to

34 Strachey, *Millicent Garrett Fawcett*, p. 40.
35 Henry Fawcett, *Manual of Political Economy* (3rd edn, London, 1869), pp. vi.
36 ibid., pp. 531–2. This passage, and the chapter in which it appeared, had been published a few months previously in the *British Quarterly Review* (vol. 49 (April 1869), p. 508). It was again reprinted in *Essays and Lectures*, pp. 70–106.
37 *Collected Works of John Stuart Mill*, vol. 15, p. 683.
38 B. L. Hutchins and A. Harrison, *A History of Factory Legislation* (3rd edn, London, 1926), p. 168.

proclaim its satisfactory results. There was no mention of the effect of the legislation on women.[39] In October 1868, however, he cautioned the Social Science Association against 'doing an injustice to women' by restricting their employment,[40] and in 1873 he delivered a strong attack on A. J. Mundella's Nine Hours Bill, in the course of which he admitted: 'When I came into this House, when I was younger and perhaps more enthusiastic than I am now, I was more in favour of legislative interference.' This speech, together with one by Sir Thomas Bazley, who had been a large cotton trades employer, was published as a pamphlet. It also contained a letter to *The Times* by Millicent Garrett Fawcett, who discerned behind the bill 'the old Trade Union spirit to drive women out of certain trades where their competition is inconvenient'.[41]

Mundella, contemplating a destruction of his bill, pointed out unhappily: 'a few years ago he was the strongest advocate for the extension of the Factory Acts to every kind of employment'.[42] Why Fawcett changed his convictions is not easy to assert dogmatically. But at the least there was in his home a sympathetic, intelligent and interested party, who supported and encouraged, if she did not initiate or determine, his revised opinions.

The similarity of the Fawcetts' thinking on economic and political matters and the value which Henry set on his wife's opinion is illustrated by the publication in 1872 of their joint *Essays and Lectures on Social and Political Subjects*. Eight of the fourteen substantial articles were by Millicent, who also edited the book. Half of her essays dealt with women's suffrage and education, while his were concerned mainly with questions of individualism and collectivism, but their common allegiance to proportional representation was the subject of two of her essays, and all of them were informed by their commitment to Liberal theories of free trade and self help. The *Englishwoman's Review* thought their styles almost indistinguishable, and to Leslie Stephen the book showed that 'their alliance implied the agreement of independent minds, not the relation of teacher and disciple'.[43] Henry's view of his wife's independent mind had already

[39] *Parl. Deb.*, 3rd ser., 189, col. 481 (30 July 1867). Mrs Fawcett's claim that his objection was not to protective legislation as such but to extending it to new trades (Leslie Stephen's manuscript biography of Henry Fawcett, Trinity Hall, Cambridge, M. G. Fawcett's comment at p. 471), is thus difficult to accept at face value.

[40] *Transactions of the National Association for the Promotion of Social Science*, 1868 (London, 1869), p. 611.

[41] *Factory Acts Amendment Bill* (London, 1873), pp. 17, 37. Henry's speech: *Parl. Deb.*, 3rd ser., 217, col. 1298 (30 July 1873); Millicent's letter: *The Times*, 9 June 1873. Their repudiation by the Trades Union Congress is reported in ibid., 16 Jan. 1874.

[42] ibid., 16 and 24 Jan. 1874. See also W. H. G. Armitage, *A. J. Mundella 1825–1897: The Liberal Background to the Labour Movement* (London, 1951), pp. 132, 134, 144, 145, 193.

[43] *Englishwoman's Review*, no. 11 (n.s.) (1872), p. 187; Leslie Stephen, *Life of Henry Fawcett* (5th edn, London, 1886), p. 127.

been expressed in his book on *Pauperism*, first delivered as lectures at Cambridge in 1870: 'Not only was the subject of the lectures suggested by her, but she has carefully revised every page, and by pointing out various alterations and improvements has rendered me most valuable aid.'[44]

The Fawcett's residence in Cambridge enabled them to play a significant role in the controversial plan to open higher education to women. Henry was more a benevolent outsider than a participant in the work of establishing a women's college, but his position was clear. He supported the movement to open the Cambridge Local Examinations to girls in the mid-1860s, urged that women should be admitted to Oxford and Cambridge to study for degrees in an intervention at the Social Science Association Congress in October 1868, and in December 1869 his home was the scene of a famous meeting held to organise support for a plan for lectures to women.[45] Soon afterwards he wrote enthusiastically about the scheme to his mother-in-law as 'one of the most sensible, and practically useful plans which has been started for promoting the education of women', and he was among the band of professors whose lectures were open to female students.[46]

Millicent's role was a typical mixture of practical organisation and careful conciliation in the pursuit of a precise aim. She agreed that the meeting in December 1869 should press unitedly for a single object, the organisation of lectures; residential accommodation, which commanded less support, could be left until a later stage.[47] She was closely involved both in organising lectures and raising money, including a subscription of £40 a year for two years from J. S. Mill and Helen Taylor. Writing to Taylor in December 1869 she explained candidly: 'All the promoters of this scheme feel that it will very probably be the means of ultimately admitting women to the University. They do not urge this publicly in favour of their scheme, because it would frighten so many excellent people who are now willing to help.'[48] Within a fortnight she informed her

---

[44] Henry Fawcett, *Pauperism: Its Causes and Remedies* (Cambridge and London, 1871), preface.
[45] Stephen, *Life of Fawcett*, pp. 173–4; *Englishwoman's Review*, no. 10 (o.s.), (1869), p. 79; Rita McWilliams-Tullberg, *Women at Cambridge* (London, 1975), pp. 32, 56.
[46] Henry Fawcett to Louisa Garrett, 24 Dec. 1869, E.G.A. Papers; Association for Promoting the Higher Education of Women in Cambridge, leaflets 1873–4 to 1879–80, Newnham College Archives.
[47] Eleanor Mildred Sidgwick in *Common Cause*, 8 June 1917, p. 100; McWilliams-Tullberg, *Women at Cambridge*, p. 56. She had argued a year earlier that women should be admitted to residence and degrees at Oxford and Cambridge ('The medical and general education of women', *Fortnightly Review*, vol. 4 (n.s.) (1868), pp. 570–1).
[48] Arthur Sidgwick and Eleanor Mildred Sidgwick, *Henry Sidgwick a Memoir* (London, 1906), p. 206; Millicent Garrett Fawcett to Helen Taylor, 4 Dec. [1869] and 4 March [1870], J. S. Mill Letters, Special Collections, Milton S. Eisenhower Library, Johns

mother: 'The lectures for women scheme is going on capitally.' The executive committee met twice at the Fawcett home. It drew up a list of lectures and subjects and arranged for the publication of a prospectus.[49] In March 1870 it was possible to claim that the success of the lectures had 'equalled the most sanguine expectations of the originators of the scheme'.[50]

The lectures continued to attract increasing numbers of students and after temporary accommodation had been outgrown, Newnham Hall, later Newnham College, was established in 1875. Mrs Fawcett continued her fund-raising activities, contributing herself substantial sums to the college's building and other special funds over a forty-year period. She also helped to recruit and retain students and served on the college council from 1881 until 1909.[51] At the same time she kept a watching brief on developments at Girton, unsuccessfully proposing a candidate for mistress in 1875 and, according to her first biographer, being offered the position herself shortly after the death of her husband.[52]

Henry Fawcett joined Mill in June 1866 in advising the organisers and presenting to the House of Commons a petition signed by 1,499 women which inaugurated the campaign for women's suffrage. The following May, shortly after his marriage, he spoke in support of Mill's amendment to the Reform Bill which would have admitted women to the franchise.[53] This action resulted in a certain notoriety, as Millicent's elder sister Alice Cowell commented in a letter from India to her mother the following month: 'I have read comments innumerable upon the woman franchise debate, Mr. Fawcett is generally treated to mild chaff upon the "lover-like ardour" with which he took up the question.'[54]

If Fawcett had been strongly influenced by Mill in his initial enthusiasm for women's suffrage,[55] by 1867 he was second to no other man in his

Hopkins University; idem to idem, 14 and 27 Dec. [1873], Mill Papers, Yale University Library, box 2, folder 36.
49 Millicent Garrett Fawcett to Louisa Garrett, 17 Dec. [1869], E.G.A. Papers.
50 Leaflet, *Lectures for Women* [March 1870], Newnham College Archives.
51 Strachey, *Millicent Garrett Fawcett*, pp. 75–83, 224; Newnham College, *Reports*; Newnham College, *Record of Benefactors* (Cambridge, 1921).
52 Strachey, *Millicent Garrett Fawcett*, pp. 106–7; Millicent Garrett Fawcett to Barbara Bodichon, 8 June [1875], Girton College Archives. The nomination of Eliza Cairnes, shortly to become the widow of the economist J. E. Cairnes, was supported by reference to her cultivation, refinement, appearance and manners, influence over those around her and the fact that she did not need the £200 annual salary – revealing qualities on which to base a recommendation to the headship of a mid-Victorian women's college.
53 Henry Fawcett to Elizabeth Garrett, 30 May 1866, Mill–Taylor Collection, 29/320; Constance Rover, *Women's Suffrage and Party Politics in Britain 1866–1914* (London, 1967), p. 5; Stephen, *Life of Fawcett*, p. 226.
54 Alice Cowell to Louisa Garrett, 27 June [1867], E.G.A. Papers.
55 As he acknowledged to the House of Commons on 20 May 1867 (*Parl. Deb.*, 3rd ser., 187, col. 835).

commitment to the cause. It now seems natural that it should have been Millicent who took the leading part in advocating women's suffrage, but Henry manifested his unwavering loyalty, speaking and voting regularly on its behalf. As in the case of India, in Millicent's view, Henry felt that women, 'being unrepresented ... were especially liable to be "put upon"'.[56] In 1884, the year of the third Reform Act, he made his support unmistakably clear, even though he was a member of a government whose leader's opposition, however delphically expressed, was undoubted.[57] In a speech in Salisbury, his birthplace, in April, he hailed the approach of the day 'when every householder, whether man or woman,' would have the vote. In his final address to his Hackney constituents the following October he declared: 'I believe the demand of women householders to be enfranchised will not rest until it is conceded.'[58] In June of the same year he, Leonard Courtney and Sir Charles Dilke took their political lives in their hands to support women's suffrage, an act sufficiently rare in the history of a struggle more often served by the lip than in the lobby to be worthy of note. All three as ministers (Dilke being in the cabinet) abstained on the women's suffrage amendment to the Reform Bill, and received Gladstone's formally expressed severe displeasure but were not dismissed.[59] Fawcett also supported the election of women to local government bodies. He spoke on behalf of Helen Taylor in 1876 when she stood for the London School Board, partly because, he told her, he believed that 'a certain number of women' should be elected.[60]

Millicent Fawcett's long career as a platform advocate of women's suffrage was preceded by a visit to the Congress of the Social Science Association in Birmingham in October 1868 where, at the age of twenty-one, she read her husband's paper on 'Economy and Trade'. Two comments were typical of many others which followed in later years: *The Times* wrote of her 'remarkable propriety', while the Earl of Carnarvon, who presided, was applauded when he referred to her 'singular clearness of

[56] Leslie Stephen manuscript biography of Fawcett, Trinity Hall, comment at p. 224.

[57] Ann P. Robson's impressive article 'A Birds' Eye View of Gladstone', in Bruce L. Kinzer (ed.), *The Gladstonian Turn of Mind* (Toronto, 1985), appears to provide a definitive, if controversial, account of the subject.

[58] *The Times*, 10 April and 14 Oct. 1884. *Pall Mall Gazette* (14 Oct. 1884) thought that the case for women's suffrage had 'seldom been put more forcibly' than in the Hackney speech.

[59] There are accounts of this incident from the point of view of each of the participants. The fullest is in Stephen Gwynn and Gertrude M. Tuckwell, *The Life of Sir Charles W. Dilke* (2 vols., London, 1917), vol. 2, pp. 6–9. See also Strachey, *Millicent Garrett Fawcett*, pp. 97–9. Dilke, who abstained reluctantly to support his colleagues, later wrote that while Courtney had been 'honest' Fawcett had acted out of political pique (B.L., Add. MS 43938, fos. 153–4). The charge seems unlikely in view of Fawcett's record of prickly – and feminist – independence.

[60] Henry Fawcett to Helen Taylor, 21 Oct. [1876], Mill–Taylor Collection, 15/60.

enunciation'.[61] At a London meeting in July 1869 she made her first short speech on women's suffrage. She was a minor star in a galaxy which included Mill, Charles Kingsley, John Morley, Dilke and Henry Fawcett, but she made enough of an impact in this early period for Mill to write at the end of the next month: 'the cause of Women's Suffrage has no more active, judicious and useful friends than Mr and Mrs Fawcett'.[62] The London meeting was followed early in 1870 by long-remembered support on the election platform of George Odger, the trade union candidate at a Southwark by-election[63] and then, in March, by a substantial lecture on women's electoral disabilities to her husband's Brighton Liberal constituents. The Conservative *Brighton Gazette* declared sniffily: 'female political orators we must regard as altogether intolerable', but the *Brighton Daily News* treated the speech as the sensational success it obviously was, spreading its report across three pages. The town hall was filled to capacity and several hundred people were turned away.[64]

Other engagements followed. The following month both Fawcetts spoke at a meeting in Ireland; Millicent was the principal speaker and made a triumphant impact. As Alice Cowell wrote to her mother, the *Irish Times* was overwhelmed. Its leading article was rapturous about her poise, knowledge and appearance: 'Mrs Fawcett's extensive reading, her speculative power, her close reasoning, her evident aptitude for social and political discussions, do not appear to have robbed her of one natural grace, nor interfered with an exquisite feminine culture except to enhance it.' The most conclusive of her arguments for women's suffrage, it asserted, was 'her own appearance at the reading-desk'.[65]

In 1871 she undertook a tour of the west of England, an event recalled many years later by the veteran suffrage worker Lilias Ashworth Hallett. She wrote that the glamour of Henry Fawcett's name and the appearance on a platform of the wife of a Member of Parliament secured

influential support . . . I had never met her before, and can always recall her girlish figure when she stopped out of the train at Bath station . . . At several meetings . . . cheers were called for by the audience for Professor Fawcett, because of his unselfish kindness in sparing his wife – on whom he was so specially dependent – to go forth and plead for this new gospel.[66]

[61] *The Times*, 7 Oct. 1868.
[62] *Englishwoman's Review*, no. 1 (n.s.) (1870), pp. 18–19; Strachey, *Millicent Garrett Fawcett*, p. 46; *Collected Works of John Stuart Mill*, vol. 17, p. 1636.
[63] *The Times*, 15 Feb. 1870, 9 Aug. 1929 (letter from Sir George Young, then aged over ninety); F. W. Soutter, *Recollections of a Labour Pioneer* (London, 1923), pp. 49–50.
[64] *Brighton Gazette*, 24 and 31 March 1870; *Brighton Daily News*, 24 March 1870. Ray Strachey's statement (*Millicent Garrett Fawcett*, p. 47) that the meeting thanked Henry Fawcett for permitting his wife to lecture was probably based on a misreading of the *News* report.
[65] Alice Cowell to Louisa Garrett, 3 June 1870, E.G.A. Papers; *Irish Times*, 19 April 1870.
[66] Quoted in Helen Blackburn, *Women's Suffrage* (London, 1902), pp. 109–10.

For women to speak in public at that time was rare. For one so young it was virtually unprecedented and called both for meticulous preparation and the full ration of Garrett 'daring', especially as Mrs Fawcett found speaking a severe ordeal.[67] She wrote in 1884, by which time public opinion had been largely overcome: 'fourteen years ago lady speakers had to endure an ordeal of ridicule from foes and remonstrance from friends such as can hardly now be conceived'.[68] In April 1870 *Punch* carried a long open letter, chiding 'Mrs Professor Fawcett' for actively promoting the 'Women's Suffrage Movement, Women's Separate Property Movement, Women's Examination Movement, Women's University Movement, Women's Admission to the Professions Movement, &c.'[69]

This was a remarkable response to an advocacy which was to encompass these and other facets of women's emancipation, but which had as yet hardly begun. It was also a milder response than many. Two years later she received a letter from a correspondent styled 'A Follower of Christ and of Paul his Apostle', who asserted that '*no Christian Woman*' should take direct part in politics nor be seen '*spouting*' on a public platform: 'You will find more truth and good sense in the writings of Paul than in those of your dearly beloved J. S. Mill.'[70] Members of her immediate family were among those who remonstrated, or were at least privately dismayed. Alice Cowell wrote to her mother in April 1870, after the news of the Brighton speech (and presumably one delivered three days later in London) had reached India: 'I share your regrets over Milly's lectures. It is a sensational way of getting one's say said, that no doubt the Brighton people will appreciate but I very much doubt it having any really good result ... And opinion in any one so young as Milly must be more like prejudices than facts I think.'[71]

His wife's suffrage activity so far from embarrassing Henry Fawcett appears to have delighted him and to have done no harm to his political career. She was especially active during the last months of his life, while he was a minister in the government which she was trying to influence, working energetically on behalf of the women's suffrage amendment to the Reform Bill of 1884. Together with other Liberal women she attempted unsuccessfully to persuade Gladstone to receive a deputation in March, she compared the supplicant women to 'starving people seated at

67 Strachey, *Millicent Garrett Fawcett*, p. 100.
68 Millicent Garrett Fawcett, 'The women's suffrage movement', in Theodore Stanton (ed.), *The Woman Question in Europe* (London, 1884), pp. 10–11.
69 *Punch*, 16 April 1870, p. 155.
70 Millicent Garrett Fawcett Papers, Manchester Reference Library, M50/2/1/6, 11 May 1872; henceforward M.G.A. Papers.
71 Alice Cowell to Louisa Garrett, 20 April 1870, E.G.A. Papers. For the anger of Henry Fawcett's mother over her daughter-in-law's appearance on Odger's platform see M. G. Fawcett, *What I Remember*, p. 59.

a banquet with our hands tied behind us' in a forceful speech in April and she declared in an article in the Liberal *Daily News* in June: 'The claim of women householders to the suffrage is upon every principle of representative government irresistible.'[72] A friend recalled many years later a visit from the Fawcetts to her father's home near York while Henry was Postmaster General: 'In those happy days she used greatly to enjoy riding on horseback, but even then she had to leave before her husband to keep an appointment on the Suffrage question.'[73]

As soon as she began to speak and write about women's suffrage Mrs Fawcett was mentioned as a future Member of Parliament. *Punch* expressed mock alarm at the prospect of two Fawcetts in the House of Commons, fearing what it termed 'normal feminine unwillingness' to accept a refusal when combined with her husband's similarly obstinate nature.[74] A more serious commentator in *St Paul's Magazine* observed two years later 'really it is hardly possible to think of her except as an absentee member of the House'.[75] Moncure Daniel Conway, the expatriate American clergyman, drew attention to the combination of capacity and propriety which enabled her to become and remain a formidable advocate of her cause in Victorian England:

Certain it is that when ladies have the suffrage, the first female member of Parliament will be the lady of whom I write – Mrs. Fawcett. Not one-half of the members of that body are so competent as she to think deeply and speak finely on matters of public policy, while not the daintiest live doll moving about London drawing-rooms surpasses her in the care of her household, her husband, and her child.[76]

The student of the Fawcett marriage is struck by the similarity of the partners' convictions and characters. As *Punch* suggested, probably more perceptively than it realised, a process of 'natural selection' appeared to have been at work in bringing them together.[77] Both were natural leaders. Conway wrote that there had been many predictions that Fawcett would one day become Prime Minister, and that his mind had 'the instinct of leadership'. But he called attention to his independence of mind, his critical faculty and his unwillingness to compromise, which might prevent him from reaching the highest office.[78] Mrs Fawcett too was a natural

[72] Copy letter Millicent Garrett Fawcett and others to W. E. Gladstone, March 1884, M.G.A. Papers M50/2/1/37; *Englishwoman's Review*, vol. 15 (1884), pp. 221–4; notes for speech, undated but probably 24 April 1884, M.G.A. Papers M50/2/4/23; *The Times*, 25 April 1884; *Daily News*, 3 June 1884.
[73] Margaret Illingworth in the *Common Cause*, 8 June 1917, p. 100.
[74] *Punch*, 16 April 1870, p. 155.
[75] Henry Holbeach, 'Literary Legislators. No. V. – Mr. and Mrs. Fawcett', *St Paul's Magazine*, vol. 11 (1872), p. 78.
[76] Conway, 'Professor Fawcett', p. 352.   [77] *Punch*, 16 April 1870, p. 155.
[78] Conway, 'Professor Fawcett', pp. 353–4.

leader and as tireless as her husband, as her long career demonstrated. The feminist writer Florence Fenwick Miller commented in 1895 that she was 'by nature and training a *stateswoman*, and one who as such might have become great'.[79] Yet she too was independent, critical and unwilling to compromise, particularly in matters of sexual morality and patriotism. She urged Elizabeth Wolstenholme Elmy, secretary of the Married Women's Property Committee, to retire from her position in 1875 because of sexual scandal before her marriage, and Mrs Fawcett's relative inactivity in this cause may well have been connected with the question of morality.[80] She launched and continued a crusade against Harry Cust in 1894–5 because of his sexual behaviour, despite being warned that she was 'the best abused woman in London' and causing great damage to the suffrage cause.[81] She risked a catastrophic split in the women's suffrage movement in the 1890s over Irish Home Rule and more seriously over the attitude of the movement to the Great War.

The Fawcetts' independence of mind meant that their party allegiance was worn lightly. Henry was neither a faithful Liberal nor a reliable radical, and the move towards collectivism in the 1880s would have left him increasingly isolated had he lived. Edward Hamilton regarded him as 'far-seeing, right-judging, fearless, and independent', but Gladstone's view of him as 'totally unable to work in concert with others'[82] was more widely held by leading Liberals. The fact that Millicent's primary loyalty was to a movement which neither political party cared about meant that she was not subject to the same strains as her husband. But her strong dislike of Gladstone and her hostility to Home Rule and collectivism meant that women's suffrage in the 1890s was in some danger of becoming a basically Liberal cause with a largely Conservative leadership, with incalculable consequences.

Both Fawcetts had the gift of inspiring confidence and love. Henry's recovery from serious illness in 1882 and death in 1884 led to remarkable demonstrations of rejoicing and grief. Edward Hamilton thought that no political leader's death, except for Gladstone himself, could have had a greater impact: 'He excited the interest and sympathy of the masses; he

---

79 *Women's Signal*, 7 Nov. 1895, p. 289.
80 Millicent Garrett Fawcett to Elizabeth Wolstenholme Elmy, 10 Dec. [1875], F.L.A.L.C.; Sylvia Pankhurst, *The Suffragette Movement* (London, 1931), p. 31. The point is speculative; neither Fawcett appears to have been active in the organised married women's property movement before or after 1875.
81 Lady Frances Balfour to Millicent Garrett Fawcett, 15 March 1894, 19 March 1895, [March 1895], 25 March 1895, Fawcett Library, City of London Polytechnic, Archives (F.L.A.), box 90A. See also letter in *The Times* signed 'FB', 7 Aug. 1929, and Ann Oakley, 'Millicent Garrett Fawcett: Duty and Determination', in Dale Spender (ed.), *Feminist Theorists. Three Centuries of Women's Intellectual Traditions* (London, 1983), p. 194.
82 Bahlman (ed.), *Hamilton*, vol. 1, p. 341.

commanded the respect of his opponents as much as his friends; he had cut a great figure in the political world both inside and outside Parliament.'[83] His view was echoed by a political outsider in another private comment; the composer Hubert Parry wrote: 'The whole nation is a sufferer. I'm sure he was the finest and truest man in the whole range of political life.'[84] Millicent, 'the sundial that recorded only the sunny hours',[85] inspired repeated demonstrations from her suffrage colleagues. Lady Frances Balfour, her antagonist in the Cust affair but long her colleague wrote after her death: 'We, her disciples, also adored her, and loved her good comradeship.'[86]

Finally, both of the Fawcetts were inspired by an obvious and unusually direct sense of purpose. Both of them early decided their beliefs and strove to achieve them without faltering or hesitation. This may in Henry's case have been partly the result of a certain intellectual incapacity to grasp fine distinctions and subtleties. Alice Cowell wrote to her father in 1872 that she had met Fitzjames Stephen at a dinner party in India: 'He told me of Harry having skated from Cambridge to Ely soon after his blindness with his brother Leslie Stephen and seemed to think the fearless way in which he went ahead regardless of holes & other people's toes typical of his whole career.'[87] Millicent fought unceasingly for a goal which must often have seemed unrealisable during a fifty-year struggle, neither losing heart herself nor allowing her fellow-workers to do so. Her leadership had been marked, a colleague wrote in 1917, by 'calm serenity and unfaltering perseverance'.[88] 'Who is the happy Warrior?' Wordsworth asked.[89] The name of either Fawcett could be supplied as an entirely appropriate reply.

Their marriage was blessed by similarity of temperament and near-identity of conviction. Conventional as Millicent was in important respects she did not hesitate to speak in public, write regularly on political subjects and play a prominent role in the cause of women's higher education, all of which were highly unusual undertakings on the part of a young married woman. Domineering and insensitive as Henry often was as a political advocate, he encouraged his wife to pursue an independent and controversial career. Their marriage brought together two remarkable individuals, sufficiently of their age to influence it, resolute in their pursuit of women's emancipation and undeterred by their failure to secure women's suffrage in the early stages of the struggle. For the young feminist movement it was a happy and effective union.

[83] ibid., vol. 2, p. 725.   [84] Hubert Parry to Alice Leith, 8 Nov. 1884, F.L.A., box 89.
[85] Helena M. Swanwick, *I Have Been Young* (London, 1935), p. 186.
[86] 'FB', in *The Times*, 7 Aug. 1929.
[87] Alice Cowell to Newson Garrett, 10 April 1872, E.G.A. Papers.
[88] 'A Member of the Executive Committee of the N[ational] U[nion of] W[omen's] S[uffrage] S[ocieties]', *Common Cause*, 8 June 1917, p. 97.
[89] William Wordsworth, *Character of the Happy Warrior* (1806), line 1.

3 *Senate House Hill: Degree Morning* (1863) by Robert Farren

(Henry Fawcett, no. 67 in the key, stands to the extreme left of the main group outside the Senate House in Cambridge. He is supported by his secretary and surrounded by a group of Trinity Hall dons, including Leslie Stephen (no. 65) and Dr Geldart (no. 66), Master of the college. Geldart is congratulating Robert Romer of Trinity Hall, Senior Wrangler in 1863.)

4 Henry and Millicent Garrett Fawcett, *c.* 1868–9

PART II

ECONOMICS

🔲🔲🔲🔲🔲🔲🔲🔲🔲🔲🔲🔲🔲🔲🔲🔲🔲🔲🔲🔲🔲🔲🔲🔲🔲🔲🔲🔲🔲🔲🔲🔲🔲🔲🔲

Henry Fawcett: the plain man's political economist

PHYLLIS DEANE

Henry Fawcett was what one would now call an applied economist: though if one could expunge from the old-fashioned term 'political economist' the ideological implications it has recently acquired, that might be the more appropriate term for him. His interest in economics was focussed directly and almost exclusively on its practical policy implications.

He came from middle-class provincial origins. His father was a politically active Salisbury draper who electioneered for the Liberals, his mother a solicitor's daughter; and Fawcett went up to Cambridge in October 1852 with his heart already set on a political career. Then, even more so than now, the would-be politician without independent means had to make his bid for Parliament from an occupation which would support him until he obtained his seat and which he could continue to hold while he served as an unpaid M.P. Fawcett's chosen route was via an academic Fellowship and a career at the bar.

For Henry Fawcett's generation of Cambridge students, as for Alfred Marshall's, only the Mathematical and Classical Triposes carried the necessary academic weight to offer an undergraduate a promising route to a college Fellowship.[1] Fawcett, being gifted with a confident, clear, logical mind and a good school record in mathematics chose that as his obvious way through the rigorous system of competitive examinations which characterised nineteenth-century Cambridge. By the time he won his Fellowship in late 1856 (bringing with it an assured income of about £250 a year) he had already learned to speak effectively on political issues at Cambridge Union debates and had entered Lincoln's Inn. He was already reading himself into his parliamentary role – taking his philosophy and economic theory more or less intact from John Stuart Mill and building upon his knowledge of current political questions from newspaper reports

[1] Leslie Stephen, *Life of Henry Fawcett* (London, 1885), p. 90.

of parliamentary debates. But in September 1858 there occurred the tragic shooting accident that totally blinded him. He was then just twenty-five, had enjoyed a severely limited undergraduate training (broadened by vigorous and sustained discussion with his Cambridge contemporaries from other disciplines, of which Leslie Stephen writes so evocatively) and had hardly begun to acquire the rudiments of legal culture. True, he had got far enough to persuade the authorities at Lincoln's Inn to exempt him from the requirement of a certificate from the Council of Legal Education, but there was evidently no solid future for a blind barrister, and in June 1860 he took his name off the books. Henceforth his ambitions were firmly turned in academic and political directions.

At a stage when most young Cambridge Fellows would have been extending their intellectual horizons into other disciplines and filling the yawning gaps in their examination-dominated undergraduate education, Henry Fawcett found himself dependant on being read to by others and on having to dictate rather than to write out his arguments. Partly from sheer force of circumstances, then, and partly, no doubt, from the nature of his own intellectual interests, he went on to develop his talents within relatively narrow confines.[2] He depended almost exclusively on Mill's *Principles of Political Economy* for the theoretical framework of his economic analysis, though he was familiar with Ricardo's *Principles* and Malthus's *Essay on Population*. He accepted Mill's *Logic* as the last word on scientific method and he was wholly convinced by Mill's writings on political philosophy. He was also, according to Stephen, deeply impressed by Buckle's *History of Civilization* (1857) and Darwin's *Origin of Species* (1859). Although his blindness must have severely narrowed the range of his grasp of contemporary research and new thinking, it did not prevent him from taking an active part in current academic debate. He regularly participated in the annual meetings of the British Association for the Advancement of Science, and in 1859, at its Aberdeen meeting, presented a paper on the drain of precious metals to the East, which (again according to Stephen) 'attracted the notice of Cairnes, Jevons and other economists'.[3] At the 1860 meeting in Oxford he attended the famous Huxley–Wilberforce debate and in December of that year published an article in *Macmillan's Magazine* where he took the Huxley–Darwinian line and attracted Darwin's approval.[4]

Most of his intellectual energies, however, were now centred on political economy, for this was a subject which both fitted in with his political concerns and offered some prospect of academic advancement

---

[2] ibid., p. 94.   [3] ibid., p. 144.
[4] Henry Fawcett to Charles Darwin, 16 July 186[1], Darwin Papers, Cambridge University Library, DAR 98, ser. ii, fo. 29.

for a blind man who was highly receptive to the current orthodoxy. Fawcett was no doubt very lucky to have been pursuing his academic ambitions in Cambridge rather than Oxford and to have had a chance to compete for the Chair of Political Economy in the early 1860s rather than in the 1870s. For, as Stephen pointed out, 'the dominant influences in Cambridge in these days were … favourable to a masculine but limited type of understanding'.[5] In contrast to Oxford, where theological controversies dominated the academic scene, Cambridge of the 1850s and 1860s was characterised by a more muscular type of Christianity, by a respect for hearty common sense and by a religious tolerance that was barely distinguishable from complete indifference. The prevailing ethos was well reflected by Fawcett. Moreover, the methodological divisions and innovations that began to erode the orthodox classical consensus in the 1870s had not yet ruffled the image of a solidly grounded science of political economy, created by Smith, extended by Malthus and Ricardo, and moderated by Mill. This was a highly congenial environment for an economist who was faithful to the paradigm embodied in Mill's *Principles*.

The professorship to which he was elected in 1863 gave Fawcett (then less than thirty years old) a respectable authority to speak on economic questions and an assured income (along with his fellowship) of about £550 a year, in return for the rather light commitment of eighteen weeks lecturing in Cambridge. As Professor of Political Economy, Fawcett's main teaching responsibility was towards the ordinary degree candidates. There was no Economics Tripos and the only honours undergraduates who might have been among his pupils were the very few who chose it as an option in the relatively new and unprestigious Moral Sciences Tripos. Those reading for an ordinary degree, however, the so-called 'poll men', were obliged to chalk up a minimum number of professorial lectures and Stephen records that 'Fawcett had a large share of the compulsory attendance'[6] – as well he might, for his *Manual of Political Economy*, published just before his election to the Chair, provided him with the material and the textbook for exactly this kind of audience.

The *Manual* indeed began quite openly as a popularisation and abridgement of Mill's *Principles of Political Economy*. In the preface to the first edition Fawcett wrote:

I think that all who take an interest in political and social questions must desire to possess some knowledge of Political Economy. Mr. Mill's treatise is so complete and so exhaustive that many are afraid to encounter the labour and thought which

[5] Stephen, *Life of Fawcett*, p. 90.
[6] When the regulation for compulsory attendance was repealed in 1876 his lectures, according to Stephen, 'were for a short period nearly deserted, but in later years he again had a respectable audience'. Ibid., p. 123.

are requisite to master it; perhaps therefore these may be induced to read an easier and much shorter work. I so well remember the great advantage which I derived from reading Mr. Mill's book that I would not publish my own work if I thought it would withdraw students from the perusal of a more complete treatise. I am, however, convinced that those who become acquainted with the first principles of Political Economy will be so much struck with the attractiveness and importance of the science that they will not relinquish its study.[7]

Whether or not his students shared his faith in the inherent attractiveness of the 'dismal science', there is no doubt of the success of his own introduction to it. The *Manual* went into six editions before he died in 1884, and his wife Millicent Garrett Fawcett saw two further editions through the press – the last in 1907. By 1884 over 22,000 copies had been sold.

The lay-out of the *Manual* corresponds closely to that of Mill's *Principles* to which it was designed as an introduction. True, it was considerably shorter, at least in the first edition. It falls into four books (instead of Mill's five) – 'Production', 'Distribution', 'Exchange' and 'Taxation'. Many of the chapter headings are the same, or similar to Mill's; they follow generally the same order and contain a number of identical bibliographical references. The first (1863) edition of the *Manual* shows no signs of diverging from the views expressed in the 1857 edition of Mill's *Principles* and is even more effective than its model in living up to the design characteristic which Mill claimed to have borrowed from Adam Smith's *Wealth of Nations*, i.e. everywhere to associate the exposition of economic principles with their applications to practical policies.[8] In effect, then, Fawcett's *Manual* is Mill's *Principles* summarised in deliberately unambiguous terms, with most of the subtle qualifications and elaborations of the argument left out, and shorn of its philosophical discussions and speculations. So, for example, Mill's Book IV, entitled 'Influence of the Progress of Society on Production and Distribution' has no obvious counterpart in the *Manual*, though there is a chapter inserted in Fawcett's Book III, 'Exchange', on 'The tendency of profits to fall as a nation advances' which effectively abridges two chapters from Mill's Book IV, and there are a number of other places where it is evident that

---

[7] Preface to Henry Fawcett, *Manual of Political Economy* (Cambridge and London, 1863). Reprinted in all subsequent editions.

[8] See Mill's preface to all editions of his *Principles of Political Economy*: 'The design of the book is different from that of any treatise on Political Economy which has been produced in England since the work of Adam Smith. The most characteristic quality of that work, and the one in which it differs from others which have equalled and even surpassed it as mere expositions of the subject, is that it invariably associates the principles with their applications'. J. S. Mill, *Principles of Political Economy with Some of Their Applications to Social Philosophy* (1848), in *Collected Works of John Stuart Mill* (25 vols., Toronto, 1963–), vol. 2, p. xci.

Fawcett is familiar with Mill's views in this area. Similarly Fawcett's Book IV, 'Taxation', sticks more closely to principles of taxation and their application, and to the social and economic effects of policies towards pauperism, than does Mill's treatment of this theme in his Book V 'On the Influence of Government'.

In short, for the student approaching the subject for the first time, with little or no interest in philosophy or abstract theory, Fawcett's *Manual* must have seemed a more relevant, clear and straightforward introduction to the current state of knowledge in political economy than Mill's discursive treatise. What it lost in intellectual depth, the *Manual* gained in direct interest to readers whose prime concern was with the applications of political economy to real world problems – and increasingly so as it went into successive editions. For once his academic position was secured by election to the Cambridge professorship, Fawcett directed most of his intellectual energies into channels opened up by his political concerns, first in researching topics appropriate to election speeches and then, after his election in 1865, in responsibly informed contributions to parliamentary debates. He saw himself, and was seen by his contemporaries, as an orthodox but determinedly non-doctrinaire political economist, pragmatically applying the principles of a well-established discipline to the practical problems of government economic and social policy. There was no obvious tension between his public and professional responsibilities, for the researches on which his parliamentary speeches were based provided the inspiration for extensions and variations in the courses of lectures he offered to Cambridge undergraduates, material for journal articles and updated illustrations or applications of principle in each new edition of the Manual.

In the 1860s, for example, trade unions and strikes inspired a lively public controversy; Fawcett, building on material already in the *Manual* (and based of course on Mill's *Principles*) gave a course of lectures on the subject in autumn 1864 which were published a year later in book form as *The Economic Position of the British Labourer* (1865), and then embodied in the next version of the *Manual*. He continued to take a keen interest in these questions, to discuss them with employers and artisans involved in actual strikes and to update the relevant chapters in his *Manual* as well as his Cambridge lectures, in the light of new ideas and events.[9] Similarly, an article he wrote for the *British Quarterly* in 1869 on Poor Law policy was expanded in a course of undergraduate lectures in autumn 1870, formed the substance of a pamphlet which appeared in the

---

[9] In the year he died Fawcett published a book on *Labour and Wages* (London, 1884), which was a reprint of five chapters from the sixth edition of the *Manual*.

following April[10] and was systematically absorbed in subsequent editions of the *Manual*. In 1877 Fawcett responded to the debate on free trade and protection with a course of lectures explaining the orthodox classical doctrine and this gave him the basis for a best-selling book that went into six editions.[11] To take another example, his interest in questions of land policy was already fully apparent in the first edition of the *Manual*, and when public controversy was stimulated in the 1880s by Henry George's land nationalisation proposals he published an article in *Macmillan's Magazine* on 'State socialism and the nationalisation of the land' (July 1883), which also appeared separately as a twopenny pamphlet and was duly embodied in the sixth edition of the *Manual*.

Looking at Fawcett's list of publications, then, one gets the impression of a policy-orientated research programme in which the choice of topics, and the range and depth of each enquiry, was determined largely by their urgency among the immediate practical problems facing the government of the day. Reading them one is struck by the extent of the repetition, not only as between items (books, journal articles and the *Manual*), but also within individual chapters or articles, where the object is clearly to maintain the coherence and lucidity of an argument for the average reader (or listener, indeed). They are direct, lively and unpolished – essays in persuasion which reflect the style of an author who is obliged to develop his ideas orally rather than to ponder them on the page. The *Manual* is the text which puts the various economic arguments into coherent analytical perspective and each new edition was carefully updated in terms of the latest information on relevant recent events and statistical evidence. It cannot have been bad for students (ordinary or honours or merely general readers) to have been thus introduced to political economy by an active politician who took his fundamental principles from the most perceptive and well educated of the mid-century classical economists and who drew his examples and illustrations from the contemporary real world. His Cambridge colleagues in other disciplines also appreciated his non-academic qualities: for example, Leslie Stephen, when defending him against the criticisms voiced by younger economists caught up in the theoretical debates of the 1870s and 1880s, asked 'whether it is not a greater advantage on the whole to secure a part of the energy of an eminent man who always keeps his studies fresh by application to outside interests, than to secure the whole energy of a purely academical student'.[12]

---

[10] *Pauperism: Its Causes and Remedies* (Cambridge and London, 1871).
[11] *Free Trade and Protection* (London, 1878). This book sold nearly 6,000 copies in six years.
[12] Stephen, *Life of Fawcett*, p. 125.

Fawcett's loyalty to the classical system of political economy and his determination to explain it as unambiguously as possible to the untutored undergraduate, or elector, or parliamentarian, has given him an undeserved reputation for being dogmatic and inflexible as well as derivative in his views. In fact, like so many applied economists, he was always concerned to relate 'pure' theory and orthodox prescriptions to empirical evidence and correspondingly ready to reword his original formulations of economic laws in the light of arguments by which they were shown to be unrealistically rigid. True, he always began by expounding the orthodox line as straightforwardly as he could. When W. T. Thornton was writing his famous attack on the classical wage-fund doctrine[13] it was Fawcett's characteristically simplistic initial formulation of it that he chose to quote and reject, viz.,

The circulating capital of a country is its wage fund. Hence, if we desire to calculate the average money wage received by each labourer, we have simply to divide the amount of capital by the number of the labouring population. It is therefore evident that the average money wage cannot be increased until either the circulating capital is augmented or the number of the labouring population is diminished.[14]

Interestingly enough, however, it was Fawcett's further discussion spelt out in the same early source that had already provoked Mill (in a letter to Fawcett) to express doubts on the orthodox doctrine, several years before the well-known review of Thornton which sparked off a general debate.[15] The thrust of this part of Fawcett's exposition is expressed more succinctly in later editions of the *Manual* thus: 'this law affirms that wages cannot generally rise or fall, unless the capital or population of the country is either increased or diminished'.[16]

But although Fawcett firmly refused to follow Mill (still less Thornton) in actually recanting the wage-fund doctrine, it is evident (from the first edition of the *Manual* as well as from later editions embodying the argument in *The Economic Position of the British Labourer*) that he did not hold the anti-union views against which Thornton was reacting and which are generally associated with a rigid adherence to the wage-fund

---

13 W. T. Thornton, *On Labour* (London, 1869). The substance of this book had already appeared as a series of articles in the *Fortnightly Review* in 1867.

14 Thornton was quoting from Fawcett's *Economic Position of the British Labourer* (Cambridge and London, 1865) but he could have found similar passages in the 1869 edition of the *Manual*.

15 J. S. Mill, 'Thornton on labour and its claims', *Fortnightly Review*, n.s., vol. 5 (1869), part 1, pp. 505–18, part 2, pp. 620–70. Reprinted in *Collected Works of John Stuart Mill*, vol. 5. See ibid., pp. 631–8. See Pedro Schwartz, *The New Political Economy of J. S. Mill* (London, 1972), pp. 94–5, for a discussion of this letter and article in relation to Mill's so-called 'recantation'.

16 Fawcett, *Manual*, (1907 edn), p. 137.

doctrine. Fawcett never found it necessary to push economic 'laws' to extreme political conclusions. The *Manual* from 1874 onwards explicitly refers to the debate on the Mill recantation thus: 'We cannot help thinking, in spite of the high authority deservedly attributed to Mr. Mill and Mr. Thornton, that too much importance has been given to the controversy and that Mr. Thornton's objections mainly rest upon a misconception of the wages-fund theory.' After quoting J. E. Cairnes's *Leading Principles* for the orthodox statement and after dismissing Henry Sidgwick's critique in a footnote, Fawcett writes: 'If, as we believe, to be the case, the view expressed in the foregoing passage is correct, it becomes obvious that *wages in the aggregate* depend upon a ratio between capital and the population.'[17]

The fact is that Fawcett used orthodox wage doctrines not as a theoretical straightjacket, or as a justification for anti-union ideology, but as a starting-point for analysing actual events. In so doing he was capable of drawing inferences that could inspire the great J. S. Mill himself. In July 1860, for example, Fawcett, then a junior college Fellow in his twenties, whose claim to fame as an economist rested on a paper contributed to the 1859 meeting of the British Association, published an article on strikes[18] which made the point that: 'Strikes exert a tendency to raise the wages of a particular class of workmen when the profits of the particular trade are temporarily raised above the present rate.'[19] and went on to develop an argument (in the spirit of Mill's optimistic chapter 'On the probable futurity of the labouring classes') to the effect that 'so long as the participation of profits is secured by an actual resort to strikes, the workman is forced upon his master as a partner'.[20] As a result of reading this article, Mill took into his *Principles* (with handsome acknowledgment to Fawcett) the idea that unionisation was altering the behaviour patterns of the labour market by encouraging workers to make a rational calculation of their chances of a successful strike. Accordingly he inserted into the 1862 edition the following passage:

The workmen are now nearly as well informed as the master, of the state of the market for his commodities; they can calculate his gains and his expenses, they know when his trade is or is not prosperous, and only when it is, are they ever again likely to strike for higher wages; which wages their known readiness to strike makes their employers for the most part willing, in that case, to concede. The tendency, therefore, of this state of things is to make a rise of wages in any particular trade usually consequent upon a rise of profits, which, as Mr. Fawcett observes, is a commencement of that regular participation of the labourers in the

---

[17] ibid., p. 136. Italics added.
[18] 'Strikes: their tendencies and remedies', *Westminster Review*, vol. 74 (o.s.), vol. 18 (n.s.) (July 1860).
[19] ibid.   [20] ibid.

profits derived from their labour, every tendency to which, for the reasons stated in a previous chapter, it is so important to encourage, since to it we have chiefly to look for any radical improvement in the social and economical relations between labour and capital. Strikes, therefore, and the trade societies which render strikes possible, are for these various reasons not a mischievous, but on the contrary, a valuable part of the existing machinery of society.[21]

In effect then, although Fawcett started from acceptance of the classical wage-fund theory as a useful tool of analysis this was not inconsistent with a sympathetically realistic view of the ability of trade unions to raise wages at the expense of abnormally large profits. 'When both the natural rate of profit is realised, and the natural rate of wages obtained, any attempt to raise wages must be either futile, or will in all probability be very injurious to the labourers themselves.'[22] But he was well aware that such a statement depended on the assumption that there was freedom to compete, and he shared the typical nineteenth-century faith in the virtues of competition: e.g. 'if employers are freely permitted to invest their capital to the greatest possible advantage, the employed may equally claim to be allowed to obtain the highest wage they can for their labour'.[23] Indeed, he saw workers' combinations as furthering the beneficent process of competition in the labour market in two ways: first, by providing a countervailing power to employers' combinations and as a means of redressing the balance of tactical advantage which so often favoured employers at the expense of employees; second, by speeding up the equalisation of wages as between occupations.[24]

Thus the policy conclusions which he drew from his basic wage theory were not that workers should be discouraged from embarking on strikes to raise wages, but that wages and profits could both be jacked up by raising the efficiency (lowering the cost) of labour, e.g. by improved education for the masses and by profit-sharing schemes. In particular, for example, he criticised the 1869 Royal Commission on Trade Unions for failing 'to appreciate the advantages resulting from co-partnership because they assumed that the share of profits received by the labourer

[21] Mill, *Principles of Political Economy*, pp. 932–3. The previous chapter referred to was evidently that on 'On the probable futurity of the labouring classes'. It is worth noticing the difference between Fawcett's direct if inelegant writing style and Mill's somewhat convoluted prose. c.f. Fawcett's own conclusion to the chapter on strikes in *The Economic Position of the British Labourer*, p. 189: 'I therefore think it has been shown, that strikes have at least one happy and beneficial tendency, because since they make labourers participate in the prosperity and adversity of the capitalist they must also tend to create a co-partnership between masters and men.'
[22] Fawcett, *The Economic Position of the British Labourer*, p. 168.
[23] Fawcett, *Manual*, p. 250.
[24] ibid., p. 253 where he discusses 'the influence which a power of combination may exercise upon wages and profits during the time which always elapses before competition can produce its equalising effects'.

was so much taken from his employer'. On the contrary, argued Fawcett: 'The fundamental advantage of these schemes arises from the circumstances that the benefit they confer is mutual; the share of profits received by the labourer is a measure of the gain secured by the employer, as a consequence of the additional efficiency given to labour and capital by introducing harmony where before there was antagonism and rivalry of interest', and he went on to make the point that supervision of an alienated labour force is costly.[25]

To questions concerning the role of government in the economy Fawcett brought the individualist ideology of a typical mid-nineteenth century Liberal. He followed Mill's *Principles* in accepting laissez-faire as the best general rule for a modern civilised community to follow, while allowing that there were a few special areas (law and order, sanitation, education, for example) where state intervention was essential. He assumed with Mill that coercion of the individual by the state was not only bad in principle, but likely to be counterproductive in its economic and social consequences. The objections to state intervention which he found most convincing were: (a) the classical argument that since individuals are a better judge of their own economic advantage than public agencies, they are likely to be more efficient in taking the relevant decisions; and (b) the argument which Mill found most persuasive, viz., that too much state intervention saps the private initiative which is a necessary condition for human development.[26] So, like Mill, he believed, for example, that a strict administration of poor relief (limiting outdoor relief to a minimum, separating man and wife in workhouses) was necessary to encourage self-help, that regulating the hours of work of adult women was an unjustifiable interference with their freedom to work, that the masses should be required to contribute to the cost of compulsory education, that state provision of housing for the poor would dry up 'the great stream of self-help' embodied in Building Societies and that compulsory workers' insurance on the lines proposed in Germany would 'lead to there being far less thrift among the labouring classes than if it had never been sought to force it on the people'.[27] However, he defended compulsory education (if not free education) and approved the establishment of a savings bank for voluntary use by the working classes. In sum: 'The conclusion above all others which we desire to enforce is that any scheme, however well intentioned it may be, will indefinitely increase every evil it seeks to alleviate if it lessens individual responsibility by encouraging the people to rely less upon themselves and more upon the state.'[28]

[25] ibid., p. 260.   [26] See Mill, *Principles of Political Economy*, p. 943.
[27] Fawcett, *Manual*, p. 306.
[28] ibid., p. 310.

Fawcett's strong bias in favour of a maximum degree of economic competition and a minimum of state intervention also set the tone of his *Free Trade and Protection* (1878) which had gone through five editions and sold some 6,000 copies by the time of his death in 1884.[29] It was a typically vigorous response to the revival of protectionist sentiment – mainly abroad but also to some extent in Britain – when the long upswing of prosperity, the 'Great Victorian boom' which lasted from 1853 to 1873 turned into recession. When the momentum of growth in world trade faltered in the mid-1870s British manufacturers became increasingly irked by high and rising tariffs in all countries but their own. Although as Fawcett said, 'scarcely anyone could now be found in England who would express doubt as to the great advantages which free trade confers'[30] a number of Chambers of Commerce passed resolutions favouring a 'policy of reciprocity', i.e. a more aggresive commercial policy using the threat of tariffs to force Britain's customers to drop their duties on British goods.

This was the challenge to which Fawcett responded in a course of lectures originally delivered to Cambridge undergraduates in autumn 1877 and then worked up into a book aimed at a much wider audience. 'As there is reason to believe that the opinions thus expressed [summed up in the view that "one-sided free trade is an absurdity"] are largely shared by many English capitalists and labourers', he wrote in the introduction, 'I shall hope in a subsequent chapter to show that, however great the injury inflicted on English industry by the protective tariffs of other countries, this injury would ... be most seriously aggravated by a policy of retaliation.' And he set out to explain in terms intelligible to the non-economist why free trade doctrines laid down so authoritatively by Smith, Ricardo and other classical economists were again being questioned; to refute each one of the arguments for protection that were currently being bandied about at home and abroad; and to spell out the practical consequences for English producers and consumers of a 'policy of reciprocity'.

Like the *Manual* Fawcett's *Free Trade and Protection* is written in a lively, direct and forceful style in which the leading arguments are hammered home by dint of frequent repetition. It contains no systematic theoretical framework – neither Ricardo's theory of comparative advantage nor Mill's theory of international trade plays any part in Fawcett's analysis. The frequent appeals to economic principles or 'general economic considerations' are presented more as self-evident propositions derived from Smith and Ricardo and modernised by the addition of contemporary real-world illustrations than as economic laws subject to

[29] A sixth edition, edited by Millicent Fawcett, was published in February 1885.
[30] Fawcett, *Free Trade and Protection*, p. 14.

logical or empirical testing procedures. In effect, Fawcett limits himself largely to a simple demand and supply analysis in which duties on imports are shown to push up prices to the immediate disadvantage of the majority of consumers and unprotected producers and to the long-run disadvantage of everyone except the landowners. While recognising the 'injury' that may be done to British producers facing foreign tariffs he exhorts both employers and employed to remember 'that the equalising force of competition is ever present to prevent an abnormally high rate of profits and wages being permanently secured by those engaged in any particular branch of industry'.[31]

Of the thirteen arguments he lists in favour of protection Fawcett finds virtue in none, not even the infant industry argument accepted by Mill, 'There is no one more ready than I am to recognise the high authority of Mr. Mill as an Economist' but 'every word which he says in support of protection rests on the supposition that when an industry has been fairly established the protective duty will be at once voluntarily surrendered by those who are interested in the particular industry.'[32] And that this was a highly unrealistic assumption he argues at length from American experience and the testimony of American economists such as William Graham Sumner and David Ames Wells. He shows that the English case was a very special one and that the political retreat from protection there was due to an exceptional concatenation of events. For Fawcett, then, any backsliding from the peculiarly English doctrine of free trade represented the thin end of a very dangerous wedge.

Directly the principle is sanctioned that certain special industries are to be fostered by the State, the trade of a country at once ceases to be regulated on purely commercial considerations and is placed under official and political guidance ... The State decides what industries shall be called into existence by protection and determines what is the exact amount of encouragement that shall be given to each particular trade. It is impossible to imagine that any government can be qualified to discharge any such functions.[33]

And even if it were, political objectives would have more influence than industrial considerations in determining the pattern of protection.

Nevertheless, wholly convinced though he was of the universality of the classical arguments for free trade, it is significant that Fawcett was prepared to allow an exception on essentially political grounds in relation to India, for which he had since 1867 taken special responsibility in the House of Commons. He defended the Indian 5 per cent duty on imports of cotton from the United Kingdom partly on revenue grounds: 'The great mass of the people of that country are so poor and live with such extreme frugality, that with the exception of salt, there is no article of general

[31] ibid., p. 148.   [32] ibid., p. 111.   [33] ibid., p. 115.

consumption which it is possible to tax; and the duty on salt has been strained to its utmost point.'[34] But the main burden of his case for allowing the Indians to retain their tariff was non-economic:

If no attempt is made to interfere with the colonies, while it is insisted on the part of England, regardless of the wishes of the Indian people, that a particular duty which is imposed on that country will not be repealed, the impression will not unnaturally be produced that India is unfairly treated and that she is sacrificed to the interests of English manufacturers. Such a feeling no doubt already exists in India.[35]

The book concludes with the following sentence:

In the appeals that are so often made that Indian cotton duties should be abolished, in order that England may consistently maintain her adherence to the principles of free trade, the mistake which may be regarded as the cardinal error of the protective system is not infrequently committed: – the interests of the manufacturers as producers, is considered; the interests of the people, as consumers, is ignored.[36]

When *Free Trade and Protection* first appeared in print, in May 1878, Fawcett sent a signed copy to Alfred Marshall who had already established his intellectual dominance in Cambridge economics and was then in his first year as Principal of University College, Bristol. Marshall was also exercised by the recent revival of protectionist sentiments at home and abroad and was then negotiating with Alexander Macmillan about the publication of his own unfinished monograph on foreign trade. Not surprisingly perhaps, Marshall did not find himself addressing the same audience as Fawcett. In a letter written to Macmillan (probably soon after receiving the signed copy of Fawcett's book) Marshall wrote: 'I find that Prof. Fawcett's book, interesting as it is, has taken up less than I thought of the ground I want to cover.'[37]

The fact is that the economic theory taught by Marshall and his disciples lecturing for the political economy options of the Moral Sciences Tripos, had already begun to develop new dimensions that could not easily be accommodated within Fawcett's classical supply and demand analysis and cost of production theory of value. It is doubtful whether many of the honours candidates reading for the political economy papers actually went regularly to Fawcett's lectures, though it is probable that most of them read his *Manual* at an early stage in their career. J. Neville Keynes, who took a first in the Moral Sciences Tripos in December 1875 worked through the *Manual* in the preceding January (along with Smith's

---

[34] ibid., pp. 115–16.   [35] ibid., p. 117.   [36] ibid., p. 173.
[37] Letter quoted in J. K. Whitaker (ed.), *The Early Economic Writings of Alfred Marshall, 1867–1890* (2 vols., London, 1975), vol. 1, p. 63. In the end Marshall abandoned his monograph on foreign trade, though some of the more theoretical chapters were printed privately by Sidgwick in 1879 as *The Pure Theory of Foreign Trade*.

Wealth of Nations and Plato's *Republic*).[38] He had already read Mill's
Principles in August 1874 and 'enjoyed it immensely' and he made notes
on Mill (now preserved in Pembroke College Library) which have marginal comments, extracted from Fawcett's *Manual*, no doubt in the following January. By the early 1880s, however, the bright young men who
were lecturing for the Moral Sciences Tripos were openly scornful of the
Manual, and even more so of Millicent Fawcett's *Political Economy for
Beginners* (1870). There are some scathing remarks in a letter from
H. S. Foxwell to Neville Keynes dated 5 April 1881 where the former
writes (in commenting on the syllabus offered by a would-be examiner for
the Examinations Syndicate): 'The Fawcetts are at the bottom of most of
his errors as invariably happens. The most curious is his almost complete
omission of any treatment of interest as distinct from profits – and his
very bad theory of wages – both thoroughly characteristic of the Fawcetts.'[39] Later that year, on 20 June 1881, Foxwell had another go at the
Fawcetts in relation to the same culprit: 'Moorsom not only founded his
teaching on Mill, but invariably on the syllabus recommended Mrs
Fawcett first. Jevons and I were talking about Mrs F.'s book yesterday.
He showed me some howling croppers in it in regard to mere matters of
fact.'[40]

What Marshall thought of his predecessor in the Cambridge Chair of
Political Economy it is difficult to say. He was not as indiscreet or as
arrogant as Foxwell. It is, however, probably safe to assume that he
thought as little of Fawcett's *Manual* as he did of his own and Mary
Marshall's book *Economics of Industry* (1879), of which, according to
Mary: 'He never liked the little book for it offended against his belief that
"every dogma that is short and simple is false" and he said about it "you
cannot afford to tell the truth for half a crown".'[41] It is perhaps sufficient,
to bring out the difference between Fawcett and Marshall to juxtapose
Leslie Stephen's comment in his *Life of Fawcett*: 'According to him, in
fact, the leading principles of political economy and those which were
really valuable, were few, simple, and therefore capable of exposition on
the level of average intelligence.'[42] In any case it does not appear that
Fawcett's *Manual* ever figured in Marshall's reading list for his students,
even as early as 1874, for (again according to Mary, though admittedly
writing much later): 'In those days books were few. There were no blue
books or Economics magazines and very few textbooks. Mill was the
mainstay with Adam Smith and Ricardo and Malthus in the background.

[38] J. N. Keynes Diaries, Cambridge University Library, Add MS 7831, entry for 9 Jan. 1875.
[39] J. N. Keynes Paper, Marshall Library, University of Cambridge, box 1.   [40] ibid.
[41] Mary Marshall, *What I Remember* (Cambridge, 1947), p. 22.
[42] Stephen, *Life of Fawcett*, p. 124.

Hearn's *Plutology* was well thought of for beginners. Later on we read Jevons' *Principles*, Cairnes' *Leading Principles* and Walker on *Wages*.'[43]

In effect, it was in the House of Commons, where he served for nearly twenty years, at the Post Office (where he was Postmaster General from 1880 until his death in 1884) and in his contacts with his constituents in Brighton and Hackney, that Henry Fawcett was most effective in applying classical economic principles as a basis for economic policy prescriptions. As an M.P. he was much more influential than J. S. Mill had been and although Gladstone often had occasion to resent his independence of the Liberal whip, and his blistering criticisms of government measures (especially in relation to India), he respected him as a force in the House. Indeed, it is arguable that a main reason for appointing him Postmaster General (in spite of the handicap of blindness) was that ministerial office would keep this energetic M.P. busy and thus mute some of his criticisms of day-to-day government policies. At the Post Office he was active in trying to improve the service offered by that department and took a personal interest in the wages and conditions of work of its army of employees. He took pride, for instance, in introducing such innovations to the counter services as parcel post, postal orders and small savings stamps, in bringing down the price of telegrams and in increasing the facilities for insurance and annuities. He was directly involved in a number of schemes to improve working conditions and performance of post office employees, for example, introducing an annual week's holiday for postmen and an incremental scale for telegraphists.

When Fawcett died, the men at the Brighton Railway Works to whom he had continued to act as personal friend and adviser (though he had not been the member for Brighton since 1874) wrote to Millicent Fawcett, offering to raise a penny subscription from the working classes to support her as his widow. 'We always thought that the Professor was a *poor man* and only had what he earned by his talents.' And when she refused on the grounds that she had been left enough to live on they replied: 'Your dear husband and our best friend has practised what he always preached to us, private thrift.'[44] The virtue of private thrift was, of course, one of the normative principles embedded in the hard core of classical political economy which survived the transition to neo-classical economic science.

Let me now conclude with an attempt to place Henry Fawcett's career as an economist into long-term perspective. The economists who figure prominently in histories of economic thought are generally of two kinds: either they have acquired a contemporary (or perhaps later) reputation for having added significantly to the theoretical or empirical stock of economic knowledge; or they have stimulated sufficient outrage among

[43] Marshall, *What I Remember*, p. 20.   [44] Stephen, *Life of Fawcett*, pp. 466–7.

leaders in the discipline to have been cited frequently in the contemporary debates. It is evident that Henry Fawcett does not qualify on either of these two counts. He was not, of course, a nonentity. As the Professor of Political Economy in Cambridge from 1863 onwards he spoke with authority on economic questions – not only in Cambridge lecture rooms, but also on election platforms and in the House of Commons where he served as a Liberal M.P. from 1865. But although he regularly participated in the annual meetings of the British Association, was an articulate member of the London Political Economy Club from 1861 and was able to give the great J. S. Mill himself some insights on labour market behaviour, it cannot be said that he was actively engaged in pushing back the frontiers of economic knowledge. Nor, indeed, did he stimulate any formal opposition from academic economists.

The fact is that the period in which he was professionally active was characterised by rising dissatisfaction with the methodological foundations and theoretical implications of orthodox political economy and by a fast developing barrage of criticisms from a variety of directions – even from within. Henry Sidgwick, for example, dated the ending of professional self-confidence in the classical orthodoxy from two 'shocks' – first Mill's recantation in 1869 of the wage-fund theory and then William Stanley Jevons's more fundamental attack in his *Theory of Political Economy* (1871).[45] In an era of methodological controversy and theoretical doubt an economist who takes no interest in such issues is unlikely to attract much attention either from the academic debaters or from subsequent historians of economic thought. More important still, a 'new economics' was in process of construction – though it did not take formal shape until after the publication of Marshall's *Principles of Economics* in 1890. Consequently, to most of those who have analysed the evolution of economic ideas in the last three decades of the nineteenth century it is the transformation of value theory associated with the names of Jevons, Léon Walras and Carl Menger in the 1890s that constitutes the dominant charactersitic of the period.

To this transition between ruling paradigms, from the classical framework of economic analysis to the neo-classical framework, Henry Fawcett made no contribution. His *Manual* expounded orthodox classical poli-

[45] Henry Sidgwick, *The Principles of Political Economy* (3rd edn, London, 1901), p. 4. It is interesting to note that Mill did not carry his recantation fully through to the relevant sections of the 1871 edition of his *Principles of Political Economy*. Jevons, by contrast, concluded his *Theory of Political Economy*, also published in 1871, with a rousing section entitled 'The noxious influence of authority' where he protested against 'deference for any man, whether John Stuart Mill or Adam Smith or Aristotle being allowed to check inquiry. Our science has become far too much a stagnant one in which opinions rather than experience and reason are appealed to.'

tical economy in the hallowed tradition of Adam Smith, as sharpened by Ricardo and broadened and updated by J. S. Mill. He wrote in the spirit of a determinedly non-doctrinaire political economist, pragmatically applying the agreed principles of a well-established discipline to the practical economic and social issues confronting government in the second half of the nineteenth century. The accident of his early blindness effectively prevented him from engaging in systematic research in applied economics; and he lacked the interest in abstract reasoning that might have drawn him to theoretical research where his blindness might have been less of a handicap. His chosen role was that of a teacher, a populariser of political economy. Accepting Mill's *Principles* as constituting the accredited theory of the subject, he set out to analyse current economic trends and policy problems in the light of that orthodoxy. The *Manual* was designed to provide a clear, relevant and uncomplicated introduction to the current state of economic knowledge and to illuminate its applicability to a changing real world.

It is evident that all Fawcett's professional writings started, if not as formal lectures, at least as dictations to an amanuensis. They are repetitious, unpolished and forthright, in the style of essays in persuasion offered by an author obliged to develop and defend his ideas orally instead of being able to read and rewrite at leisure. At the same time, however, these simplistic, unpedantic interpretations of economic theory were married to a realistically informed appreciation of the contemporary economic scene. No doubt because he never considered it necessary to push economic 'laws' to extreme conclusions Fawcett was immune to the anxieties which bothered contemporary theorists (such as Mill) who felt that when the abstractions of pure theory were leading to manifestly unacceptable policy prescriptions, it became necessary to recast the theory in more acceptable form. Indeed it is fair to describe him as a practitioner of what his contemporaries categorised as the 'art of political economy' rather than the economic science which the theorists aspired to create.[46] Applied economists must generally resign themselves to the knowledge that in focusing on the contemporary real world their writings acquire a relatively ephemeral quality by comparison with those that deal with fundamental principles. What would Marshall's reputation have been had it depended solely on his *Industry and Trade* or his *Money, Credit and*

---

[46] J. Neville Keynes, for example, in writing the treatise which marked the end of the methodological debates of the 1870s and 1880s distinguished three types of economic enquiry: (a) 'a positive science ... a body of systematized knowledge concerning what is' (b) 'a normative or regulative science ... a body of systematized knowledge relating to criteria of what ought to be and concerned therefore with the ideal as distinguished from the actual', and (c) 'an art as a system of rules for the attainment of a given end'. *The Scope and Method of Political Economy* (London, 1891), pp. 34–5.

Commerce? Or Walras's had it depended on his books on social economics or applied economics? In addition, of course, Fawcett's publications were largely didactic in style and intention and few economists can expect to impress posterity with their textbooks, still less with popularisations of the textbooks of others.

Within his own time, however, Fawcett's impact on economic opinion in and out of Parliament was not negligible. His currently relevant attempts to explain the substance and policy implications of elementary economic analysis to non-professionals (students, politicians and general readers seeking an understanding of contemporary economic problems) almost certainly influenced a wider audience than the writings of any other English professor of economics. We cannot know whether Fawcett's *Manual* induced more students to read economics than did Mill's *Principles* which it was designed to popularise. But if there was any virtue in teaching the rudiments of classical political economy to the plain man of the 1860s, 1870s and 1880s that was where Henry Fawcett outshone his fellow economists.

5

The plain man's political economist: a discussion

DONALD WINCH

When approached from the perspective normally adopted by historians of economic thought, as Phyllis Deane makes abundantly clear, Henry Fawcett appears to have been unfortunate in being an unquestioning populariser of John Stuart Mill's position, an uncritical contemporary of William Stanley Jevons and an academically undistinguished predecessor of Alfred Marshall in the Cambridge Chair. He might have fared better if he had been one of the many critics of orthodox political economy who flourished in the 1870s and beyond, the vigour or even existence of whose criticisms might have ensured resuscitation by those modern opponents of economic orthodoxy who set some store by genealogy. In these respects, historians of economic thought, of divergent persuasion, have amply revenged themselves on a man who once sounded out Mill on the desirability of writing a history of political economy himself, only to receive the following reply from his mentor:

A History of Political Economy is not a kind of book much wanted on its own account, but it would afford an opportunity for interesting discussions of all the contested points, and for placing them in the strong light which results from the comparison of conflicting opinions and from a study of their origins and filiation. Though, therefore, it is a work I should hardly suggest to anyone, yet if any competent political economist with a talent for philosophical controversy feels spontaneously prompted to undertake it, the result is likely to be useful and interesting to those who care for the subject.[1]

With such lukewarm encouragement it is hardly surprising that no centennial assessment of Fawcett's efforts as a historian of economic thought is called for. In view of his problems in reading widely dispersed sources, and the fact that his knowledge of earlier political economists seems to have been confined to Adam Smith, David Ricardo, Thomas

---

[1] Mill to Fawcett, 4 Dec. 1863, in *Collected Works of John Stuart Mill* (25 vols., Toronto, 1963–), vol. 15, p. 907.

Tooke's *History of Prices*, and Mill, we have probably not lost a good deal.[2] Mill himself, though more widely read and certainly not lacking 'a talent for philosophical controversy', did not venture far beyond anecdote and polemic in his own forays into this kind of historical territory.

Once more it has to be said that Fawcett's failure in the eyes of those whose attention is often largely focussed on theoretical innovation and methodological novelty lies in his literal-minded fidelity to Mill's priorities. Mill himself possessed and displayed the skills of an economic theorist, but he encouraged others to believe, as he put it, that 'the purely abstract investigations of political economy ... are of very minor importance compared with the greater practical questions which the progress of democracy and the spread of socialist opinions are pressing on'.[3] Whereas Mill's wildly incautious statement that 'happily there is nothing in the laws of value which remains for the present or any future writer to clear up' acted as a spur to the ambitious and disaffected young Stanley Jevons, and later drew an embarrassed apology from Marshall, Fawcett accepted it as a comforting reflection. His own treatment of value in the *Manual* was so foreshortened that even Mill felt that by 'going at once to money prices without first discussing the general laws of exchange value' under conditions of barter, Fawcett was perhaps cutting one corner too many in his efforts to simplify the subject.[4]

With all the benefits of hindsight and a knowledge of contemporary developments in economic thinking that were often unknown to Fawcett, no economist worthy of his calling is likely to forgive Fawcett's blithe complacency on theoretical matters. This leaves the memorialist who is also an economist with the restricted task of pointing out that Fawcett was only guilty of making stronger practical claims for the guidance offered by the orthodox version of his discipline than he ever made for himself as its expositor; and that his qualities as an applied economist who never shirked the opportunity to tackle major controversial issues were by no means as negligible as might be supposed. Phyllis Deane has performed this task so admirably that were I to attempt to follow her it would only be to underline a point or two. Instead, I shall attempt to broaden out the discussion in one direction by making a few strategic comparisons between Fawcett and Jevons, treating them as near-contemporaries and

[2] Leslie Stephen, *Life of Henry Fawcett* (London, 1885), p. 97.
[3] Mill to Karl D. Heinrich Rau, 20 March 1852, in *Collected Works of John Stuart Mill*, vol. 14, p. 87.
[4] Mill to Fawcett, 17 May 1863, in ibid., vol. 15, p. 859. Let me confess, however, to a liking for Fawcett's characteristic choice of an athletic illustration when making a familiar point about the impossibility of a simultaneous rise or fall in the value of all commodities: 'This is as impossible as it would be for each one of six rowers to row faster or slower than the other five. A cannot row faster than his companions except by each of them rowing slower than A.' *Manual of Political Economy* (6th edn, London, 1883), p. 312.

fellow-economists who pursued divergent courses which say something about changes that were occurring to the discipline they both professed in the 1860s and 1870s.

Fawcett's career is an interesting reminder of the way in which a command of the principles of the relatively novel science of political economy could furnish a means of advancement for those lacking more conventional social and academic advantages. An earlier and appropriately Scottish example would be Francis Horner, one of Dugald's Stewart's pupils at Edinburgh, the first British university to offer a course on the subject during the early 1800s. Quite self-consciously, Horner set about using his expertise in political economy as a means of furthering political ambitions that would have otherwise seemed fruitless without fortune or family contacts. It was partly as a result of this expertise that he entered Parliament under the patronage of a Whig magnate, and was held in sufficient esteem to make it seem likely that he would have become Chancellor of the Exchequer in any Whig ministry formed in the 1820s.[5] As in Fawcett's case, Horner's obituarists devoted much of their space to praise for what they regarded as a triumph of 'character' over circumstances – the theme of Stefan Collini's paper in this volume. But Jevons – another person for whom the new science was to become a personal if not political vehicle for security and advancement – furnishes more interesting points of contrast with Fawcett which I shall present, oversimply, as differences between intellectual and political radicalism.

Blindness apart, it would not be difficult to show that Jevons, the intellectual radical of the pair, was less favoured by circumstances than Fawcett, whose Cambridge connections, support from Mill and sheer good luck in the way in which his opponents bungled the professorial election in 1863 enabled him to achieve a measure of independence and financial security by the age of thirty. At the same time, Jevons, admittedly Fawcett's junior by two years, was being appointed as a tutor at Owen's College, Manchester, thereby putting an end to a period of insecurity which had found him during the previous year hawking his services in London as a researcher for others at 3 shillings an hour. When Fawcett was drawing his £550 for lecturing on political economy in Cambridge for eighteen weeks each year, Jevons was receiving £100 a year for giving six lectures a week, together with evening classes on four nights, and having to cover logic, and mental and moral philosophy, as well as political economy. Fawcett's appointment was based on sympathetic support from friends in Cambridge and the publication of a popularisation of Mill's

[5] For further discussion of Horner from this point of view, see Stefan Collini, Donald Winch and John Burrow, *That Noble Science of Politics. A Study in Nineteenth-Century Intellectual History* (Cambridge, 1983), pp. 47–52, 58–9.

Principles. Jevons, on the other hand, in a highly self-conscious bid for scientific fame and reputation, had shifted his efforts from chemistry and meteorology towards political economy, and had already formulated what he believed to be 'the true Theory of Economy' based on the principle of diminishing marginal utility. His first public account of his new mathematical theory was delivered to the British Association in 1862, probably in Fawcett's presence, and had been received, he felt, 'without a word of interest or belief'.[6] Jevons had also completed various statistical studies, one of which, on the fall in the value of gold, had appeared in 1863, to be followed two years later by his book on *The Coal Question,* the first of his works to draw widespread public recognition. This work on the exhaustion of British coal supplies was immediately seen to have implications for debt and taxation policy, but for Jevons it was chiefly of importance for its value in helping to establish his reputation as an economic scientist capable of bringing the higher standards of statistical and empirical research which prevailed in the natural sciences to bear on economic problems.

Along with everybody else, Jevons could pay tribute to Fawcett's capacity 'to state and discuss the most difficult, dry, and intricate scientific arguments' in 'a profound, lucid, and yet agreeable manner', especially when dealing with a subject of common interest, namely the gold question. But in private he exalted in the fact that on this subject Fawcett had been converted by, and was heavily dependent on, his own researches.[7] By 1870, when the *Theory of Political Economy* was published, Jevons included 'Professor Fawcett' alongside Mill in his bitter attack on 'the noxious influence of authority' in political economy, an influence which he believed to be absent in natural science.[8] By that time, of course, Jevons was one voice among many raised in criticism of the hold exercised by the Ricardo–Mill school on economic thinking, and it merely serves to underline what Phyllis Deane has clearly hinted at, namely that for most of his tenure of the Cambridge Chair Fawcett was regarded by many who were committed to the revitalisation of economic studies as an intellectual survival from an earlier age.

As Stefan Collini shows, much the same might be said of Fawcett's political views. He retained all the original anti-aristocratic opinions of the early Philosophic Radicals, especially on questions of land tenure. He also belonged to a Cambridge republican circle which pledged hostility 'to the hereditary principle as exemplified in monarchical and aristocratical

6 R. D. C. Black and R. Könekamp (eds.), *Papers and Correspondence of William Stanley Jevons* (7 vols., London, 1972–81), vol. 1 (1972), p. 188.
7 ibid., vol. 3 (1977), pp. 42–3.
8 *Theory of Political Economy* (2nd edn, London, 1879), pp. 298–300.

institutions, and to all social and political privileges dependent upon sex'.[9] Indeed, Fawcett's set of political causes, together with the enthusiasm he brought to his advocacy of almost all of Mill's 'crotchets', makes him a useful test of historical understanding – especially to those who bring twentieth-century categories and sympathies to the study of nineteenth-century alignments. Hence we find in Fawcett a leading exponent of free trade, laissez-faire and self-help, an apologist for neo-Malthusianism and the Poor Law Amendment Act, who also adopted republican postures, was a fervent supporter of feminist principles, of conservationism in the interests of the unpropertied mass and of the extension of the cooperative principle to industry. Fawcett also lectured on the International in 1871/2 and – to end on another *apparently* incongruous note – was an advocate of a policy of subsidising the travel costs of urban workers which bears some resemblance to that pursued by the Greater London Council before its recent demise.[10]

By contrast with all this Jevons appears to have been made a middle-of-the-road Gladstonian Liberal who, in the period of agitation leading up to the Second Reform Bill, confided the following statement of his political inclinations to his journal:

What side am I to take ... or can I take both? I cannot consent with the radical party to obliterate a glorious past – nor can I consent with the conservatives to prolong abuses into the present. I wish with all my heart to aid in securing all that is good for the masses, yet to give them all they wish and are striving for is to endanger much that is good beyond their comprehension. I cannot pretend to underestimate the good that the English monarchy and aristocracy with all the liberal policy actuating it, does for the human race, and yet I cannot but fear the pretensions of democracy against it are strong and in some respects even properly strong. This antithesis and struggle perhaps after all is no more than has always more or less existed but is now becoming more marked. Compromise perhaps is the only resource. Those who rightly possess the power in virtue of their superior knowledge must yield up some that they may carry with them the honest but uncertain will of those less educated but more numerous and physically powerful.[11]

These are hardly the tones of a confident partisan, and they sound more like wealth and brains versus numbers than the programme endorsed, say, by the authors of *Essays on Reform*.

[9] See Stephen, *Life of Fawcett*, p. 286.
[10] See *The Economic Position of the British Labourer* (Cambridge and London, 1865), pp. 69–70.
[11] Black and Könekamp (eds.), *Papers and Correspondence*, vol. 1, entry for 1 Nov. 1866, pp. 207–8; see also his comment in a letter dated 28 Dec. 1866 (vol. 3, p. 150) that: 'It is very difficult to know what view to take of this Reform agitation. I am not a democrat as perhaps you know and don't much care to adopt popular views to please the mob. However, I don't think any reform bill that is likely to pass will really upset our system here, while it may lead to many real improvements.'

It is significant that this journal entry was made just after Jevons had got himself into considerable trouble with Manchester radicals for a lecture on trade unions in which he stated that 'our working classes, with their growing numbers and powers of combination, may be led by ignorance to arrest the true growth of our liberty, political and commercial'.[12] The labour question certainly provides another example of convergence and divergence between the positions of Fawcett and Jevons considered as political and intellectual radicals. The main point of convergence lies in the fact that this was a case where Jevons endorsed one of Mill's 'crotchets', the idea of cooperation and industrial copartnership as the best long-term solution to the conflict between capital and labour. The belief that trade unionism might provide a stepping-stone to cooperation undoubtedly helped Mill and Fawcett to adopt a sympathetic position towards trade union activities – though it is worth underlining Phyllis Deane's view that neither before nor after Mill's recantation of the wage-fund theory did this doctrine stand in the way of general sympathy for trade unions. The doctrine was largely employed not as a means of attacking trade union activities but for the quite different purposes of stressing the long-run damage that could be done by increases in unproductive consumption and any failure to heed basic Malthusian warnings on population.[13]

What then can we say about Jevons, for whom the wage-fund doctrine was simply part of the dogmatic rigmarole associated with the dominant Ricardo–Mill–Fawcett school of thought on fundamental questions of economic theory? The *Theory of Political Economy* leaves no doubt as to his opposition to this doctrine, and while he did not apply his value theory to trade unions in that book, the implications for the analysis of wages are fairly clear. Jevons himself spelled out most of them in lectures and articles on strikes and trade unions, and more especially in his book on *The State in Relation to Labour*.[14] The issues are complex and by no means clear-cut, but a brief summary judgement would run as follows: a theory which makes the demand for labour depend on the prospective market value of the joint product of capital and labour raises questions about the effect of higher wages on the prices of final goods which, though clearly recognised, cannot perhaps be so clearly posed by earlier modes of

[12] See ibid., vol. 7, (1981), pp. 37–54, and vol. 3, pp. 128–38, for the criticisms of Jevons's lecture and his replies.

[13] For fuller documentation on this issue see F. W. Taussig, *Wages and Capital* (London, 1896), chs. 11 and 12; Pedro Schwartz, *The New Political Economy of J. S. Mill* (London, 1972), ch. 5; and D. P. O'Brien, *The Classical Economists* (Oxford, 1975), pp. 111–18, 284.

[14] See *Primer of Political Economy* (London, 1878), chs. 7–9; *Methods of Social Reform* (London, 1883), pp. 98–118; and *The State in Relation to Labour* (London, 1894). See also, Black and Könekamp (eds.), *Papers and Correspondence*, vol. 6 (1977), pp. 68–79.

analysis. It enabled Jevons, for example, to give greater substance to the view that the real clash of interests entailed in trade union action to raise wages was between one group of workers and another rather than between capital and labour. Higher wages were, in most cases, achieved not at the expense of profits so much as at the expense of those consumers/fellow-workers who were obliged to pay higher prices. In other words, wage disputes were best seen as examples of conflict between the organised minority producing interest groups and the unorganised majority consuming interests. Jevons's approach to these matters also dramatised the contrast between measures which benefited all by means of increased production at lower cost, and those that benefited the minority through higher wages based on protected or monopoly powers available to both workers and capitalists – though available only on a differential basis.

Hence in large part Jevons's far cooler analysis of strikes and trade unions, and the otherwise surprising conclusion that the new wage theory supported a more negative verdict on trade unions than the wage-fund doctrine was ever alleged to have done: 'On the whole, then, we conclude that it is quite impossible for trade unions in general to effect any permanent increase of wages, and that success in maintaining exclusive monopolies leads to great loss and injury to the community in general.'[15] It was for this reason, presumably, that Philip Wicksteed ('the only Jevonian theorist of note', according to Joseph Schumpeter) wrote that 'Jevons had a strong dislike and suspicion of trade unions, based on economic theory', where the final clause is as important as the main statement.[16]

This antagonism to the wage-fixing activities of trade unions does not mean, of course, that Jevons, in contrast to Mill and Fawcett, was espousing the cause of capital as opposed to that of labour. Nor does it mean that Jevons, by virtue of being one of the founders of the body of thought which later became known as neo-classical economics, was, as some Marxian interpreters would hold, inexorably committed to an apologetic approach to the problems of capitalist society, despite claims to be pursuing purely abstract and apolitical truths. As has already been mentioned, Jevons was as much of an enthusiast for profit-sharing schemes and worker-owned cooperatives as Mill and Fawcett were, despite the fact that his economic theory relating wages, profits and prices supported stronger negative conclusions on one of the main activities of trade unions and might well have served to increase his fears concerning

---

[15] *State in Relation to Labour*, p. 109.
[16] See P. H. Wicksteed, *The Common Sense of Political Economy* (2 vols., London, 1938) vol. 2, p. 807.

the effect on consumers of monopoly powers gained through closer collaboration between workers and their employers. For if the real conflict is between producers and consumers, one has to ask how this could be resolved in a socially beneficial way by a system which adds to the capacity of producers to act as monopolists. The answer to this question is that Jevons, in common with Mill and Fawcett, presupposed that cooperation would work at the enterprise rather than the industrial level, with competition being maintained between the different enterprises within an industry.[17]

But even when the reformist policy conclusions, or rather in this case, perhaps, hopes, were similar, differences between Fawcett and Jevons remain. Fawcett was more of a political economist in every sense, employing simplified versions of an established theory to propose solutions to political problems, where the faith of an intellectual conservative enabled him to make confident applications of his knowledge. As an old-style political economist who differed from Mill's other chief disciple, John Eliot Cairnes, in not wishing to treat the discipline as an abstract science, Fawcett drew no rigid distinctions between science and art. Wherever a gap existed between economic analysis and policy conclusions, it was legitimate to attempt to bridge it by invoking political hopes. Lawrence Goldman's contribution to this volume suggests that, compared with some other contemporary middle-class sympathisers with working-class aspirations, Fawcett's answers to the labour question contain incoherences and reveal damaging gaps of a moral and intellectual kind between his politics and his political economy. It may be interesting to close this comment with a discussion of just why what may be a cogent criticism of someone like Fawcett is far less appropriately levelled at Jevons, despite the fact that both men shared a common utilitarian background.

Jevon's sympathies were tempered by a different kind of professional ideal as well as by a more general and precise form of economic analysis. He had chosen the path of *scientific* rebel, and while this did not prevent him from pronouncing on policy questions, it modified his mode of doing so. In common with other political economists of the period Jevons sought a more neutral stance for the economist, one that would enable him to occupy the difficult, but professionally defensible position of standing above the more extreme partisan positions, while at the same time contributing to policy debate. The biographical evidence seems to show that as Jevons became more deeply engaged in the business of being a

---

[17] For an interesting treatment of this question which takes Wicksteed's characterisation of Jevons's opinions on labour questions as its starting-point, see Ian Steedman, 'Trade interest versus class interest', *Economia Politica*, vol. 3 (Aug. 1986), pp. 187–206.

professional economist so his willingness to pronounce on the larger political questions associated with laissez-faire individualism and collectivism gradually faded.[18] A devastatingly frank sentence in the *Theory of Political Economy* confesses that 'the usefulness of the theory is a different question from that of its truth, and is one upon which I am not quite so confident'. Unfortunately, for my purposes at least, the sentence was removed from subsequent editions. But anybody who has read the opening and concluding pages of *The State in Relation to Labour* on the reasons why 'there can be no royal road to legislation' will recognise the same mentality – that of an intellectual radical who could not in good conscience go beyond a mixture of Cartesian doubt and examination of the piecemeal results of Baconian experiment to endorse a full-blooded and interlinked political programme.

If Jevons was in this respect one of the first of a new professional breed, Fawcett becomes one of the last amateurs. In the absence of other evidence that would establish this contrast decisively, I will close with a counterfactual hypothesis which indicates my belief. It is not simply a matter of saying that whereas Fawcett might well have been troubled by Lawrence Goldman's charges, Jevons would not: I conjecture that Jevons would increasingly have been worried only by arguments which showed that his economic theory of wage-determination was lacking in logical consistency and/or empirical content.

[18] The best of recent work on these matters depends on Black and Könekamp's edition of Jevons's *Papers and Correspondence*. See R.D.C. Black's chapter on Jevons in D. P. O'Brien and J. R. Presley (eds.), *Pioneers of Modern Economics in Britain* (London, 1981); and T.W. Hutchinson, 'The politics and philosophy in Jevons's political economy', *Manchester School*, vol. 50 (Dec. 1982), pp. 366–78. I am grateful to Professor R.D.C. Black both for his comments on an earlier version of this comment and for allowing me to see two unpublished Special Lectures on Jevons given at Manchester University in 1982 on 'Transitions in political economy'.

6

*Henry Fawcett and the labour question in mid-Victorian Britain**

GIACOMO BECATTINI

If [a] student had been talking with an Englishman acquainted with the subject in 1870 he would have said that the leading authorities of the day were disciples of Mill. Perhaps he would have set Cairnes above all but some might have looked to the less critical and constructive disciple, the blind Henry Fawcett of Cambridge University, who held the chief academic chair of political economy at the time.

> Wesley C. Mitchell, *Types of Economic Theory. From Mercantilism to Institutionalism*, ed. J. Dorfman (2 vols., New York, 1967–9), vol. 2, p. 7.

A suitable starting-point for the reconsideration of the life and thought of Henry Fawcett is the curious disparity between his contemporaries' appraisal of his role as a politician and an economist and the lack of attention he has received at the hands of many historians. Fawcett was certainly not an outstanding figure as a scholar or as a politician. All the same, he fulfilled a special role of his own in mid-Victorian Britain. He stood out in the anonymous crowd of M.P.s. His interventions, whether written or oral, were always granted careful attention by politicians and trade unionists.

Mr. Fawcett [wrote *The Economist*] can hardly be regarded as the leader of any section of the Commons, and yet he is received on rising as no mere borough member ever is received. A scholar, a doctrinaire and at the same time member for the Radical majority of one of the most Radical constituencies in the Kingdom,

* I should like to thank Dr Jonathan Steinberg who first had the idea of making this reassessment of Fawcett and helped me, together with Dr Maud Tyler, to make my laboursome thoughts on this subject understandable to the English-speaking world.

Special thanks are due to Marco Dardi, with whom I discussed several versions of this paper. I owe much more than can be said to his original and inspiring book *Il Giovane Marshall. Accumalazione e Mercato* (Bologna, 1984), but he is in no way responsible for the argument advanced here. I am also very grateful to Trinity Hall, Fawcett's college, for providing me with the best academic atmosphere one could wish for, and to the Italian Consiglio Nazionale delle Ricerche for financial help.

Mr. Fawcett is listened to by Tories of the 'highest' type and his speeches frequently tell distinctly on divisions.[1]

And as Postmaster General in the Gladstone government, 1880–4, he made a distinct mark. Several important innovations in the British postal service were due to his initiatives.[2]

In his capacity as a professional economist (Professor of Political Economy in Cambridge from 1863 to 1884) Fawcett was known to his contemporaries as a loyal but somewhat limited follower of John Stuart Mill, whose *Principles of Political Economy* he had summarised (some said 'diluted') in his very popular *Manual of Political Economy*.[3] Many contemporaries criticised him harshly, and some made fun of him for his simplifications of Mill's theories, but everybody considered him one of the most representative and influential exponents of the dominant economic doctrine.

In a series of lectures given in the year 1870 William Stanley Jevons is reported to have said:

Some students have a great opinion of Fawcett's *Manual*, and Fawcett is no doubt a great man: and if any student wishes to read his *Manual* he will find it a very clear and readable digest of Mill's system; but at the same time it contains comparatively few opinions *but* those of Mill. It has been publicly described as 'Mill and Water' and it is not altogether an inapt expression.[4]

It is L. L. Price, however, who gives us the most representative picture of how the economist Fawcett was considered by his contemporaries, in his lively historical profile of British economic thought. 'It would be incorrect', he writes, 'to say that he made any considerable contribution to the development of economic theory. His strength seems to have lain rather in the domain of practice. Those chapters of his *Manual* in which he dealt with the practical facts of the Poor Law, or of Cooperation, were the more original.'[5] On the grounds of this judgement, Price includes him, together with Arnold Toynbee – a very strange bedfellow! – among the economists devoted to a reform of society. If we accept this setting of the man and the scholar – and in a sense we must accept it – we come to the conclusion that those features of social commitment which have always marked the

[1] *The Economist*, 7 Feb. 1873.
[2] Howard Robinson, *The British Post Office. A History* (London, 1948). For an extensive exposition of Fawcett's innovations see: Leslie Stephen, *Life of Henry Fawcett* (London, 1885), pp. 402–9.
[3] Henry Fawcett, *Manual of Political Economy* (Cambridge and London, 1863).
[4] R. D. C. Black and R. Könekamp (eds.), *Papers and Correspondence of William Stanley Jevons* (London, 1977), vol. 6, pp. 3–4.
[5] L. L. Price, *A Short History of Political Economy in England*, (1st edn, London, 1891: 7th edn, London, 1911), p. 179.

economic school of Cambridge, down to its most recent exponents, were already present before Alfred Marshall came on the scene.

If it is true, as W. E. Gladstone once wrote of Fawcett, that 'there has been no public men of our days whose remarkable qualities had been more fully recognised by his fellow countrymen and more deeply embedded in their memories',[6] then the question arises as to how it could have happened that only a few years after his death, by the beginning of the new century, the image of Fawcett had completely faded away. Indeed, had it not been for the intense political activity of his wife, Millicent Garrett Fawcett, a leading suffragist, and for the spectacular academic performance of his daughter Philippa (classified, albeit informally, above the Senior Wrangler in the Mathematical Tripos of 1890), his name would have sounded, at the beginning of the new century, that is just sixteen years after his death, like the feeble echo of a political and cultural season long passed away.

The sudden loss of fame at the time of death of a figure who had been important in life is not so uncommon an event, but every time it happens, it raises the question: was it true fame? In other words, what conjunction of events first determined the success, and then the sudden oblivion? I do not pretend to give a full answer to such a question, which involves aspects that lie outside the area of knowledge of the economist and even of the historian of political economy; I intend in this paper to offer some comments, and perhaps some clues, in the hope that others, better equipped for the enterprise, will want to consider and complete them.

The opinion that Fawcett was not worth much as a theoretical economist, which we have seen expressed by Jevons and Price, is certainly well founded if we consider his own specific contributions to a rigorous solution of the problems left open in the Millian version of the classical theory. Fawcett was apparently not aware of what those problems were, nor of what conditions were needed to solve them within the methodological limits of the classical economic theory. Yet we cannot agree to dispose of him hastily as a vulgar epigone of the classical school. The evolution of economic thought should not be conceived as a succession of final answers to fundamental questions raised once and for all. It is rather to be conceived as a social process which engages successive generations of economists, each of which derives, both from the preceding generation and from the surrounding world, the questions which must be answered.[7]

---

6 Stephen, *Life of Fawcett*, p. 465.
7 'The substance of economic thought', wrote Alfred Marshall to L. L. Price, 'cannot well be to any great extent the work of any one man: it is the product of the age. Perhaps an exception should be made for Ricardo: but everything of importance that was said in the five generations 1740–65, 1765–90, 1815–40, 1865–90 seems to me to have been thought

Within such a view of the evolution of economic thought, a place may also be found for those authors who accept the challenge of the problems which their own contemporaries and fellow-countrymen believe to be relevant, whether or not they lie within or without the boundaries of their field of studies, strictly defined. When an economist gathers the questions which emerge from common discourse and persuades his colleagues that some problem, thus far considered external to the discipline, is in fact part of it, he contributes to a redefinition of its boundaries, and indirectly forces its conceptual reorganisation.

In the words of a Marshallian scholar:

Perhaps all writings in economics, as in political philosophy – a very large part of it at any rate – in the last analysis is topical. It appears that contemporary economic problems suggest the subject, and the available framework of economic science provides the way in which the problem is approached and analysed. Very often during the process of this scientific examination, the theoretical frames of the science, and its tools of analysis, receive an enlargement, refinement or an overhaul.[8]

From the point of view just sketched, the activity that Fawcett carried on vigorously – to bring within the scope of enquiry of the theoretical economist social phenomena such as combinations of workers and strikes – contributed, as we shall see, to that metamorphosis of British economic thought in the second half of the nineteenth century, which is conventionally called the marginalistic 'revolution', or 'counter-revolution'. In order to understand what actually happened in nineteenth-century British economic thought, we must take together British economic, social and intellectual history. The 1860s and the 1870s were not characterised by a frontal battle between the 'classical' troops and the 'Jevonian' ones on the theme of the theory of value, but instead by a host of skirmishes – a kind of guerrilla warfare, full of surprising developments and not devoid of theoretical and methodological implications – on more specific issues, especially the economic and social conditions and the political prospects of the working masses. Let us not forget that we are considering the years that witnessed the maturation and the realisation of the great electoral reform of 1867, which opened the electoral rolls to a good number of ordinary people.

Now, the most pressing question of the period, and therefore the driving force behind the reflections of economists (who were still barely professionalised), was not the labour theory of value. The main subversive consequences of this had long before been defeated and expelled from the

out concurrently more or less by many people.' A. C. Pigou (ed.), *Memorials of Alfred Marshall* (London, 1925), p. 379.

[8] N. Jha, *The Age of Marshall. Aspects of British Economic Thought, 1890–1915* (2nd edn, London, 1973), p. 13.

common sense of the masses and would reappear only when the Marxian message had been, to some extent, absorbed. Rather, the issues of the moment concerned the answers that 'social science'[9] could offer to explain, and possibly foster, the adaptation of traditional values and behaviour in Britain to the new, all-pervading force of industrialisation. One aspect of such a process which worried observers was the incidence of strikes. The newspapers reported them frequently and underlined how often they failed. Failures generally cost the workers more than they gained. Was such behaviour rational? Strikes posed a dilemma for 'heartless' economists whose claims to have discovered the 'natural' laws of social organisation clashed with the spontaneous reaction of working people in the real world. Strikes also threatened the deferential order of society in which each subject knew 'his place'. They subverted the 'natural' order of superiority and inferiority and hence, in the eyes of alarmed conservatives, what they considered the inner structure of Victorian society.

Trade unions, pressed between pathetic reminders of the 'good old solidarity' between social ranks and the stern injunctions of the economic laws, found themelves pushed into an awkward position, right on the fringe of civil society: either societies for mutual aid among poor souls, or semi-criminal associations of rebels. This, in broad terms, was the cultural situation of Britain, with regard to the social problems and perspectives of the working population, at the end of the 1850s when Fawcett made his debut as a student of social phenomena and as a would-be politician.

Fawcett's original contribution to the evolution of political economy and, as we shall see, at one and the same time to the political and social compromise of mid-Victorian Britain[10] emerged in the earliest stage of his career and was connected with the labour question. In fact the labour question, and not just the wages question, constantly recurs throughout Fawcett's entire works as is proved by several lecture courses which he gave in Cambridge from 1864 onwards. These lectures formed the basis of a number of volumes which had some effect on the public opinion of the time: *The Economic Position of the British Labourer* in 1865, *Pauperism* in 1871, *Essays and Lectures on Social and Political Subjects* (with

[9] Lawrence Goldman, 'The origins of British "social science", 1830–1835: political economy, natural science and statistics', *Historical Journal*, vol. 26, no. 3 (1983), pp. 587–616; and idem 'A peculiarity of the English? The Social Science Association and the absence of sociology in nineteenth-century Britain', *Past and Present*, No. 114 (Feb. 1987), pp. 131–71. For a different view, cf. Reba N. Soffer, 'Why do disciplines fail? The strange case of British sociology', *English Historical Review*, vol. 97 (1982), pp. 767–802.
[10] The flexible 'Gramscian' notion of hegemony for an interpretation of the mid-Victorian compromise is used with remarkable results by Trygve R. Tholfson, *Working Class Radicalism in Mid-Victorian England* (London, 1976).

Millicent Garrett Fawcett) in 1872, *State Socialism and the Nationalisation of the Land* in 1883.

In 1859 Fawcett, by then twenty-six years old, attended the annual meeting of the Social Science Association, which that year was held in Bradford. The subject of the talk he delivered could not have been more topical, nor the title bolder: 'The theory and tendency of strikes'. As a speaker the young man certainly could not match the polished style of Lord Brougham, nor the pathos of Lord Shaftesbury, regular attenders at the meetings of the Social Science Association. Fawcett's style was simple, direct and unburdened by any unnecessary show of erudition. His words could be understood by everyone, intellectuals, businessmen, clerical workers or middle-ranking trade unionists.

Fawcett's talk began with a vigorous denunciation of current opinions. 'Personal recriminations can avail nothing',[11] he said. Bad masters on the one side and ruthless agitators on the other do not suffice to explain the growth of combinations and strikes. The power that binds tens of thousands of men on strike, with their starving families and holds them for months, cannot be reduced to deceit or delusion. 'To bandy accusations from masters to men will not get rid of the fact that 12,000 men can combine.'[12] The main road, in fact the only road, to the discovery of the deep causes and to the analysis of the effects of these new social phenomena consists in the application of the methods of investigation proper to social science. Due to the backward state of the other social sciences this meant, in practice, turning to political economy. By this expression Fawcett understood essentially, if not exclusively, the Millian version of English political economy and not what he considered the pseudo-theoretical bastard creatures produced by the so-called inductivist school, led in Cambridge itself by no less an authority in the field of history and methodology of science than William Whewell.[13] On the other hand Fawcett was not satisfied with the way in which many true or presumed economists tackled the theme of strikes:

When the subject of strikes is discussed political economy is seldom employed for any other purpose than conveniently to dispose of the whole question in some such outburst of outraged science as this: 'How contrary to political economy to seek

[11] Henry Fawcett, 'The theory and tendency of strikes', *Transactions of the National Association for the Promotion of Social Sciences*, 1859 (London, 1860), p. 635.
[12] ibid.
[13] L. Goldman, 'The origins', pp. 594–600. See also Salim Rashid, 'Richard Jones and Baconian historicism at Cambridge', *Journal of Economic Issues*, vol. 13, no. 1 (March 1979), and idem, 'The growth of economic studies at Cambridge: 1776–1860', *History of Education Quarterly*, vol. 20 (Fall 1980), pp. 281–94.

ten hours wages for nine hours work. This cannot be; the immutable laws of demand and supply forbid it.'[14]

Words which would not have sounded amiss on Marx's lips.

'In order to gain an object', the combinations, said Fawcett, 'use the most perfect system of political organization; they act with mutual forbearance, they have recognised leaders, who make speeches, often showing a great power of reasoning; the provinces are visited by deputations, and the movement is supported by subscriptions throughout the length and breadth of the land.'[15] Fawcett was clearly enjoying this vivid portrait of the great conspiracy. His provocative intention becomes more explicit later in his talk, when after attributing the frequency of strikes to the 'growing intelligence of the working classes' he gleefully adds that 'many philanthropists are deeply distressed' by this interpretation of strikes. This is Fawcett at his best: lucid, ironic, sarcastic.[16]

We can easily imagine the reactions of a hall full of intellectuals and politicians committed in their various ways to doing good: surprise, irritation, maybe anger. But at the end of the speech there was a great burst of applause and Fawcett was warmly congratulated. News of the performance spread rapidly. Thomas Hare wrote to Mill; J. M. Ludlow wrote to F. D. Maurice; Sir James Kay-Shuttleworth extended an invitation to Fawcett to present his ideas at a special meeting at St Martin's Hall; even the oracle of the time, England's glory, George Eliot, was impressed. In short it was a triumph for the young Fellow of Trinity Hall; and it was on this triumph that he was to build his political career, a truly remarkable achievement for a blind man.

The ideas Fawcett expressed at that Bradford meeting have reached us through the abstract reproduced in the *Transactions* of the Social Science Association, and more diffusely through an unsigned review article that Fawcett published in the *Westminster Review* of July 1860. It was through the manuscript of this article, sent him by the author, that J. S. Mill came to appreciate fully Fawcett's intelligence. The same ideas were repeated by Fawcett in his subsequent writings, practically for the whole of his life, but after 1865, when Fawcett published *The Economic Position of the British Labourer*,[17] not only did they not develop, but rather tended to shrink or recede into the background of the Fawcettian discourse. In the following pages we shall be concerned mainly with those

[14] Henry Fawcett, 'Strikes: their tendencies and remedies', *Westminster Review*, vol. 74 (o.s.), vol. 18 (n.s.) (July 1860), p. 4.
[15] Fawcett, 'The theory', p. 635.   [16] ibid., p. 639.
[17] Henry Fawcett, *The Economic Position of the British Labourer* (Cambridge and London, 1865).

early writings, and especially with the articles in the *Westminster Review* and the *Transactions*, for a reconstruction of Fawcett's theses.

The first substantial point made by Fawcett in his paper is methodological in character: Fawcett believed that economic science, as he saw it, was fully qualified to deal with complex social phenomena such as combinations of workers and strikes. In particular he believed that these phenomena had their scientific explanations, or at least a beginning thereof, in that chapter of economic theory (a nearly empty chapter, indeed!) which studied the gravitation of market wages around 'natural' wages.

Tendencies, therefore [writes Fawcett] are constantly acting to bring wages into a position which may be described as their natural rate, and as these tendencies act with increasing force the more wages are disturbed from their natural rate, the position may be regarded as one of stable equilibrium. Similarly it is often stated that the planets revolve in ellipses ... the paths of the planets are disturbed by an infinity of causes ... The explanation of many most important phenomena must be sought entirely amongst these disturbances. In precisely a similar manner the phenomena of strikes must be considered with reference to those causes which disturb wages from their natural rate.[18]

Fawcett takes for granted the forces that produce, so to speak, the 'wages' ellipses' and concentrates his analysis on those that prevent market wages following these 'ellipses' strictly. Saving and investment decisions of the capitalists define rigorously the amount of resources being devoted to the subsistence of the workers during the production period conventionally defined; the average wage cannot therefore exceed the ratio between that amount and the number of employed workers. The number of employed workers, due to the active competition for work among the workers, will coincide with the totality of the labour supply. The same active competition between workers distributes the total amount of the wages fund in such a way that the average wages are made actual.

If the actual intensity of the competition among workers were equal to that assumed by the theory, coalitions and strikes to increase the wages of some sections of workers would be absolutely useless.[19] But if that competition is not adequate, due, for instance, to their ignorance of the conditions of their labour in different places or to their irrational attachment to their birthplace, then they will get less than the whole amount of the wages fund. A part of it will remain in the hands of the capitalists who face workers who are 'ignorant' or not keen to move. In this case, there is room for combinations of workers and strikes, as a means of affecting the distribution of the total product. In fact, if the

---

[18] Fawcett, 'Strikes', p. 6.   [19] ibid.

coalition of workers demands wage increases from the capitalists, the latter may find it convenient to share some of their extra profits because they may not be able to find other workers equally well fitted to the organisation of their firms, or because, due to full employment, they will have to attract workers from other employers. The action of the unionised workers will thus have the effect of accelerating the realisation of the distribution pattern established by the economic theory.[20] The argument is not entirely new among economists: J. R. McCulloch, for instance, had used it already in his *Essays on Wages* (1833), but in the context of the late fifties it must have sounded rather unusual and provocative.[21]

The second original idea contained in Fawcett's essay is, at first sight, only an extension of the first. Fawcett distinguished between disturbances which act permanently (the unwillingness of workers to leave their homes) and 'those of a temporary nature'.[22] In Fawcett's view the ignorance of the workers about the demand for labour in other districts is matched by the ignorance of all workers about the demand for the final products in their industry. The workers do not know the state of the market as well as the capitalists do, and therefore miss the opportunity of participating fully in the extra profits derived from booming trade. If the unionised workers were to know what capitalists know, they would be able to tune their wage demands precisely to the fluctuations in demand for the final product.

This idea of an information gap between masters and men and of its effects on distribution was widely discussed in labour newspapers of that period. It is interesting to find an echo of it in a text of a few years later. In 1873, that is right in the middle of Fawcett's tenure of the Chair of Political Economy, Alfred Marshall gave six lectures to women students on the labour question. We have the notes taken at these lectures by his pupil Mary Paley. Mary's notes include the following: 'Some of the unions have formed the brilliant idea of starting co-operative stores expecting to lose by it; but expecting to obtain better knowledge than they do now of the state of trade and the current rate of profit in different branches, as the masters are not in the habit of revealing the circumstances of trade.'[23]

In the case of workers' knowledge of the state of the market for their products, and for reasons very like those already seen, the capitalists will find it convenient to give up a portion of their extra profits. That widening

20 ibid., pp. 7–8.
21 D. P. O'Brien, *J. R. McCulloch. A Study in Classical Economics* (London, 1970), p. 369.
22 Fawcett, 'The theory', p. 637.
23 Perhaps we should add that in the margin beside the quoted passage there is the following comment in Alfred Marshall's hand: 'I have not heard that much has come of this.' 'Some economic questions directly connected with the welfare of the labourer', May term 1873, lecture notes taken by Mary Paley, MS copy, 1873, Marshall Library, Cambridge.

of social distance which characterised the period of great mid-Victorian prosperity, and which threatened the compactness of the social body, would thus be avoided. We should perhaps add that according to Fawcett, 'profits [in normal circumstances] are the reward of abstinence, in the same manner that wages are the reward of physical exertion'.[24] In his view what mostly hurts the sense of justice, and must therefore be removed, if one aims at orderly social progress, is the continuous widening of the gap between the well-being of different regions of the country and different social classes. In this view unions and strikes appear, on the one hand the symptom of, and on the other the endogenous remedy for, such a socio-economic pathology.

What Fawcett failed to understand is that this sharing out of profits not yet realised, is, at least implicitly, founded on a game of expectations (on the future state of the market and the actual power of the opposing combinations) which goes beyond the traditional theoretical framework. In the previous case we considered a redistribution of a fund already formed at the beginning of a specified period; now we bargain over the share of a flow of expected profits over a period of unspecified length.

The third original idea is that of the 'perfect strike'. Let us see, in the words of Fawcett, how he conceives it. He pictures a deputation 'of combined thousands' urging their case to masters in the following terms:

We examine all the prices of your trade as carefully as you do for yourselves ... we therefore know that you can afford to raise your wages ... We have calculated exactly the sacrifices we shall be compelled to make; we consider that what we hope to gain renders it worth our while to make these sacrifices; our combination is supported without compulsion.[25]

If the workers are ready to endure any sacrifice for their cause, they will be able to demand from the capitalist what the economic laws guarantee them. The capitalist – by definition a rational agent – will grant it to them without giving rise to an open conflict. 'A perfectly organized strike', writes Fawcett, 'must tend to give the labourers increased wages, whenever the employers' profits are by some temporary cause advanced above the ordinary rate.'[26] The capitalist, in fact, knows what damage he can suffer from an open conflict in such a period and has no reason to go into one, provided the requests of the workers are not such as to put him in a position of disadvantage in comparison to the other masters in his sector or district. At this very stage an important qualitative change in the social relationships occurs: open conflicts between opposing coalitions are superseded by a situation of collective bargaining aimed at establishing

---

[24] Fawcett, *Manual* (2nd edn, 1865), p. 173. [25] Fawcett, 'Strikes', pp. 8–9.
[26] ibid., p. 9.

'that natural rate of wages towards which wages must have a constant tendency to approach'.[27]

The point Fawcett misses is that the substitution of compact social bodies, such as the perfect combinations of employers and employees in each sector, for the mass of individual workers and capitalists assumed by the classical theory, makes the 'natural wage level' established by the theory quite irrelevant. Here we enter a world of bilateral monopolies, or at least of multilateral oligopolies that lies clearly outside the boundaries of classical economics.[28] It is interesting to observe that some of Marshall's early writings, namely those where he attempts to apply the theory of international trade to so-called 'economic nations', that is, compact unions of workers and capitalists, start with a similar view of industrial relations.[29]

From an 'ideological' point of view, Fawcett's idea is so novel as to border on genuine subversion. It certainly goes against the common feeling of the time, which viewed unions as the cause of strikes, and strikes as a threatening sign of a collapsing social cohesion. If a strike breaks out, it means, in Fawcett's terms, either that at least one of the parties was imperfectly informed about the state of the market (for products or for factors) or that it was equipped with a wrong theory for the interpretation of the available information, or that a mistake was made in the evaluation of the determination and/or the powers of endurance and retaliation of the opponent. But once everybody is equally well informed and equipped with the same theory, the agreement must be reached on those same terms that the theory proves to be necessary and therefore 'right'.

The strike is, on the one side a sign of the failure of the market to do the job assigned to it by the classical theory, and on the other a temporary, riotous substitute for a peaceful and civilised bargaining process aimed at discovering the levels fixed by the theory. What better 'theoretical' foundation could be conceived for the movement toward arbitration committees, which then was becoming fashionable, than Fawcett's argument?[30]

[27] Fawcett, 'The theory', p. 639.
[28] Pedro Schwartz, *The New Political Economy of J. S. Mill* (London, 1972), pp. 87–8: 'His presentation of the idea that both employers and workers weighed the inconvenience of a strike against the advantages which might be gained by it, is a step forward in the time when workmen were generally believed to engage upon strikes out of sheer perverseness, and foreshadows later analytical developments such as Professor Hick's "concession curve" of the employers and "resistance curve" of the unions.'
[29] J. K. Whitaker (ed.), *The Early Economic Writings of Alfred Marshall, 1867–1890*, (2 vols., London, 1975), vol. 2, pp. 123–8.
[30] On arbitration and conciliation boards see V. L. Allen, 'The origins of industrial conciliation and arbitration', *International Review of Social History*, vol. 9 (1964), pp. 237–54, and W. H. G. Armitage, *A. J. Mundella 1825–1897: The Liberal Background to the Labour Movement* (London, 1951).

Fawcett's fourth idea is that once both combinations have experienced a sensible sharing of extra profits for a period of time that is to everybody's advantage, it seems reasonable to expect that they will proceed to attempt to give an institutionalised form to their experience. A new, standard type of contract will then take shape out of everyday practice: one based on profit-sharing.

Fawcett does not make it clear whether he means only a regular, institutionalised, sharing of the profits or whether he also means a participation of the 'hands' in the running of the firm. Sometimes he speaks of profit-sharing, sometimes of copartnership. But even when he speaks of simple profit-sharing he means something essentially different from the piece-work wage system. In this latter the worker is only interested in the quantity of the production; in the profit-sharing system he is also interested in the quality of it, at least so far as it is considered relevant by the buyer.

The proposal was not altogether new.[31] In the past certain agricultural contracts, for example *métayage*, had rested on a kind of partnership or product-sharing. Even its theoretical contribution was not entirely new: Charles Babbage, in fact, had written on the issue in the 1830s. Yet the proposal can be considered, in a sense, original and revealing. Take the case of *métayage*: this had already been declared by the economists of the English school as an inefficient system of land tenure. In particular, this contract discouraged the landowner's investment, since it granted him only a portion of the resulting increase of product. Now, Fawcett knew all this very well, as is clearly shown in his *Manual of Political Economy*.[32] The fact that nevertheless he advocated a contractual form (profit-sharing), implicitly considered inefficient by the central body of the economic doctrine to which he subscribed, raises some problems. Fawcett knew very well that nineteenth-century social (and economic) theory was based on the idea that the line of progress consisted of what Henry Sumner Maine later summed up as 'general movement from status to contract'. He knew also that both *métayage* and profit-sharing went against that general tendency insofar as they reintroduced elements of custom in a world of free, untrammelled, competition. The different solution he gave the two problems (*métayage* and profit-sharing) suggests he came close to under-

---

[31] On these matters, see R. A. Church, 'Profit-sharing and labour relations in the nineteenth century', *International Review of Social History*, vol. 16 (1971), pp. 4–16; see also Sedley Taylor, *Profit-Sharing Between Capital and Labour, Six Essays* (London, 1884) (the work was dedicated to Fawcett), and Charles R. Fay *Co-partnership in Industry* (Cambridge, 1913). For a critical survey of the recent wave of discussions on profit-sharing, see D. C. Blanchflower and A. J. Oswald, 'Profit-sharing – can it work?', *Oxford Economic Papers*, vol. 39 (1987), pp. 1–17.

[32] Fawcett, *Manual* (2nd edn, 1865), p. 233.

standing that competition does not act only by destroying custom, but also by solidifying in new institutions aspects of the competitive strife that could otherwise strain and disintegrate the moral fabric which holds contemporary society together.

It is worth pausing for a moment to note how even the supposedly driest and most mechanical version of classical political economy, for such is the reputation which Fawcett's *Manual* has, contains fascinating insights and impulses which carry it out to the edge of acceptable theory and even beyond. Underlying Fawcett's arguments in the *Manual*, but much more in the earlier work I have considered here, is a view that the capitalist system contains an embodied tendency to produce institutions for the protection of the interests of the weaker members of society.

The last idea contained in the 1859 essay, one taken up again and developed in the subsequent writings – the profit-sharing system as a bridge to cooperation – goes well beyond the point just mentioned. The sharing out of extra profits (there is no extensive discussion about the fate of extra losses), and the eventual share of workers in the running of the firm, in fact, are supposed to provide the workers with the financial means and the direct experience of the business world which may be used to facilitate the creation of permanent cooperatives.[33] Now, having passed through the hard school of resistance to the repression of illegal combinations, of self-discipline in pay requests, and having learned the inner logic of the firm, the workers can enter the ideal state of social relations where the associated labour hires capital, rather than the other way round.

If one considers Fawcett's argument as a whole, one cannot avoid being struck by the force of the underlying political vision. Fawcett leads us, with an apparently irresistible syllogism, from a present of strikes and harsh conflicts to a future of peaceful social cooperation, without resort to interventions from outside the system of economic forces. In his own words:

We have pointed out tendencies which we believe will act irresistibly to introduce cooperation, and yet no one circumstance has been mentioned which can make either our aristocracy tremble or our constitution fear. Without the aid of legislation, which would prove as injurious as it is certainly needless, all can be affected by the peaceful workings of advancing intelligence.[34]

Forces and relationships already included in the system, apparently contradictory and disharmonious, simply unfold their potential. Fawcett claims that their inner nature has come to light by virtue of the application

[33] In fact most cooperatives, kept alive by injections of money by well-off philanthropists, were short-lived. See Philip N. Backstrom, *Christian Socialism and Cooperation in Victorian England. Edward Vansittart Neale and the Cooperative Movement* (London, 1974), for the best treatment of the subject.
[34] Fawcett, 'Strikes', p. 23.

of economic reasoning to that system. But we already know that in fact Fawcett had to go beyond classical political economy to link the different fragments of his argument. What actually guided him was not classical economic theory, which was rather silent in the face of complex social phenomena like combinations and strikes, but his alert political intuition. In order for mid-Victorian society to realise those conditions of orderly progress that constituted the strongest aspiration of the middle classes of whom Fawcett was an expression, a 'theory' had to be found, no matter whether strictly economic or socio-economic, that made legitimate the 'sensible' action of the working classes. The embryo of such a theory was given precisely in Fawcett's 1859 essay, rightly applauded at the Social Science Association meeting.

At this point, we have to pause to take a more general view of Fawcett's 'infringements' of the classical code. Too much history of economic thought is purely unilinear. Some historians scan texts of the nineteenth century for those linear developments leading from the darkness of classical error to the light of Walrasian truth; others trace the decline from an essentially 'correct' theory, which had alarming social implications, to an 'incorrect' theory, which suited the interests of the ruling classes. This sort of approach does not produce a real history of economic thought in all its meandering, uncertain, unfinished, temporarily determined and irrecoverable reality. Of course, one generation takes up problems its predecessors have left unsolved, but often in so doing it misreads or transforms them, tearing them out of context or reading them without the background of that set of assumptions which the previous age so took for granted that it had no need to spell them out.

The interesting question, historically speaking, is the extent to which the classical theory came to be questioned by problems felt in the real world. There can be no doubt that the birth of organised, permanent, connected trade unions, raised new questions. They were no longer casual, temporary and local aggregates of the labouring poor, but new social institutions which were part and parcel of the 'actual constitution' of the country. The classical theory could disregard the accidental explosions of anger and resentment of the 'poor souls' or the 'dangerous classes' of previous ages, but it had now to explain the economic role of organisations that were, in Marshall's terms, authentic 'economic nations' capable of arousing feelings of loyalty in persons now called 'members', provided with strategies and tactics of their own.

At least two escape routes opened. One reduced the classical theory to emptiness by so diluting its laws that they became hazy and hence indeterminate. The other was to include the new social reality into the old system without apparently weakening its rigour. Where the former preserved the system as a whole, opening it to new developments, the latter preserved a kind of formal clarity but at the cost of contradictions and paradoxes. Fawcett chose the second route, taking up questions which a strictly classical economist might well have refused to answer.

The general sense of Fawcett's 'transgressions' is ambiguous. There is an element of abstract rationalism in them which seems to link a sort of (James) Millian 'dryness' to 'pure' economics as practised by scholars like Jevons or F. Y. Edgeworth. But, as we have seen, under the surface and against all appearances, there are also elements of a more historico-sociological approach, which leads directly to Marshall. This ambivalence shows itself most clearly in the implicit revision of the central concept of competition.[35] The classical theory rests on an undeveloped concept of competition. This is because competition can only be defined in ways consonant with the theoretical structure of which it is part, where it must guarantee the gravitation of market prices (and hence also of market wages) around the natural ones. Introducing the propensity to combine into the classical theory and arguing that it is as rational as individual action,[36] Fawcett slid, without knowing it, from one approach to another. But in this new approach rational behaviour no longer guarantees the gravitation of market prices around natural prices. The way to 'normal' prices is clearly open.

Fawcett's brilliant performance would not have had much effect if it had not caught Mill in an appropriate stage of his intellectual evolution. In 1859 Mill was in the middle of implementing his project of refounding a reformist alliance.[37] His sentimental and intellectual intimacy with the late Harriet Taylor had rekindled his interests in issues of social reform. In 1859 he was living with Harriet's daughter, Helen, surrounded by a group of disciples and admirers. In the words of his biographer: 'He gradually drew about himself a small, politically insignificant [sic] coterie. Fawcett, McLaren, Buxton, Amberley, Torrens, W. E. Forster, Thomas Hughes,

35 Kenneth G. Dennis, Competition in the History of Economic Thought (New York, 1977).
36 This idea is shared by other writers of the period, as for instance Francis D. Longe, A Refutation of the Wage Fund Theory of Modern Political Economy as Enunciated by Mr. Mill, M.P. and Mr. Fawcett, M.P. (London 1866), p. 17: 'combination or association on the part of either labourers or employers ... should be regarded as a force ... of the same natural and normal character as competition itself'. By stretching the concept we could even consider it as foreshadowing one of the favourite Marshalian tenets. See Alfred Marshall, Principles of Economics, 9th (Variorum) edition, ed. C. Guillebaud (2 vols., London, 1961), vol. 1, p. 5: 'the fundamental characteristic of modern industrial life is not competition but self-reliance, independence, deliberate choice and forethought ... They may and often do cause people to compete with one another: but on the other hand may tend, and just now indeed they are tending, in the direction of cooperation and combination of all kinds good and evil.'
37 Michael St John Packe, The Life of John Stuart Mill (London, 1954), pp. 414–17.

and P. A. Taylor. With their help, and with expert advice from outside Parliament, he was able to raise projects which he knew well were too far before their time.'[38] Mill had only known Fawcett for a short time, but he had already appreciated the man for his resources of intellectual vigour (if not subtlety), and for his complete devotion. Fawcett stood with him along the whole range of his political projects: with him and Hare on electoral reform; with him in the cause of women's emancipation; and he was to be beside him through all the major events in the years to follow. But perhaps what raised Fawcett most in Mill's eyes was the fact that Fawcett enjoyed the trust of important groups of trade unionists, with whom he mixed very naturally. Mill's political design of this period included a great alliance of all the forces of progress which encompassed the remains of Benthamite radicals, the left-wing Liberals and, above all, the 'respectable' working classes. Mill saw beyond the contingent situation in which they had no vote, to an age when they would be enfranchised. Within this political design there was certainly a place for Fawcett, right from the beginning of their relationship. But it is doubtful if Mill expected any intellectual gains to flow from this friendship, and he must have been pleasantly surprised, therefore, to discover that Fawcett could provide him with a contribution that was both ideologically and theoretically useful. By 1860 the most vexing problem for Mill was that of shaping the character of the working classes in such a way that they could fulfil their destiny, and so, up to a point, the destiny of modern society. Mill saw that two of the most formative institutions of capitalist society – the market for labour and for commodities – tended, both of them, to reduce the moral and cultural level of the working masses. On the other hand Mill had already explored – as an exchange with Harriet Taylor shows clearly – the narrow limits of the possibility of inculcating 'right principles' through the educational system.[39]

The problem had two sides: first of all, Mill wanted economic institutions which could mould, by their daily, pervasive action, the kind of character fit for the purpose. But, on the other hand, he had to explain away all those doctrines that prevented the working classes from taking their share in the process of advancing civilisation. To understand this point we must go back to the most important chapter of the sixth book of Mill's *Logic*, the one on liberty and necessity. There Mill writes: 'To think that we have no power of altering our character and to think that we shall not use our power unless we desire to use it, are very different things, and have a very different effect on the mind ... it is of great consequence that

[38] ibid., p. 457.
[39] F. A. Hayek (ed.), *John Stuart Mill and Harriet Taylor. Their Friendship and Subsequent Marriage* (London, 1951), pp. 145–8.

we should not be prevented from forming such a desire by thinking the attainment impracticable.'[40] In order to overcome the situation of a working population without a say in political matters we need, Mill argued, truly free agents, that is, persons freely balancing the different hypothetical outcomes of their behaviour, in the market for labour and for commodities as well as in the political arena.

It was just when Mill had these problems at the back of his mind that Fawcett's article for the *Westminster Review* arrived. As soon as he read it, he wrote about it to Helen Taylor in enthusiastic terms. 'I have just been reading a manuscript on strikes by Fawcett: it is the best thing I ever read on the subject, with some new lights even to me.'[41] What was it, in particular, that struck him in that article? A letter to J. Chapman of August 1861 tells us:

I believe I agree entirely with the view taken in Mr. Fawcett's article. But I do so specifically on the ground stated, I believe, for the first time by him, viz. that the power of striking tends to bring about something approximating to what I consider the only right organization of labour, the association of the workpeople with their employers by a participation of profits.[42]

He then adds, with clear polemical intent against Frederic Harrison and the trade unionists fighting against the piece-work system: 'I regard the payment of a fixed sum per day as essentially demoralizing.'[43] This is the crucial point: Mill believed that the right solution to the social problems of the age should combine the requirements of an efficient production system with an uplifting of the spirit of the agents involved. Profit-sharing seems to him 'moralising' and, according to the Fawcettian argument, directly conducive to his ideal state, cooperation.

We have another proof of how Mill's expectations were fulfilled by Fawcett's paper, when in 1862 the new edition of his *Principles of Political Economy* came out. Here Mill employed fully the Fawcettian argument. He started by absorbing the first point made by Fawcett, and giving it its classical form: 'I do not hesitate to say that associations of labourers, of a nature similar to trade unions, far from being a hindrance to a free market for labour, are the necessary instrumentality of that free market.'[44] But most of all he stressed the 'ideological core' of Fawcett's argument.

The tendency, [he wrote] of this state of things is to make a rise of wages in any particular trade usually consequent upon a rise of profits, which, as Mr Fawcett observes, is a commencement of that regular participation of the labourers in the

[40] *Collected Works of John Stuart Mill* (25 vols., Toronto, 1963–), vols. 7 and 8; see vol. 8, p. 841.
[41] ibid., vol. 15, p. 686.   [42] ibid., p. 735.   [43] ibid.,
[44] J. S. Mill, *Principles of Political Economy*, 7th edn, ed. W. J. Ashley (London, 1909), p. 937.

profits derived from their labour, every tendency to which ... it is so important to encourage, since to it we have chiefly to look for any radical improvement in the social and economic relations between labour and capital. Strikes, therefore, and the trade societies which render strikes possible, are for these various reasons not a mischievous, but on the contrary, a valuable part of the existing machinery of society.[45]

From a political point of view what is relevant in Mill's subsequent, much publicised, 'recantation' is already contained in these very strong statements. But if this is true it is not the whole truth. Mill had some reservations on the strictly economic foundations of the Fawcettian argument, as it is shown by the fact that the passage quoted is not inserted in Book Two, devoted to distribution, but in Book Five, devoted to what would nowadays be defined as social and economic policy. The matter begins to clarify itself in 1866, when Mill wrote to Fawcett to thank him for sending a copy of *The Economic Position of the British Labourer*. Mill wrote:

I need hardly say how highly I approve your chapter on cooperation ... The chapter which on the whole I least like is the one on wages, though it will probably be more praised than any of the rest: but I think I could shew that an increase of wages at the expense of profits would not be an impracticability on the true principles of political economy.[46]

Here Mill showed he had realised that his own wages-fund theory, at least as it was perceived through Fawcett's version, could constitute an obstacle to his great political design. Two more letters can help to clarify the point. On 19 October 1867 he wrote to W. T. Thornton: 'the book [the book *On Labour* that Thornton was then preparing] will be very serviceable in carrying on what may be called the emancipation of pol. economy, its liberation from the kind of doctrines of the old school (now taken up by well to do people)'.[47] And on 22 December he wrote to Chadwick: 'If they [trade unions] limit their attempt within reasonable bounds, I do not see why they should not in many cases succeed, both in raising wages, and in (what is equivalent) diminishing the hours of labour ... so long as there is any margin of profit to take the increase from.'[48]

It is in this same span of time that a number of criticisms of the wages-fund theory (mostly attacked in Fawcett's simplified version) appeared: for example F. D. Longe's pamphlet and W. L. Sargant's book.[49] Mill never deigned to answer them nor would he ever quote them in his works. If my interpretation of Mill's motives at this stage of his life is

[45] ibid., pp. 937–8. [46] *Collected Works of John Stuart Mill*, vol. 16, p. 1130.
[47] ibid., p. 1320.
[48] ibid., p. 1335.
[49] Longe, *A Refutation*; William Lucas Sargant, *Recent Political Economy* (London and Birmingham, 1867).

correct, this negligence appears understandable. Longe and Sargant had
attacked the wages-fund theory in an ideologically different direction
from the one shared, more or less, by Mill, Fawcett and Thornton. The
first one to attack it in what Mill considered the relevant light was
Thornton, who started from a criticism of Fawcett's version of the
wages-fund theory but ended much in accordance with Fawcett's and
Mill's political perspectives. This gave Mill the opportunity to remove
once and for all that theory of the wages fund that blocked the way to his
political hopes. And he did it with his usual elegance, by taking upon
himself the criticisms that he could have easily shifted onto Fawcett's
simplifications.

᠊ The significance of Mill's famous 'recantation' is too complex an issue
in the evolution of political economy to be discussed here.[50] What
interests us is that Mill (whether rightly or wrongly is another issue)
argued that the fund (which is no longer a fund but rather a flow) from
which striking labourers can draw their improvements is not the amount
of resources destined, at the beginning of the period, for the payment of
wages, but something larger and vaguer which includes profits (net of the
maintenance of the capital and the capitalists) flowing into the enterprise,
as well. He adds, in a provocative way, that the workers have no moral
obligation to the employers, at least in the distribution of the income,
since 'the employers are quite capable of taking care of themselves'.[51] The
only restraint which workers need to observe is not 'to kill the goose to get
at the eggs'.[52] As far as the long-run theory of wages is concerned, Mill
recants nothing; it remains unaltered as the background to an argument
which floats in-between the short and the long run.[53]

Mill knows perfectly well that only the short-run theory of the wages

[50] See F. W. Taussig, *Wages and Capital*, (London, 1896); W. L. Breit, 'The wages fund
controversy revisited', *Canadian Journal of Economics and Political Science*, vol. 33
(Nov. 1967), pp. 509–28; S. Hollander, 'The role of fixed technical coefficients in the
evolution of the wages fund controversy', *Oxford Economic Papers*, vol. 20 (Nov. 1968),
pp. 320–41; Schwartz, *The New Political Economy*, ch. 5; R. B. Ekelund, 'A short run
classical model of capital and wages: Mill's recantation of the wages fund', *Oxford
Economic Papers*, vol. 28 (March 1976), pp. 66–85; E. G. West and R. W. Hafer,
'J. S. Mill, unions, and the wages fund recantation: a reinterpretation', *Quarterly Journal
of Economics*, vol. 92 (Nov. 1978), pp. 603–19. On the side of the historians see
R. V. Clements, 'British trade unions and popular political economy, 1850–1875',
Economic History Review, vol. 14 (n.s.), no. 1 (1961–2), pp. 93–104; Eugenio Biagini,
'British trade unions and popular political economy, 1860–1880', *Historical Journal*,
vol. 30, no. 4 (1987), pp. 811–40.
[51] J. S. Mill, 'Thornton on labour and its claims', *Fortnightly Review*, n.s. vol. 5, part 1
(May 1869), pp. 505–18, part 2 (June 1869), pp. 620–700. Reprinted in J. S. Mill, *Essays
on Economics and Society*, ed. J. M. Robson, and *Collected Works of John Stuart Mill*,
vol. 5. See ibid., p. 662.
[52] Mill, 'Thornton on labour', p. 657.
[53] On this point see Dardi, *Il Giovane Marshall*, pp. 43–64.

fund has an immediate cash value in political terms, but, of course, the probable feed-back of temporary workers' gains on to the level of natural wages also marches in the political direction which pleases him.

By putting the weight of his exceptional prestige in matters of economic theory (and by this stage he has no rivals) on the side of the trade unions, Mill altered the balance of forces which made up public opinion. And public opinion according to him plays a crucial role in determining the distribution of wealth: 'The rules by which it is determined are what the opinions and feelings of the ruling portion of the community make them.'[54] It was as if political economy itself seemed to be changing its position on an absolutely central question of contemporary debate. It may be worth pointing out that this change in the 'theoretical' basis of the current debate on wages took several years to be accepted even by those, the trade unions, who were its main beneficiaries.[55]

It would be arbitrary to attribute to Fawcett the merit (or the demerit, depending on one's point of view) of causing Mill's recantation, not least because Mill takes up a conception of the wages fund that leaves Fawcett behind, attached to conservative theoretical positions that he himself had contributed to render untenable. On the other hand, if my reconstruction of the matter is correct, one cannot deny to Fawcett a certain influence in the process of thought which in ten years time was to lead Mill to recant.[56]

To conclude, what answers can be given to the questions posed at the start of this paper? Unlike the 'heartless economists' (Fawcett himself has sometimes been called one, but we have seen that this is not correct) who regard capitalism as a 'natural' form of society, which can be extended to 'backward' countries, and perfected but not transformed into something different, Fawcett, in the wake of Mill and in accordance with the 'progressive' opinion of the late 1850s, considered the hired labour contract, that is, the hard core of the capitalistic mode of production, as an imperfect and unstable solution to the production–distribution problem. It tended to generate from inside itself a succession of forms (profit-sharing and, then, cooperation) ending up in a possible cooperative mode of production. This idea of a society which is unfair and unstable in itself (but not radically so) and yet contains the seed of a different society, which is fair and stable, allows one to identify capitalism not as the end of history in the way pure apologists do, nor as the negation of humanity, as

---

[54] Mill, *Principles*, p. 200.

[55] 'What seems strange is that it took them [the trade unionists] five or six years to introduce the new arguments into their ideological arsenal.' Biagini, 'British trade unions and popular political economy', p. 830.

[56] The impact of Fawcett's paper on the thought of Mill has been extensively commented upon, albeit in a different light, by Schwartz: cf. *The New Political Economy*, pp. 87–103.

radical critics think. To sum up, it depicts a theoretical middle position on which it is possible to base a progressive political design, yet not a subversive one, capable of solidifying the consensus of the middle classes and of the so-called working-class aristocracy. Fawcett was, for a period of his life, say until Mill's death, the living proof that this interpretation of capitalism reflected the prevailing opinion. In February 1873 *The Economist*, having praised his 'hard common sense' and his shying away from the 'pulpiness and sentimentality' so common among radicals, concluded that 'he makes radicalism intelligible and tolerable to men who have something to lose'.[57] Less than one year later, in January 1874, in a very different journalistic location, *The Bee Hive*, Frederick Harrison wrote: 'Of all the professed economists of our time, no one, not even Mr. Mill himself, has done so much to break down the narrow sophisms of the older school as Henry Fawcett.'[58] And he concluded by urging the workers to vote again for him, despite all the recent, harsh disagreements between Fawcett and the organised workers.

The subsequent years witnessed the gradual deepening of the gap between Fawcett and the trade unions: Fawcett's uncompromising individualism identified his position more and more with those of the middle classes. His obsession with the principle of self-help and the minimisation of the role of the state made him unpopular with a growing proportion of 'progressives'. With the arrival of the 1880s the situation changed rapidly. The new economic difficulties of Great Britain – caused by factors including competition from the United States and Germany, the increased responsibilities of an imperial power, the transformation of the trades union movement, the birth of political movements more similar to continental ones, the reemergence of socialist themes in Georgian and Marxian versions, the change of the philosophical climate under the influence of the neo-Hegelians – produced an economic, social, political and cultural setting in which ideas like Fawcett's no longer belonged. A few years after his death, Fawcett's name remained only a memory: the memory of a blind man whose will-power overcame even the most disabling of physical handicaps.[59]

The memory of Mill did not vanish as rapidly as Fawcett's because his system of thought, obviously much more complex and sophisticated than Fawcett's, contained in itself elements which could be part of the new cultural mix. The ideology of self-help, which joined Mill to Fawcett, can evolve into that of 'self-realisation', and the responsibility for the latter can be, at least partially, transferred from individual shoulders to those of

[57] *The Economist*, 7 Feb. 1873.   [58] *Bee-Hive*, 31 Jan. 1874.
[59] Winifred Holt, *A Beacon for the Blind. Being a Life of Henry Fawcett, the Blind Postmaster General* (London, 1915).

the state.[60] In Mill, unlike in Fawcett, there are embryonic elements of this metamorphosis of one of the cornerstones of political individualism into an 'element of para-socialist collectivism'. If he had lived ten years longer, Mill would have probably been one of the first Fabians; Fawcett would certainly have not.

[60] The point has been well put by Stefan Collini, *Liberalism and Sociology. L. T. Hobhouse and Political Argument in England 1880–1914* (Cambridge, 1979), pp. 28–32.

5 Professor Henry Fawcett

PUNCH, OR THE LONDON CHARIVARI.—April 15, 1882.

PARCELS POST
OFFICE

REPLY
POSTCARDS

THE MAN FOR THE POST.

6 The Postmaster General, from *Punch*, vol. 82 (15 April 1882), p. 175

PART III

POLITICS

7

Henry Fawcett and the Social Science Association: Liberal politics, political economy and the working class in mid-Victorian Britain

LAWRENCE GOLDMAN

I

Our friend H. Fawcett intends making every effort to get into the House, and I hope there is a chance of success for him ultimately as his determination is great and he will not be discouraged by one or two defeats.[1]

Thus wrote C. B. Clarke of Queen's College, Cambridge, to Thomas Hare in November 1860. Clarke, 'the most intimate of all Fawcett's friends in college days'[2] and an important source for Leslie Stephen's biography, was merely expressing a general view of Fawcett in the early 1860s, for everyone noted that here was a young man in a hurry, complete with almost inordinate political ambitions, 'looking out in every direction for an opening into political life'.[3] And yet, as Bernard Cracroft explained in 1867 in *Essays on Reform*, 'not less than 500 Members in the House of Commons are either County members, or, if representing boroughs, either peers or relations of peers, or landowners or under landowners' influence', constituting, therefore, 'one vast cousinhood'.[4] And Fawcett was not a part of this extended family. From a relatively humble background he had neither connections nor money, and in the 1868 election the average borough contest cost a candidate nearly £1,000, the average county over £3,000;[5] Fawcett's £250 a year as a Fellow of Trinity Hall would not go far.[6] But he could speak in public and write in the journals in a direct and

---

[1] C. B. Clarke to Thomas Hare, 8 Nov. 1860, Hare Papers, St John's College, Oxford, MS 356.

[2] Leslie Stephen, *Life of Henry Fawcett* (London, 1885), p. vii.   [3] ibid., p. 188.

[4] Bernard Cracroft, 'The analysis of the House of Commons, or indirect representation', in *Essays on Reform* (London, 1867), pp. 164–5.

[5] The precise figures were £988 and £3,011. See H. J. Hanham, *Elections and Party Management. Politics in the Time of Disraeli and Gladstone* (London, 1959), p. 251.

[6] Stephen, *Life of Fawcett*, p. 33.

forthright style, and on the basis of this talent, and with the encouragement of others, he constructed a political strategy: as Mill explained it in
April 1860, soon after meeting Fawcett for the first time, 'anything which
tends to make you known as a public speaker without looking like a desire
on your part to push yourself into notice, is useful for your ulterior views'.[7]

The Social Science Association, by providing a platform and an
audience for the discussion of a host of social and political issues,
attracted many young men like Fawcett with an 'ulterior view' in mind.
They came to capture the attention of the many hundreds of participants
who actually attended the meetings of the S.S.A., and the many thousands
more who read verbatim reports of the speeches and proceedings in the
provincial and metropolitan press. According to *The Times*, indeed,
'self-seeking men' found social science 'the surest road to personal
reputation'.[8] *Blackwood's Magazine*, always hostile to the Association in
its backwoods Tory way, contemptuously linked it with 'a crowd of
ambitious and active individuals, who climb up out of respectable chaos
by that shining ladder of Public Beneficence and University Charity', and
it picked out for its special scorn 'the rising young man, whose clever
paper at a Social Science Meeting, or skilful reformatory project, draws
the attention of a minister'.[9] It was an accurate observation of the way in
which the S.S.A. was employed to further Liberal careers in general and
Fawcett's career in particular. Frequent interventions at a variety of the
Association's meetings brought Fawcett's name and opinions before the
public and brought him the patronage and the support of other Liberal
politicians and intellectuals who were also taking part. The records of the
Association thus provide a type of commentary on Fawcett's political
progress from his first entry into public life, only recently blinded, in 1859,
until 1868, when, having established himself in the House of Commons
following his election for Brighton in 1865, he last attended one of its
meetings. And they also contain some detailed statements of Fawcett's
views, which, because advanced in the give and take of debate on matters
of immediate practical relevance, rather than carefully composed for
publication, are of considerable interest in setting Fawcett 'in context' – in
assessing his positions on political and social issues in relation to the
whole range of Liberal opinion in the 1860s, and in situating his

[7] *Collected Works of John Stuart Mill* (25 vols., Toronto, 1963–   ), vol. 15, p. 692. Mill
  and Fawcett met for the first time on 8 February 1860. See also Mill to Fawcett, 26 Feb.
  1860: 'You have only to take every fair opportunity of making yourself known as a public
  speaker and lecturer' (ibid., p. 688), and Mill to Fawcett, 24 Dec. 1860: 'You will be your
  own best helper if you go on making yourself known by well-considered writings' (ibid.,
  p. 716).
[8] *The Times*, 25 Sept. 1882, p. 7.
[9] [Margaret Oliphant], 'Social Science', *Blackwood's Edinburgh Magazine*, vol. 88 (Dec.
  1860), p. 703.

economics against a somewhat wider background than the doctrines, derived from Mill's *Principles*, which dominated orthodox political economy in the mid-nineteenth century.

II

In the autumn of 1856 'it was suggested to Lord Brougham that he should take the lead in founding an association for affording to those engaged in all the various efforts now happily begun for the improvement of the people, an opportunity for considering social economics as a great whole',[10] and after a year's preparation the National Association for the Promotion of Social Science held its inaugural Congress in Birmingham in October 1857. This was the first of twenty-eight successive annual meetings, held each autumn, that the Association organised up to 1884. During these years the Social Science Congress, as it was known, convened for a week at a time in a major British city and offered its services as an open forum for the discussion of all aspects of social policy and reform. Each Congress was a grand civic occasion in each locality in turn: meetings were attended by thousands, and the comings and goings, discussions and debates, commanded national attention in the daily press and journals. The Association cultivated a parliamentary image and was variously referred to as a 'supplementary parliament'[11] and a 'parliament out of session'[12] that was staffed, according to the *Spectator* in June 1862, by the 'volunteer legislators of Great Britain'.[13] It was an 'amateur parliament'[14] where aspiring professionals like Fawcett could try out their ideas and perfect their techniques for moving minds and winning useful friends. According to the Social Science Association's first secretary it had three aims: 'facilitating discussion on matters of high social import', 'spreading information thereupon' and 'influencing the work of the government and legislation in the people's interest'.[15] The Association brought 'before the public mind a more general and scientific view of social and political questions'.[16] By 'gathering together the experience of the nation'[17] it bridged 'the interval between the speculation of the philosopher and the proposals of the statesman' and so prepared 'the legislator's

[10] *Transactions of the National Association for the Promotion of Social Science*, 1857 (London, 1858), p. xxi.
[11] *Daily News*, 30 Sept. 1869, p. 4.
[12] Lord Houghton at the Concluding Meeting of the 1873 Congress, *The Times*, 9 Oct. 1873, p. 7.
[13] *Spectator*, 14 June 1862, p. 657.   [14] *Western Daily Press* (Bristol), Oct. 1869, p. 2.
[15] G. W. Hastings, 'Address of the Chairman of the Council, 1870', *Transactions*, 1870, p. 106.
[16] *The Times*, 21 Sept. 1882, p. 6.   [17] *Glasgow Daily Herald*, 2 Oct. 1860, p. 2.

way'.[18] As *The Times* concluded in 1882, it was 'entitled to be fairly reckoned among the powers of modern English life'.[19]

The S.S.A. initially structured its work in five 'departments' on legal reform, penal policy, education, public health and 'social economy' (concerned with industrial and commercial affairs). In addition to the annual Congress, its members met regularly for discussion in meetings held in London during the parliamentary session, and it maintained a central office in the capital to organise its lobbies of Parliament and the administration. The Association could count on some influential members. It attracted the active participation of three Liberal Prime Ministers: Lord John Russell, who was on the platform at its inaugural meeting in the Birmingham Town Hall in 1857 and who presided over the Liverpool Congress in the following year; Gladstone, who visited the Congress in 1858 and 1863 and who later chaired its Committee on Labour and Capital in 1868; and the young Earl of Rosebery who presided at the Glasgow Congress in 1874. It caught up a number of cabinet ministers in its work: Carlisle and Stanley, Bruce and Forster, Northcote and Carnarvon and others sat on committees and attended its meetings.[20] And it linked itself to earlier traditions of social reform through associations with Shaftesbury, President of the Manchester Congress in 1866, and the aged Brougham who was its chief patron and first President. The S.S.A.'s inaugural General Committee included eighteen peers, twenty-eight M.P.s and those so-called 'statesmen in disguise', Edwin Chadwick, William Farr, John Simon and James Kay-Shuttleworth from that most influential group of mid-Victorian civil servants.[21] John Stuart Mill attended a number of meetings and gave his views to the Association on electoral reform, the 1870 Education Act and the contentious Contagious Diseases Acts.[22] F. D. Maurice addressed the London Congress in 1862 and sent a paper to the Sheffield Congress three years later.[23] Charles Kingsley, President of the Department of Education

18 *Daily News*, 3 Oct. 1881, p. 5; 2 Oct. 1873, p. 4.
19 *The Times*, 19 Aug. 1882, p. 9.
20 Stanley was President of the Department of Public Health in 1857; Carlisle, when Lord Lieutenant of Ireland, presided over the Department of Punishment and Reformation in 1858; Bruce was President of the Education Department in 1866 and of the whole Congress in 1875; Forster was a member of the committee responsible for producing the S.S.A.'s report on *Trades' Societies and Strikes* in 1860; Carnarvon was President of the Birmingham Congress in 1868; and Northcote presided over the Bristol Congress in the following year.
21 *Transactions*, 1857, pp. xv–xvi.
22 See *The Times*, 11 April 1865, p. 10; *Sessional Proceedings of the National Association for the Promotion of Social Science*, 1869–70; pp. 349–51; 1870–1, pp. 234, 269–70.
23 F. D. Maurice, 'Working men's colleges', *Transactions*, 1862, pp. 293–7; idem, 'What better provision ought to be made for the education of the girls of the upper and middle classes?', *Transactions*, 1865, pp. 268–74.

at the Bristol Congress of 1869, commended an organisation that 'drew together so many congenial minds upon points of the greatest possible interest to the nation'.[24] John Ruskin sent a paper to the Liverpool Congress in 1858.[25] The Social Science Association thus brought together components of the political, administrative and intellectual elites of mid-Victorian Britain, and, as a 'movable and unofficial Parliament'[26] was to act as an intermediary between government and public opinion, a link between politicians and an expanding political nation before and after the Second Reform Act.

For a generation and more before it expired in 1886, the S.S.A. was singularly successful in this role. It sponsored and encouraged social research, it brought contending parties together for debate and it exerted considerable influence over successive governments. Though its claims were sometimes inflated and though it was far more successful at initiating government action rather than directing policy once the preliminary measures had been taken, there is no doubt that its representations secured the Taunton Commission of 1865 from which followed the Endowed Schools Act in 1869 and the reform of secondary schooling, and the Royal Sanitary Commission of 1869 which led to the reforms of the early 1870s, culminating in the great consolidating Public Health Act of 1875. It dictated the terms of the 1869 Habitual Criminals Act and the 1871 Prevention of Crimes Act after a decade of campaigning for changes in the English penal system. It was instrumental in securing the Married Women's Property Act of 1870. And its extensive research into trades unionism, published in 1860 as *Trades' Societies and Strikes*, and described by the Webbs as 'the best collection of Trade Union material and the most impartial account of Trade Union action that has ever been issued'[27] – superior, indeed, to all the nineteenth-century Royal Commission reports – led the way to public acceptance and legal recognition of trade unions in the 1860s and 1870s. The list of achievements, great and small, could be much extended for there was hardly a social question which the S.S.A. excluded from its platform. When the Association celebrated its twenty-fifth anniversary by publishing a summary of its work, *The Times* commended 'an extraordinary compass of enterprise and achievement'.[28] As one M.P. wrote in the year the S.S.A. disbanded, 'It would not be an exaggeration to say that there is hardly a subject relating to any branch of national life which the Association has not

---

[24] *Western Daily Press*, 6 Oct. 1869, p. 3.
[25] John Ruskin, 'Education in art', *Transactions*, 1858, pp. 311–16.
[26] *Daily News*, 2 Oct. 1873, p. 5.
[27] Sidney and Beatrice Webb, *History of Trade Unionism* (London, 1892), pp. 227–8.
[28] *The Times*, 19 Aug. 1882, p. 9. See J. L. Clifford-Smith, *A Manual for the Congress with a Narrative of Past Labours and Results* (London, 1882).

touched, always with some effect more or less, and sometimes with considerable success.'[29]

III

Fawcett attended six S.S.A. Congresses (in 1859 at Bradford, 1860 at Glasgow, 1863 at Edinburgh, 1865 at Sheffield, 1866 at Manchester and 1868 at Birmingham), as well as a number of its smaller meetings held regularly during the parliamentary session in London. He delivered five papers to the Association in all, the last, in 1868, as President of the Department of Economy and Trade,[30] and he made frequent contributions in discussion such that the S.S.A.'s *Transactions* preserve his views on subjects as diverse as emigration and immigration; trade unions, strikes and the arbitration of industrial disputes; cooperation; elementary education; the administration of railways; the employment of women; international law and taxation. He was also a belated addition in 1859 to the committee set up in the previous year that was responsible for the production of the report on *Trades' Societies and Strikes* – a committee that also included William Farr, James Kay-Shuttleworth, W. E. Forster, F. D. Maurice, J. M. Ludlow, Thomas Hughes, Godfrey Lushington, Richard Holt Hutton and G. J. Shaw-Lefevre – although there is no indication that Fawcett contributed anything distinctive to its extensive research in the field and to its conclusions based on the information obtained.[31] Leslie Stephen related that Fawcett preferred the meetings of the British Association for the Advancement of Science where the participants in its Section F for 'Statistical Science' could debate a range of similar issues 'to those of its younger rival', the S.S.A.[32] But there is no direct evidence to support the claim – indeed Fawcett seems to have relished the opportunity that the S.S.A. provided for holding forth in public – and it is perhaps more probable that Stephen was giving his own opinion. Stephen certainly attended the S.S.A.'s 1860 Congress at Glasgow, following in the footsteps of his father who had presided over

[29] 'Social science in England', in Sir Richard Temple, *Cosmopolitan Essays* (London, 1886), p. 124.
[30] 'The theory and tendency of strikes' and 'The protection of labour against immigration', *Transactions*, 1859, pp. 635–40, 704–5. 'On the disadvantages of restricting Fellowships in the English universities to members of the Church of England' and 'How the condition of the labouring classes may be raised by cooperation', *Transactions*, 1860, pp. 438, 871–3. 'Address on economy and trade', *Transactions*, 1868, pp. 113–24.
[31] *Trades' Societies and Strikes. Report of the Committee on Trades' Societies, Appointed by the National Association for the Promotion of Social Science. Presented at the Fourth Annual Meeting of the Association at Glasgow, September 1860* (London, 1860).
[32] Stephen, *Life of Fawcett*, p. 184.

the Department of Social Economy in 1858 at Liverpool,[33] but it seems likely that he had far less patience than Fawcett with the provincial middle class who flocked to listen to the debates, and with the endless round of soirées and dinners which were part and parcel of a week with the Social Science Association.

Fawcett's success at the S.S.A. was assured from the first. The impression made by two papers read at the Bradford Congress in October 1859 apparently won him 'several friends', some of whom, in Leslie Stephen's words, 'were so impressed by his abilities as to consider the possibility of procuring an invitation for him to stand for some Northern borough'.[34] Kay-Shuttleworth commended his paper on 'The theory and tendency of strikes',[35] and J. M. Ludlow, writing to F. D. Maurice after the Congress made special reference to 'a blind Trinity Hall M.A. named Fawcett, who earned great kudos by divers papers of a theoretical character'.[36] A year later, in November 1860, following his contributions to the Glasgow Congress in the previous month, 'with singular audacity', as Leslie Stephen recalled, 'he proposed himself as a candidate for the borough of Southwark ... He brought a letter from Brougham who had seen him at the Social Science Association' and 'was otherwise completely unknown to the constituency'[37] – a letter Fawcett applied for on the strength of his success at the S.S.A. Fawcett explained to Brougham that he had been encouraged to seek a political career by 'several gentlemen who have heard me speak at the meetings of the Social Science Association' and that he was intending to put himself forward for a vacant seat at Newcastle. He reminded Brougham of 'the difficulty of a young man like myself first getting into Parliament' and assured him that 'nothing would so much promote my return as a few written words of recommendation from you'. 'I believe', he continued with characteristic immodesty, 'it is generally admitted that there is at the present time a singular absence of rising young men in the House of Commons. It would be my great ambition to promote those Liberal principles, and those measures of social reform, of which your Lordship has always been so eminent a champion.'[38]

Fawcett's opportunism was well timed. The death of Sir Charles Napier on 6 November 1860 created a vacancy at Southwark, and three days later, with what might be considered indecent haste, Fawcett presented

[33] The *Glasgow Herald*, 25 Sept. 1860, p. 2, contained a list of visitors to the S.S.A. which included 'Henry Fawcett, Esq., Cambridge; Rev. Leslie Stephen, Cambridge'.
[34] Stephen, *Life of Fawcett*, p. 184.   [35] ibid.
[36] J. M. Ludlow to F. D. Maurice, 19 Oct. 1859, Ludlow Papers, Cambridge University Library, Add, 7348/17/33.
[37] [Leslie Stephen] 'Henry Fawcett', *Dictionary of National Biography*, vol. 18, p. 254.
[38] H. Fawcett to Brougham, 7 Nov. 1860, Brougham Papers, University College, London, B.MS 14273

himself to a committee of local Liberals 'appointed to look out for some independent candidate who would stand upon principles of purity',[39] bringing 'as his credentials [the] letter from Lord Brougham'.[40] On the following evening the precious document was read to the assembled electors of Southwark at a meeting at the St George's Tavern, Lambeth Road, where the worthy citizens learnt that in Brougham's judgement, 'the good cause of liberal opinion and generally of social progress would receive a great advantage by Mr. Fawcett's return as member for Southwark'.[41] Kay-Shuttleworth sent a letter of support and the radical Liberal, Duncan McLaren, who had heard Fawcett at the S.S.A. in Glasgow, came unannounced to an election meeting and 'spoke of him in the warmest terms'.[42] The calm of High Table at Trinity Hall thus gave way to the commotion of the Royal Oak Tavern in Bermondsey where Fawcett addressed a meeting on the 12th of November; to the Brown Bear Tavern on the 13th; the Europa Tavern, Rotherhithe, on the 15th; the Ship Tavern on the 16th; the Horse and Groom on the 17th; and the Woolpack Tavern, Bermondsey, on the 21st.[43] And night after night, with evident vigour and enthusiasm for the rough and tumble of electioneering, Fawcett laid out his political programme, declaring himself 'a thorough Liberal – a supporter of free trade – of vote by ballot and of the franchise being extended so as to admit within its pale the great body of the respectable working classes'.[44] A political career had thus begun: as Mill wrote to Fawcett when the ultimately unsuccessful campaign was over, 'I can see that a great point has been gained, that you have made a very favourable impression generally, and that people are familiarised with the idea of you as a candidate. The compliments paid you, and the great support you received, will tell much for you at any future election.' Richard Cobden also followed the campaign. In a letter to the eventual victor, H. A. Layard, he expressed his 'strong sympathy for poor young Fawcett. I know his father who is a good politician at Salisbury, and was aware of the sorrowful circumstances under which his son lost his sight ... I sincerely hope he may yet find some field for the employment of his energy. But Southwark was not a proper field.'[45] Others were less charitable. The sheer audacity of Fawcett's enterprise were obviously a talking point: as James Bryce later recalled, 'His first attempts to get into

[39] Stephen, *Life of Fawcett*, p. 189.   [40] ibid.
[41] 'The representation of the borough of Southwark', *Morning Star* (London), 12 Nov. 1860, p. 2.
[42] Stephen, *Life of Fawcett*, p. 194.
[43] Fawcett's campaign can be traced in daily reports in the *Morning Star*.
[44] *Morning Star*, 13 Nov. 1860, p. 2.
[45] Mill to Fawcett, 24 Dec. 1860, in *Collected Works of John Stuart Mill*, vol. 15, p. 716; R. Cobden to H. A. Layard, 20 Dec. 1860, B.L. Add MS 38987 fo. 12.

Parliament without the help of money or local connections were thought absurd, and would have been publicly ridiculed but for the sympathy which his blindness excited.'[46] And G. C. Brodrick caught the absurdity of the shoestring campaign in Southward in some anecdotes that he included in his memoirs in 1900.[47]

In the midst of the electioneering, Fawcett wrote again to Brougham to express his 'sincere obligations': 'Owing to your most kind letter of introduction, I have met with a most favourable reception at Southwark.'[48] No doubt this was an exaggeration, but the episode is an interesting example – or rather, a symbol – of the way in which Fawcett gathered political patronage and support at the S.S.A. And his success at the Association brought more than merely political rewards: at Bradford in 1859 he came to the attention of Thomas Hare, the tenacious advocate of a system of proportional representation, and through Hare was soon intimate with Mill, his intellectual and spiritual mentor for the rest of his life.[49] Like Ludlow, Hare was evidently impressed by Fawcett's entry into public life and mentioned him to Mill, who in turn 'was very much interested by your account of Mr. Fawcett. So active an interest in progress in a man early afflicted with such a misfortune as blindness is very rare and meritorious. Is the recovery of his sight quite hopeless?'[50]

IV

At this early stage in Fawcett's career his opinions were, to say the least, fluid. As Christopher Harvie has pointed ouid, in June 1860 in a pamphlet entitled *The Leading Clauses of a New Reform Bill* he advocated enfranchising only those who had saved more than £60 – an eminently conservative proposition. But five months later at the St George's Tavern in Southwark he declared in favour of both the £6 household and lodger franchises.[51] His support for proportional representation in the first pamphlet he published obviously endeared him to both Hare and Mill – indeed, to ensure that Mill fully appreciated the labours of his new disciple, Fawcett sent him three separate copies[52] – but thereafter his

46 [James Bryce], 'The late Mr. Fawcett', *Nation* (N.Y.), vol. 39 (Nov. 1884), p. 457.
47 G. C. Brodrick, *Memories and Impressions, 1831–1900* (London, 1900), p. 265.
48 Fawcett to Brougham, 17 Nov. 1860, Brougham Papers, B.MS 14275.
49 Stephen, *Life of Fawcett*, p. 82.
50 Mill to Hare, 30 Oct. 1859, in *Collected Works of John Stuart Mill*, vol. 15, pp. 642–3.
51 Christopher Harvie, *The Lights of Liberalism. University Liberals and the Challenge of Democracy, 1860–1886* (London, 1976), p. 118. See also Stephen, *Life of Fawcett*, pp. 186, 191; *Morning Star*, 12 Nov. 1860, p. 2.
52 See H. Fawcett, *Mr Hare's Reform Bill, Simplified and Explained* (London, 1860); see also Mill to Fawcett, 14 July 1860, in *Collected Works of John Stuart Mill*, vol. 15, p. 701.

enthusiasm seemed to wane a little, to Mill's consternation.[53] Here was a young man jumping on and off the political and intellectual bandwagons of the moment. Thus a year after the famous confrontation at Oxford between Bishop Wilberforce and T. H. Huxley, Fawcett tried to align himself at the following British Association meeting in Manchester in 1861 with the party of progress in a paper 'On the method of Mr. Darwin in his treatise on the Origin of Species'. But the difficulties involved in adopting a new mentor while remaining faithful to an older one got the better of him, and many of the audience may have been surprised to discover from Fawcett that 'Mr. Darwin had strictly followed the rules of the deductive method as laid down by John Stuart Mill.'[54]

But of one thing Fawcett was certain: he was a Liberal. As Leslie Stephen explained to the electors of Brighton in February 1864 in an eminently obscure publication that Stephen wrote and edited himself whilst electioneering for his friend, 'it would be easier to doubt that Mr. Wilberforce was an abolitionist, or that Mr. Cobden is a free-trader, as for those who know him to doubt that Mr. Fawcett is a liberal, staunch to the backbone'.[55] Fawcett went one better; with evident relish he described himself to a meeting of the S.S.A. at its Birmingham Congress in 1868 as 'an extreme politician' whose 'opinions were very advanced'.[56] We can be a little more precise than this in placing Fawcett in a political context: he was one of the 'university Liberals' of the 1860s that we associate with two symbolic texts of generational discontent, both published in 1867, *Essays on Reform* and *Questions for a Reformed Parliament*. Fawcett did not actually contribute to either of these collections of essays written by individual academic Liberals, and he was not to be found at the centre of this group of young dons, journalists, briefless barristers and aspiring politicians, whose institutional and intellectual affiliations were more with Oxford than Cambridge. But he knew many of them personally, dined with them regularly in their select gatherings and clubs, and

[53] Following a speech Fawcett gave in Brighton on 13 Sept. 1864, on parliamentary reform, Mill wrote to Cairnes that he was 'disagreeably surprised not so much by Fawcett's saying nothing about representation of minorities, but by his saying things which are repugnant to the most obvious argument for it'. Mill to Cairnes, 3 Oct. 1864, in ibid., p. 958.

[54] *Report of the Thirty-First Meeting of the British Association for the Advancement of Science*, 1861 (Manchester), Transactions of Sections, p. 142.

[55] *Brighton Election Reporter*, 13 Feb. 1864 (no. 4), p. 1. The six numbers of the *Reporter* are held in the British Library. Bound with them is a letter from Millicent Garrett Fawcett explaining that 'When my husband was first a candidate for Brighton in 1864, none of the existing Brighton papers would put in anything in his support: and his friend Mr. Leslie Stephen started and edited and in the main wrote, a little paper called the *Brighton Election Reporter*. It only ran to 6 numbers.'

[56] Fawcett was addressing the S.S.A.'s annual Working Men's Meeting. See the *Birmingham Daily Post*, 3 Oct. 1868, p. 5.

concurred with much of their politics, though the internal coherence of a group encompassing 'positivists, Christian Socialists, idealists and utilitarians'[57] could never be very great and can easily be exaggerated. University Liberals supported parliamentary reform, Italian nationalism and the cause of the North in the American Civil War, the legal recognition of trade unions, cooperative production and distribution, the codification of the law and the systematisation of legal procedure, the redistribution of educational endowments and the religious and educational reform of the universities. Indeed, their formative campaign, prosecuted throughout the 1860s, was for the abolition of the university tests, and Fawcett declared his membership of the group by organising in 1862 a 'petition signed by 74 resident fellows and tutors at Cambridge, praying for the abolition of the assent to the Act of Uniformity on election to a Fellowship',[58] which was presented to the House of Commons by the M.P. for Kilmarnock, Edward Pleydell-Bouverie.

In the late 1850s and early 1860s these academic Liberals came to the Social Science Association. Of twenty-one 'reform essayists' who contributed to the two volumes published in 1867, ten addressed the S.S.A. – indeed, as a group they contributed twenty-seven papers in all.[59] They came because the Social Science Association had been founded in the mid-1850s to combat the hiatus in domestic reform that distinguished Palmerston's political ascendancy in the mid-nineteenth century and which so frustrated these young radicals. They came because the Social Science Association was an essentially Liberal forum: behind a rhetoric of political neutrality – a necessary strategy for an organisation hoping for consistent influence over successive governments of varying ideological composition – lay a commitment to the reform of social institutions and social policies which attracted few Conservatives before the late 1860s and early 1870s. And they also came because the Social Science Association held out the prospect of uniting in John Morley's famous formula of 1867, 'Brains and Numbers'.[60]

---

[57] Harvie, *Lights of Liberalism*, pp. 20, 141. On academic Liberalism, see also Christopher Kent, *Brains and Numbers: Elitism, Comtism, and Democracy in Mid-Victorian England* (Toronto, 1978).

[58] Harvie, *Lights of Liberalism*, p. 79.

[59] G. C. Brodrick, Richard Holt Hutton, Lord Houghton (Richard Monckton Milnes), John Boyd Kinnear, Goldwin Smith, Frank Harrison Hill, Godfrey Lushington, Frederic Harrison, J. Thorold Rogers and J. M. Ludlow. In addition, Albert Rutson, the editor of the volumes, delivered his views on university reform to the 1868 Birmingham Congress (See the *Birmingham Daily Post*, 2 Oct. 1868, p. 6) and attended several of the Association's meetings in London. And A. V. Dicey was a number of one of the organisations from which the S.S.A. developed, the Law Amendment Society.

[60] 'The extreme advanced party is likely for the future to have on its side the most highly cultivated intellect of the nation, and the contest will lie between brains and numbers on

Although the S.S.A. was an essentially middle-class forum which attracted the industrial and commercial bourgeoisie to its Department of Social Economy, the legal profession to its Jurisprudence Department and doctors to the Public Health section, it also played host in its debates on trade unionism to another section of the developing Liberal coalition, the labour aristocracy as represented by some of the leading trade unionists of the period: to William Newton[61] who with William Allan founded the Amalgamated Society of Engineers; to Alexander Campbell of the Glasgow Trades Council;[62] to T. J. Dunning of the London Bookbinders;[63] to Robert Applegarth of the Carpenters and Joiners;[64] to William Dronfield of the Sheffield Association of Organised Trades,[65] and to Alexander Macdonald, President of the Miners' National Association from its foundation in 1863 until his death in 1881, and the first working man elected an M.P. in 1874.[66] J. M. Ludlow and Lloyd Jones in their famous study of the *Progress of the Working Class*, published in 1867, noted how working men had 'taken part repeatedly in the proceedings of the Social Science Association, either by contributing papers to its transactions or by joining in its discussions'.[67] The German political economist, Lujo Brentano, explained in a brief history of the Amalgamated Society of Engineers that was published in 1870 that the union took

one side, and wealth, rank, vested interest, possession in short, on the other.' *Fortnightly Review*, vol. 1 (n.s.) (1867), p. 492 (a review of *Essays on Reform*).

[61] Newton delivered an unpublished paper to the S.S.A. in 1861, 'The origins, progress and recent position of the Amalgamated Society of Engineers', *Transactions*, 1861, p. 680. He also took part in discussion at Bradford in 1859 and London in 1862. See *Transactions*, 1859, p. 721; 1862, p. 798.

[62] Campbell presented a paper to the S.S.A. in 1863 on 'Co-operation: its origins, advocates, progress, difficulties and objects', *Transactions*, 1863, p. 752. He also took part in the discussion at Glasgow following the submission of the report on *Trades' Societies and Strikes*: see p. 611.

[63] Dunning wrote two papers for the S.S.A.: 'Some account of the London Consolidated Society of Bookbinders', *Trades' Societies and Strikes*, pp. 93–104, and 'Labour in connexion with trades' unions', *Transactions*, 1861, pp. 682–3. For his contributions to discussion, see *Transactions*, 1859, pp. 716–19; 1862, pp. 796–7, and *Trades' Societies and Strikes*, pp. 612–13.

[64] Applegarth was employed by the S.S.A.'s 'Committee on Labour and Capital' in the early 1870s, and, in this capacity, was involved in the S.S.A.'s attempts to settle the London Builders' Strike of 1872 and the Barnsley Weavers' Strike of 1873. See *Sessional Proceedings of the National Association for the Promotion of Social Science*, 1867–8, p. 389; 1871–2, p. 389; 1872–3, pp. 211–2.

[65] William Dronfield, 'Trades' Societies and a working man's view of them', *Sheffield and Rotherham Independent*, 6 Oct. 1865, p. 5. The paper was never printed in the *Transactions* for 1865 and so spurred Dronfield to the organisation of a Social Science Association for working men, the Trades Union Congress (see n. 69). For his views on elementary education and the 'Revised Code', see *Transactions*, 1865, p. 370.

[66] Macdonald contributed to a discussion on elementary education and the regulation of child labour at the Sheffield Congress. See *Transactions*, 1865, pp. 366–7.

[67] J. M. Ludlow and Lloyd Jones, *Progress of the Working Class*. (London, 1867), p. 283.

'every opportunity of arguing its case before the world': in 1859 its executive 'resolved to send a delegate' to the Bradford Congress 'that no misrepresentation of their society, or of other trades-unions might remain unanswered'.[68] The S.S.A. provided a forum where the mid-Victorian trades union movement could put its case for social acceptance, though the suspicion, following the Sheffield Congress in 1865, that the Association's organisers were unfavourably disposed to pro-union contributions was a spur to the foundation of the Trades Union Congress itself which was initially conceived as a working men's Social Science Association where the organised working class might discuss all relevant social issues.[69] The T.U.C. was sometimes seen as an offshoot of the S.S.A. in these years – it represented to *The Times* in 1882 'social science from the working man's point of view'[70] – which is not surprising given that the circular distributed among unions in 1868 inviting them to send delegates to the inaugural Trades Union Congress in Manchester made an overt comparison with the Social Science Association.[71] Despite the S.S.A.'s ambivalence to organised labour – its leaders were welcome as physical symbols of class harmony but their message was often ignored or edited out of the *Transactions* – the very presence of such men at the Association's debates and the S.S.A.'s valuable investigation of 'new model unionism' provided opportunities for meeting with and learning about the working class. So Frederic Harrison acclaimed *Trades' Societies and Strikes*: it was 'the most valuable blue book respecting industry ever composed' and 'the opinion of such a committee may fairly be considered as authoritative, and to outweigh a hundredfold the general notions of any one man based on partial experience'.[72] The S.S.A. brought together Liberal M.P.s, trades unionists, 'advanced' employers like A. J. Mundella, Thomas Brassey, Samuel Courtauld and Samuel Morley who were sympathetic to the claims of the unions, and the intellectual 'friends of labour', the Christian Socialists and Positivists. It thus helped to build the inter-class alliances, many of them dependent on personal contact, which laid the foundations of the distinctive Lib-Lab politics of the sixties,

---

68 [Lujo Brentano], 'The growth of a trades-union', *North British Review*, vol. 53 (Oct. 1870–Jan. 1871), p. 113.
69 See 'The origins and establishment of the Trades Union Congress', in A. E. Musson, *Trade Union and Social History* (London, 1974), pp. 40–5; R. M. Martin, *TUC: The Growth of a Pressure Group, 1868–1976* (Oxford, 1980), p. 43.
70 *The Times*, 25 Sept. 1882, p. 7.
71 The circular is printed in Musson, *Trade Union and Social History*, p. 43. It was 'proposed that the Congress shall assume the character of the annual meetings of the British Association for the Advancement of Science and the Social Science Association, in the transactions of which societies the artizan class are almost entirely excluded'.
72 Frederic Harrison, 'The good and evil of trade-unionism', *Fortnightly Review*, vol. 3 (Nov. 1865–Feb. 1866), p. 37.

seventies and eighties – a political configuration to which Fawcett contributed.

During this period, organised labour gained legal recognition under the trade union legislation of 1871 and 1875, and, in return, accepted the guidance of these middle-class Liberals who brought the trade unions into the Liberal political fold. But those who would guide had also to obtain a prior knowledge of the organisation, customs and aspirations of the industrial classes and thus Fawcett came to the S.S.A. both to learn from, and to lecture to, the working class.

The first of these postures was evident in 1865 when he attended the S.S.A.'s Congress at Sheffield. He held up a discussion on the relation of industrial labour to elementary education in order to secure a clear statement from Alexander Macdonald on the miners' long and unsuccessful campaign to ensure 'that no child shall work more than eight hours out of the 24, and that he shall go to school for a certain number of hours until he is 14 years of age'. Fawcett, evidently surprised by the miners' concern for the education of their children, had 'never listened to any statement in [his] life with more interest' and found it 'astonishing' that 'this admirable request should have been made for so many years without receiving more attention than it has yet done from the House of Commons'.[73] Four days later Fawcett met with the Sheffield Filesmiths' Union at their quarterly meeting in the local Temperance Hall in what Leslie Stephen described as 'a remarkable conference'[74] on union intimidation, the introduction of machinery into the file trade and the employment of children in Sheffield's factories. In the course of some lengthy exchanges Fawcett made his own position clear: he denounced the supposed 'trade outrages' for which Sheffield was notorious in the mid-nineteenth century and he warned that opposition to mechanisation would only drive capital elsewhere.[75] But he came before the union as an enquirer whose 'great object' was 'to obtain information': 'my sole object', he declared, 'is to ascertain the truth, and if I do ascertain it, and it redounds to your credit, you shall find that I will make a great deal of use of it'. It was, he concluded, 'one of the most instructive evenings which I have ever spent'.[76]

But Fawcett's personality had a marked strain of didacticism running through it, and if at the S.S.A. he was brought into contact with the

---

[73] Transactions, 1865, pp. 366–7; Sheffield Independent, 7 Oct. 1865.
[74] Stephen, Life of Fawcett, pp. 158–9.
[75] 'The Sheffield Filesmith's Union. Conference of the Workmen with Professor Fawcett, M.P. Trade Outrages and Machinery', Sheffield and Rotherham Independent, 12 Oct. 1865, p. 6.
[76] ibid. See also 'The introduction of machinery into the File Trade', Sheffield Independent, 11 Oct. 1865, p. 5, and an editorial, 'Professor Fawcett, M.P., and the Filesmith's Union', 14 Oct. 1865, p. 6.

working class and learnt from them, he was always most comfortable when he could assume a pedagogic role. And so the Association's annual Working Men's Meeting became his favoured forum. At each Congress the Working Men's Meeting, held on a single evening, attracted thousands of the respectable working class to hear the leading figures of the Social Science Association lecture to them on the need for self-restraint and moral rectitude – on 'temperance, intelligence and thrift', as A. J. Mundella formulated the message to 3,000 working men in the City Hall in Leeds in 1871.[77] The meetings were devised to promote social solidarity, uniting those on the platform with those in the body of the hall. But though the working men cheered, they were never allowed to speak. The presence of the eminent, the speeches from participants in the Congress proper and an expansive rhetoric that emphasised the bonds and obligations linking rich and poor reinforced the Association's claims to be a truly national forum that could bring the classes together. 'We open our doors to all sects, all classes, all parties and all conditions of men': thus Brougham in 1860 when, in the words of the *Glasgow Daily Herald*, men 'of lofty name and standing' met 'in social communion with the working men of Glasgow'. The delegates sent 'from the various trades in the city' saw before them on that occasion Lord Brougham and the Lord Provost seated with 'about 200 of the leading citizens of Glasgow and leading members of the Association, and above 50 representatives of the working men of the city'. The evening's theme was clear: the working classes were to be included 'as fellow-workmen in the great cause of Social Science' because this science of reform was 'of general interest, and all class distinctions should be kept out of sight in its consideration'.[78] The Working Men's Meetings were thus symbols on a grand scale of the reconciliation of the classes that we associate with the mid-Victorian 'age of equipoise' and they gave Fawcett – who actually addressed this meeting in Glasgow – an opportunity to indulge in populistic rhetoric and develop a reputation as a friend to the working man. In the City Hall in Glasgow and the Dunedin Hall in Edinburgh, in the Music Hall in Sheffield and the Town Hall in Birmingham,[79] Fawcett commended consumer cooperation, an extension of the franchise, 'a compulsory system of education based on unsectarian principles'[80] and industrial copartnerships between employers and their workforce. And the working men who listened and

77 *Leeds Mercury*, 7 Oct. 1871, p. 5.
78 For a report of this meeting see the *Glasgow Daily Herald* 27 Sept. 1860, p. 4. For an editorial reflecting on the social significance of this meeting see ibid., 29 Sept. 1860, p. 5.
79 For full reports of these four Working Men's Meetings, see the *Glasgow Daily Herald*, 27 Sept. 1860, p. 4; *Daily News* (London), 12 Oct. 1863, p. 3; *Sheffield Independent*, 6 Oct. 1865, p. 8; *Birmingham Daily Post*, 3 Oct. 1868, p. 5.
80 The phrase is from the *Birmingham Daily Post*, ibid.

cheered might well have been surprised to meet with a Professor of Political Economy, who, in his own words, 'sometimes tried to place himself in the position of a labourer, and to think what his thoughts would be in that position';[81] who 'would never estimate the greatness or the civilisation of a nation by the amount of its accumulated wealth';[82] who believed, as he explained at Sheffield, that the British 'concentrated too much attention upon the production of wealth, and did not sufficiently consider how wealth was to be distributed';[83] and who contrasted the 'magnificence and expenditure' of 'fashionable London' with 'the wretchedness and poverty' of Bethnal Green and Whitechapel.[84]

With these easy words Fawcett developed a political identity as a middle-class advocate of the claims of the working class. As he explained to the Sheffield filesmiths in 1865, 'I have been looked upon in the Association for the Promotion of Social Science that I was too ready to believe the working men, and that I have pandered to their prejudices.'[85] In 1863, The Daily Telegraph noted that he was 'a great favourite with the working classes' of Edinburgh;[86] in 1867, Mill used the argument that he was 'much trusted' by working men to try to win him a place on the Royal Commission on Trades' Unions.[87] When it looked as if Fawcett might have difficulty in securing the Liberal nomination at Brighton in 1868, George Howell of the Reform League wrote in his favour to the secretary of the League's Brighton branch, for 'the working men of England' could not 'afford to lose the services of one of their best and most uncompromising champions': Fawcett was a politician 'who understands the questions of capital and labour, and whose sympathies are with the mass of toilers rather than the employers'.[88] And in the subsequent campaign, George Odger, the shoe-maker secretary of the London Trades Council from 1862 until 1872, came to Brighton to aver that there was 'not a better man in the house'. Fawcett, he explained, was always available to meet with working men, and 'no man did more' in the passage of the Master and Servant Act of 1867 which mitigated the iniquity of the Master and Servant Laws under which breach of contract by an employer was a civil, but by an employee, a criminal

[81] Sheffield Independent, 6 Oct. 1865, p. 8.
[82] Birmingham Daily Post, 3 Oct. 1868, p. 5.
[83] Sheffield Independent, 6 Oct. 1865, p. 8.   [84] ibid.
[85] ibid., 12 Oct., 1865, p. 6.
[86] The Daily Telegraph, 10 Oct. 1863, p. 3.
[87] Mill to Spencer H. Walpole (Home Secretary), 29 Jan. 1867, Collected Works of John Stuart Mill, vol. 16, p. 1232.
[88] George Howell to J. Thompson, 28 Oct. 1868, quoted in Royden Harrison, Before the Socialists, Studies in Labour and Politics, 1861–1881 (London, 1965), p. 173; F. M. Leventhal, Respectable Radical, George Howell and Victorian Working Class Politics (London, 1971), p. 109.

offence.[89] As Odger explained, 'Mr. Fawcett was applied to; we took counsel with him, and he never rested till he had obtained equality between the employer and the servant in the eye of the law.'[90]

V

There were, of course, a very large number of Members of Parliament who shared Fawcett's opposition to the Master and Servant Laws – so many, indeed, that 'a successful meeting of legislators was held in the "tea room" of the House of Commons itself' in 1864 at which a trade union delegation 'impressed their desires upon all the friendly members'.[91] But it would be difficult to argue with this appreciation of Fawcett from one of the outstanding leaders of the labour movement in the mid-nineteenth century, who, in his own words, 'had a hundred conversations with him in the lobby of the House' during the session of 1867.[92] As Bryce explained after Fawcett's death, 'There was, perhaps, nobody in England, except Mr. Gladstone himself, whose advice [the working class] would have been so willing to take, believing it to be absolutely honest and straight-forward.'[93] But if Fawcett really was an 'uncompromising champion' of the working class, then it would be legitimate to expect that his economics would have complemented his politics: that Fawcett, like other components of university Liberalism – the Positivists and Christian Socialists most obviously – would have challenged some of the orthodox positions of political economy that were hostile to working-class organisation and wage-bargaining. The S.S.A. made occasional gestures in the direction of economic heterodoxy. Its secretary, George Woodyatt Hastings, elected a Liberal M.P. in 1880, was himself on the fringes of academic Liberalism, and, as he explained in 1868, social science was 'not confined to economics, to the principles regulating the creation and distribution of wealth, however, important those may be; it does not deal only with material interests; it deals with the whole well-being of man and the progress of society, with those moral aims and aspirations which the

89 'Reform League Meeting in Brighton – Address of Mr. George Odger', *Brighton Guardian*, 8 Nov. 1868, p. 6.
90 ibid. The Act of 1867 'did not entirely satisfy the unions ... because it still permitted criminal actions against workmen for breach of contract in "aggravated cases", whatever they might be'. Henry Pelling, *A History of British Trade Unionism* (3rd edn, Harmondsworth, 1976), p. 64.
91 S. and B. Webb, *History of Trade Unionism*, p. 253.
92 *Brighton Guardian*, 18 Nov. 1868, p. 6.
93 [Bryce], 'The late Mr. Fawcett', p. 457.

Association was established to further'.[94] 'Social science' offered an alternative type of social explanation to this radical intelligentsia – an alternative that was more in accord with their social ideals and their political commitments. If political economy could find no place in its theory for trades unions, those 'unnatural' interventions in the perfect market for labour whose efforts to increase wages could only, under the terms of the wage-fund doctrine, diminish the amount of capital available for investment and so impoverish the working class – then 'social science' had gone out to investigate these growing institutions and the Social Science Association began a movement for their social acceptance. As Hastings affirmed towards the end of the S.S.A.'s career, the members of the Association were 'not to moon after what are termed the strict principles of political economy, whatever that phrase may mean, but to inquire, investigate, reason for ourselves; to find out the facts, make true inductions, and leave the principles of the science, as they can well afford, to take care of themselves'.[95]

But Fawcett's public profile as an economist, within and without the S.S.A., encompassed none of these subversive intentions and unorthodox positions. If he sometimes played the role of honest broker – at Sheffield in 1865 he believed he could discuss the issues dividing labour and capital 'calmly and with an unprejudiced mind'[96] – he also enjoyed his position as an authority on political economy and an exponent of its axioms. He prefaced many of his contributions at the S.S.A. with the economic doctrine relevant to the point at issue[97] and he was ever vigilant to answer 'the statement so often repeated about political economy being hard-hearted' which 'was about as unreasonable as if they were to say that a proposition in Euclid, or any physical fact, was hard-hearted or selfish'.[98] He had a talent for summary and simplification – for making things plain, perhaps too plain, to the average reader – and his success at the S.S.A. when addressing middle-class audiences was based on his exposition of a 'plain man's political economy' to relatively uninstructed audiences. To Ruskin, therefore, he was the 'dismal science' incarnate, who had taught the acceptance, throughout his public life, 'of the great Devil's law of Theft by the Rich from the Poor, in the two terrific forms either of buying men's tools, and making them pay for the loan of them – (Interest) – or buying men's lands, and making them pay for the produce of them –

[94] 'Address by G. W. Hastings, Chairman of the Council', *Transactions*, 1868, p. 133.
[95] G. W. Hastings, 'Opening address', ibid., 1882, p. 2.   [96] ibid., 1865, p. 519.
[97] His contribution on 'The protection of labour against immigration' (ibid., 1859, pp. 704–5) began with a statement of the relationship between wages, capital and population.
[98] ibid., 1863, pp. 749–50. Fawcett made a similar point in his 'Address on economy and trade', ibid., 1868, pp. 114–15.

(Rent)'.[99] The very popularity and simplicity of Fawcett's *Manual* made him an obvious target for Ruskin's bitter invective and ridicule,[100] and Fawcett was consequently charged 'with having insufficiently investigated the principles of the science he is appointed to teach',[101] and with having written 'stark idiotisms' in 'defence of the theory of interest on money',[102] and he was challenged by Ruskin, both in public and private, to defend his ideas – invitations he declined.[103]

But Fawcett was never the sole object of Ruskin's contempt, which was evenly distributed among all the 'professors of political economy'.[104] And Ruskin's 'challenge to the nineteenth century system of production, and the "laws of political economy" which supported it'[105] came from too far outside accepted economic discourse to have troubled the orthodoxies of the age. Fawcett's outlook was never idiosyncratic but merely a faithful reflection of 'the implicit acceptance of "classical" economics as the basis of social life'[106] on the part of most university Liberals, such that Leslie Stephen's summary of his political economy as presented in the *Life*, constitutes, in Christopher Harvie's judgement, 'probably the best account of the economic beliefs held by Fawcett's generation'.[107]

But can there be any safety in numbers? Can Fawcett's doctrines be explained (and, indeed, defended) on the grounds that a majority of those from similar backgrounds thought as he did? Ruskin's critique may have been too raw and radical to have merited a response. But there were others like Frederic Harrison and J. M. Ludlow, Edward Beesley and Godfrey Lushington, from a comparable milieu, who were strident in their more reasoned disagreements with consensual economics. And if Fawcett and some of his generation found it hard to accept Thornton's refutation of

99 *Fors Clavigera. Letters to the Workmen and Labourers of Great Britain*, Letter 78 (June 1877), in E. T. Cook and Alexander Wedderburn (eds.), *The Works of John Ruskin* (39 vols., London, 1903–12), vol. 29,. p. 136.

100 See Cook and Wedderburn (eds.), ibid., vol. 17, pp. 138–9; vol. 27, pp. 188–9; vol. 27, pp. 314–16.

101 *Fors Clavigera*, Letter 22 (Oct 1872), Proposition II, in ibid., vol. 27, p. 378.

102 ibid. See also Ruskin to H. E. Luxmore, 15 May 1873, in ibid., vol. 37, p. 67.

103 ibid., vol. 27, p. 378, and vol. 29, p. 136. As Stephen explained, 'Mr. Ruskin once challenged Fawcett to a discussion upon the first principles of political economy. Fawcett sensibly declined a discussion which would at most have been an amusing illustration of argument at cross purposes, with an utter absence of common ground.' Stephen, *Life of Fawcett*, pp. 136–7.

104 On 4 July 1868, at one of the S.S.A.'s most interesting debates on industrial relations, chaired by Gladstone, Ruskin interrupted the proceedings to lay before the meeting a series of ten questions on 'the natural law of wages' which 'he wished to put to professors of political economy'. See 'Wages and capital', *Sessional Proceedings*, 1867–8, pp. 405–6.

105 Raymond Williams, *Culture and Society, 1780–1950* (Harmondsworth, 1961 edn), p. 148.

106 Harvie, *Lights of Liberalism*, p. 159.   107 ibid., p. 305 n. 82.

the wage-fund doctrine in the late 1860s, then there were many others, including Mill himself, who were prepared to admit that they had been wrong. Fawcett's adherence to the outmoded doctrine is of the highest importance: it illustrates Leslie Stephen's description of 'an intellect wanting in versatility and less open to new ideas than powerful in its grasp of the old'[108] – there is no escaping Fawcett's essentially conservative mind[109] – and it begs certain questions about his commitment to the interests of the organised working class. For the wage-fund doctrine was in constant use in the mid-nineteenth century as an ideological weapon against trade unionism: indeed, to accept the wage-fund doctrine implied a simultaneous belief in the redundancy of unions, for the short-term gains in remuneration that they might secure could only be bought at long-term cost to the working class: if unions did succeed in temporarily increasing wages above their 'natural level' (and there were many who contended that this was impossible) then either the flight of capital or the consequent increase in population would ultimately result in their impoverishment.[110] But it is by no means the only example of Fawcett's zealous attachment to the orthodoxy that he assimilated in the late 1850s and early 1860s and stayed faithful to thereafter. For at the Social Science Association he was involved in a number of exchanges in which aspects of this orthodoxy were questioned, and what is so striking about his performance in response is his consistency in defending these orthodox positions even when the evidence available to him, and his political affiliation to working-class causes, might have been expected to have prompted a quite different approach.

Fawcett actually came to public attention at the S.S.A. in 1859 and at the British Association in 1860 by his strident defence of orthodox economic methodology. One aspect of unconventional political economy as developed across successive generations in the nineteenth century was a critique of orthodox deductivism.[111] Richard Jones in the 1830s, the Positivists in the 1860s, the Historical School – T. E. Cliffe Leslie, W. J. Ashley and William Cunningham – in the 1870s and 1880s, and the

---

[108] Stephen, *Life of Fawcett*, p. 125.

[109] R. V. Clements, 'British trade unions and popular political economy, 1850–1875', *Economic History Review*, vol. 14 (n.s.) (1961–2), p. 93.

[110] On Fawcett's satisfaction with 'the substantial truth of the wage-fund theory' see Stephen, *Life of Fawcett*, pp. 155–8. On the rejection of the theory, see W. Hamish Fraser, *Trade Unions and Society. The Struggle for Acceptance, 1850–1880* (London, 1974), pp. 176–80.

[111] For studies of the interplay of the methodologically orthodox and unorthodox, see Stefan Collini, Donald Winch and John Burrow, *That Noble Science of Politics. A Study in Nineteenth-Century Intellectual History* (Cambridge, 1983), and Lawrence Goldman, 'The origins of British "social science", 1830–1835: political economy, natural science and statistics', *Historical Journal*, vol. 26, no. 3 (1983), pp. 587–616.

Webbs and others at the end of the century, all founded their disagreements with substantive economic doctrines on a fundamental opposition to what Beatrice Webb termed 'a Self-Contained, Separate, Abstract, Political Economy'[112] and advocated an inductive economics able to take account of the totality of moral and social as well as economic factors, instead. But Fawcett would have none of it. If the Committee on Trades' Societies and Strikes had found, as they explained in an interim report in 1859, 'so many differences between the operation of trade societies and so many things in which they vary from the ordinary received views as to their nature and working, that they are convinced that no safe conclusion can be arrived at, except by induction from a very extensive body of facts',[113] then Fawcett, zealous in his open opposition, called instead for a 'theory of strikes' without which 'conclusions must be vague and empirical'. 'Deductive principles', he contended, were 'necessary to explain the observations of physical science, to connect them one with another, and to bring out their relative importance', and 'social science requires the same mode of investigation as physical science'.[114] Battle resumed in the following year at the British Association in Oxford where Fawcett delivered a critique, 'in a masterly manner'[115] of 'Dr. Whewell on the Method of Political Economy'.[116] It must have been a fascinating confrontation: the venerable Master of Trinity had just published an edition of Jones's political economy, complete with an introduction vindicating his old friend's inductivist project,[117] and he was apparently beaten by his upstart combatant on a point of detail.[118] Their differences continued into the 1860s: after the *Manual* was published they exchanged letters on Jones's ideas,[119] and Fawcett's inaugural lecture as Professor at Cambridge began with a vindication of 'deductive reasoning' in explicit opposition to Jones and the 'inductive method'.[120]

---

[112] Beatrice Webb, *My Apprenticeship* (London, 1926), Appendix D, 'On the nature of economic science', p. 437.

[113] 'Report of the Committee on Trades' Societies', *Transactions*, 1859, p. 659.

[114] H. Fawcett, 'The theory and tendency of strikes', ibid., 1859, p. 635.

[115] *Oxford Chronicle*, 30 June 1860, p. 5. The paper was delivered to Section F of the British Association on 29 June. Unfortunately, no report of the session can be traced.

[116] *Report of the British Association for the Advancement of Science*, 1860, (Oxford), Transactions of the Sections, p. 191.

[117] See Whewell's 'Prefatory notice' in William Whewell, D.D. (ed.), *Literary Remains Consisting of Lectures and Tracts of the Late Rev. Richard Jones* (London, 1859).

[118] Fawcett apparently quoted a sentence from Whewell's preface which Whewell disavowed. When the sentence was then read to the meeting by the chairman, Nassau Senior, 'the common impression was that Whewell had been defeated by his junior'. See Stephen, *Life of Fawcett*, p. 119.

[119] Fawcett to Whewell, Whewell Collection, Trinity College, Cambridge, Add. MS a. 203 135, 21 May 1864.

[120] H. Fawcett, 'Inaugural lecture on political economy' (delivered before the University of Cambridge, 3 Feb. 1864), *Macmillan's Magazine*, vol. 9 (April 1864), pp. 497–8.

Fawcett was arguing a case with which very few of those who professed political economy at this time would have disagreed.[121] But occasionally his rigorous conventionalism provoked controversy. In 1863, the S.S.A.'s Congress at Edinburgh discussed 'the Position of the Cotton Districts' of Lancashire, then enduring the 'cotton famine' as a consequence of the American Civil War. Edmund Potter M.P., owner of the largest calico-printing works in the world,[122] delivered a paper paying tribute to 'the character of the people' and 'their morals and behaviour under most trying circumstances',[123] which ended with two questions:

Does the importance of the cotton trade, in connexion with Imperial interests, justify measures on its behalf for securing by legislation ... the safety and progress of the trade, and thus keeping up the physical and moral health of the workers? Or is it economically sounder to leave a large population to sink for an undetermined period, before it can be parted with, either by costly emigration, or absorbed into other employments at a much lower rate of wages?[124]

Fawcett took this as an appeal for state aid for the industry on the part of the masters, and in response had cold comfort to dispense to both employers and employees. As 'the manufacturers had entered into a speculative trade' then 'they themselves must take the consequences of any change'.[125] As for the workforce, he advocated that they emigrate and 'he hoped that every farthing of the money that would be subscribed by the nation to assist the Lancashire operatives would be diverted to that purpose'.[126] This may have been strict economics, but it won Fawcett few friends. On the one hand, Kay-Shuttleworth, who, in his daughter's words, 'did not intend to speak, but ... was obliged to make a short speech',[127] was provoked into an angry defence of 'the Lancashire proprietors' who, he claimed, had never asked for government assistance.[128] And on the other, Fawcett's remarks were at odds with the spirit of the meeting and the more general middle-class sympathy for the privations of the Lancashire operatives: their fortitude was taken as an

[121] Marshall claimed that Jones's 'influence, though little heard of in the outside world, largely dominated the minds of those Englishmen who came to the serious study of economics after his work had been published by Dr. Whewell in 1859'. See A. C. Pigou (ed.), *Memorials of Alfred Marshall* (New York, 1956 edn), p. 296. For a contrary (and probably more accurate) view of Jones's importance, see Salim Rashid, 'Richard Jones and Baconian historicism at Cambridge', *Journal of Economic Issues*, vol. 13, no. 1 (March 1979).
[122] Fraser, *Trade Unions and Society*, pp. 84–5.
[123] Edmund Potter, M.P., 'On the position of the cotton districts', *Transactions*, 1863, p. 659.
[124] ibid., p. 660.   [125] ibid., p. 757.   [126] ibid., p. 758.
[127] Janet Kay-Shuttleworth to Ughtred Kay-Shuttleworth, 9 Oct. 1863, Papers of Sir J. P. Kay-Shuttleworth, John Rylands Library, University of Manchester, item 668.
[128] *Transactions*, 1863, p. 758.

illustration of their social maturity and political responsibility and used to justify an extension of the franchise in 1866 and 1867.[129] Though Fawcett, along with the generality of mid-Victorian political economists, saw emigration as a solution to the problems of so-called 'surplus labour' – indeed, Fawcett's very first appearance in public ended with the declaration 'that there can be no agency so powerful as emigration to effect a great change in the material condition of the poor'[130] – it is doubtful in the extreme if the organised working class who were to do the emigrating had such enthusiasm for, and confidence in, this supposed panacea. As R. V. Clements has put it, 'few trade unionists' gave the idea of emigration 'more than passing attention or more than a most subordinate position in their system of thought'.[131] And Fawcett's solution had little to recommend it in the particular circumstances of the 1860s. As John Pender M.P., the Manchester cotton textiles merchant, pointed out in the same discussion, emigration 'would not do, for the very ships which took the emigrants out would bring them all back again':[132] it was very poor economics to send away an experienced workforce to employment in the competing textile industries of other countries when at some stage in the future the Civil War would end, the trade would revive and the labour would once more be required. In this case, Fawcett's orthodox laissez-faire was out of place; it was economically irrational and out of harmony with prevailing sentiment.

The members of those working-class audiences who cheered Fawcett in the 1860s might well have reconsidered their enthusiasm had they been able to afford a ticket to the Association proper, and had they heard their champion advise them to seek their livelihoods elsewhere. They might also have begun to doubt the word of a man who could glibly contend 'that labour ought to be considered as a commodity, to be regulated like every

---

129 Ironically, Fawcett himself used this argument before the House of Commons in 1866. *Hansard*, clxxxii, 13 March 1866, 203–4.

130 H. Fawcett, 'On the social and economical influence of the new gold', *Report of the British Association for the Advancement of Science*, 1859 (Aberdeen), Transactions of the Sections, p. 209. See also H. Fawcett, *Manual of Political Economy* (Cambridge and London, 1863), pp. 158–61.

131 R. V. Clements, 'Trade unions and emigration, 1840–80', *Population Studies*, vol. 9 (Nov. 1955), p. 167.

132 See the report of the discussion in *The Daily Telegraph*, 12 Oct. 1863, p. 5. Pender maintained 'that the wisest course was to retain the operatives at home, as the trade would speedily recover, and be better than it had ever been'. *Transactions*, 1863, p. 757. As Potter himself explained, 'I think suggestions for broadcast emigration schemes as a necessity, are as yet unsound. Emigration is the natural safety-valve of an overplus population, one sinking and starving on a non-productive soil, or hanging on a trade decaying for want of demand for some superseded commodity; but a harsh, mischievous, and costly remedy wherewith to meet what may be classed as the temporary disruption of a trade.' 'On the position of the cotton districts', ibid., p. 659.

other commodity'.[133] Was labour just an economic category like any
other, or was 'the living labour of the living man', as Thomas Hughes put
it in 1860, to be considered in the light of 'higher laws' than those
propounded by the political economists?[134] The issue recurred in a
number of the Association's debates since the humiliation of being
categorised as a 'commodity' in 'the cruel jargon of the Economists', as
Frederic Harrison once put it,[135] was more than leading trades unionists
and their intellectual advocates could tolerate in a period which saw them
make concerted attempts to win middle-class recognition for the social
claims and moral worth of organised labour. Thomas Hughes, evidently a
different type of university Liberal, protested at Glasgow that the masters
'treated the labour of their men, which was in fact the lives of their men,
on the same principles as those on which they treated a dead commodity':
that they placed 'the living man and inanimate things on the same
footing'.[136] But Fawcett, echoing the views of the employers in the same
discussion,[137] took refuge with the textbooks, for 'everyone who had read
a passage of political economy must be aware that the existence of
political economy depended upon the supposition that labour in all
questions of demand and supply was to be treated identically the same as
any other commodity'.[138] It was good, strict economics but it did not
correspond to the spirit of Fawcett's *political* rhetoric at this time which
was full of the dignity of labour and the legitimate rewards – the vote and
education to the fore – which were its due.

VI

This disjunction betwen Fawcett's economics and his politics is similarly
evident in his attitude to trades unionism and in his panacea for industrial
relations, copartnership. For if Fawcett accepted the legitimacy of trades
unions – as he explained at Birmingham in 1868, 'there could be no doubt
if a man liked to enter an association of his fellow-labourers for their
mutual benefit, he had a right to enter into such a combination'[139] – then
he had none of the enthusiasm of other university Liberals who saw

[133] 'An account of the discussion at Glasgow on Thursday, Sept. 27, 1860', *Trades' Societies and Strikes*, p. 605.
[134] ibid., p. 622.
[135] See Frederic Harrison, *Autobiographic Memoirs* (2 vols., London, 1911), vol. 1, p. 253.
[136] *Trades' Societies and Strikes*, p. 599.
[137] Edmund Potter asked if it was 'sound economical opinion that labour is like any other commodity, and to be treated as such?', and contended in response 'that they could not treat labour in any other way'. Henry Ashworth 'was very unwilling to speak of human labour in any terms that might be deemed a disparagement of it; but he could not regard it in any other light than as a commodity'. Ibid., pp. 603, 606.
[138] ibid., p. 605.   [139] *Birmingham Daily Gazette*, 7 Oct. 1868, p. 7.

unions as an embodiment of the moral advance of labour and a means to its social and economic integration. In *Essays on Reform*, Richard Holt Hutton paid tribute to 'the power of sustained sacrifice for a common purpose, the fortitude in suffering, the self-denial in prosperity, the nobleness of individual self-devotion for the common cause' which trades unionism exhibited.[140] But Fawcett's references to 'social terrorism' and 'great social tyranny' in the relevant chapter of the *Manual*[141] would suggest that his views were rather different from those of some of his collaborators on *Trades' Societies and Strikes* – like Hutton – who had specifically set out to dispel the prejudices that these emotive terms encouraged. And it is impossible that Ludlow or Hughes would have 'agreed so entirely' as Fawcett said he did with an attack on trades unionism contributed to the Sheffield Congress by an embittered ex-unionist.[142] Fawcett accepted trades unions and strikes as inevitable – as a 'natural outgrowth of our modern industrial system'[143] – but he looked beyond that system,[144] and beyond the first attempts at the organised conciliation and arbitration of disputes in the 1860s that gave unions an enhanced status through their very participation in formal wage-bargaining,[145] to cooperation and profit-sharing between masters and men as the ultimate solution to industrial strife. For if strikes were 'primarily due to a separation between capital and labour, it is evident that we must seek a remedy in schemes which will create some identity of interest among all persons engaged in any industrial undertaking'.[146]

Profit-sharing – the distribution of a fixed portion of the profits of an enterprise to the employees, in addition to normal wages and salaries, and copartnership, by which employees were able to buy shares in the enterprises that employed them – were a distinctive middle-class enthusiasm of the 1860s and 1870s.[147] And Fawcett was one of the loudest advocates of these schemes both because of the more harmonious industrial relations and the gains in productivity that they seemed to promise. As he explained in Edinburgh in 1863, their 'great and important

[140] R. H. Hutton, 'The political character of the working classes', in *Essays on Reform*, p. 37.

[141] Fawcett, *Manual*, pp. 258, 260. The 'great social tyranny' merely referred to the efforts of trade unions to limit apprenticeships.

[142] *Sheffield Independent*, 6 Oct. 1865, p. 5. See John Wilson, 'What are the best means of establishing a system of authoritative arbitration between employers and employed in cases of strikes and lock-outs?', *Transactions*, 1865, pp. 476–80. It was because William Dronfield's pro-union paper on the same subject was not eventually published in the *Transactions* of 1865 that Dronfield set out on a path that eventually led to the foundation of the T.U.C. See n. 65.

[143] Fawcett, 'Address on economy and trade', *Transactions*, 1868, p. 118.

[144] Fawcett, 'The theory and tendency of strikes', ibid., 1859, p. 639.

[145] Fawcett, 'Address on economy and trade', ibid., 1868, p. 120.   [146] ibid., p. 118.

[147] G. D. H. Cole, *A Century of Cooperation* (Manchester, 1945), p. 159.

advantage' was 'that increased energy and increased intelligence were
evoked from the labourer by giving him a direct interest in the work in
which he was employed, by making him feel that the more prosperous
the concern was, the larger would be the share of profit which would be
allocated to him'.[148] Fawcett's special enthusiasm – and that of the sympathetic middle class more generally – was reserved for one enterprise in
particular, the collieries at Whitwood and Methley Junction, near Nor-
manton in the West Riding, that were owned by the Messrs Briggs and
which were turned into a copartnership in 1865. Fawcett had a particular interest in the scheme, given that one of his articles in the Westminster Review in 1860 had apparently given Henry Briggs, the company's chairman, the idea of transforming his business.[149] The virulence
of mid-century mining disputes made the progress of the enterprise an
object of great interest, and the Social Science Association listened to a
number of papers from the Briggs family and from others which
monitored the progress of the scheme.

Under it, the joint-stock limited liability company of Henry Briggs and
Sons was capitalised at £90,000. The Briggs family retained two-thirds
of the nine thousand £10 shares issued, and the remaining three thousand were offered for sale with 'a preference to applications from
officials and operatives employed in the concern'.[150] As Fawcett
explained the working of the scheme in 1869, 'when the profits exceed
10 per cent, after setting aside a fair amount to reimburse capital,
one-half the remaining surplus should be distributed amongst the
labourers, and ... each individual's share of this bonus should be pro-
portioned to the aggregate wages which he has earned during the
year'.[151] The experiment seemed to be a great success: at the end of the
first year, 12 per cent of total profits amounting to £1,800 was divided in
bonuses, giving an average bonus of 7.5 per cent on annual earnings.[152]
And Fawcett went to 'a commemorative meeting of the shareholders,
workmen, and friends of Henry Briggs, Son, and Co. Limited' at the
Leeds Town Hall 'to celebrate the successful completion of their first
year's working under the principle of cooperative partnership of employers and employed' where he commended 'the blessed example of the
Messrs Briggs' as marking 'a new and blessed era in the industrial history

[148] *Transactions*, 1863, p. 755. For a similar, profit-oriented justification from Fawcett, see ibid., 1866, p. 781.
[149] Stephen, *Life of Fawcett*, p. 164. See H. Fawcett, 'Strikes: their tendencies and remedies', *Westminster Review*, vol. 74 (o.s.), vol. 18 (n.s.) (1860), pp. 1–23.
[150] Archibald Briggs, 'The Whitwood Collieries', *Transactions*, 1866, p. 703.
[151] Fawcett, *Manual*, (3rd edn, 1869), p. 239.
[152] H. C. Briggs, 'Industrial partnership as carried into practice by Henry Briggs, Son & Co., at the Whitwood Collieries', *Sessional Proceedings*, 1867–8, p. 322.

of this country'.[153] As he told the S.S.A. in May 1868, 'He had personally visited the Whitwood Collieries since the industrial partnership scheme had been in operation, and had made inquiries of the workmen, and could testify to the success of the experiment.'[154]

But by 1875 the experiment was over and the enterprise had reverted to its earlier form. And an explanation of its failure is a study in Fawcett's gullibility – though it was a characteristic he shared with many other middle-class enthusiasts and even leading trade unionists. For the Briggs's scheme was no exercise in philanthropy but 'a new form of enlightened commercial shrewdness which pays' as G. J. Holyoake told the S.S.A. in 1865,[155] with a number of highly unattractive ulterior motives as well. The copartnership was introduced after a decade of vicious industrial strife in the Briggs's collieries, encompassing four strikes and seventy-eight weeks without any coal production at all, 'besides innumerable minor disputes and consequent interruptions to work'.[156] And Henry Briggs, the chairman of the local employers' association who never hid his desire to break the South Yorkshire Miners' Federation, founded during the dispute of 1858, had come to personify, as one historian has put it, 'exploitation and repression' in the eyes of his workforce.[157] If the members of the S.S.A. had wanted to get a flavour of industrial relations on the Yorkshire coalfield at this time, they had only to turn to Ludlow's 'Account of the West Yorkshire coal strike and lock out of 1858', contributed to *Trades' Societies and Strikes* and highly critical of the employers.[158]

The copartnership ended these disputes, but old prejudices died hard and, as Holyoake put it, the masters 'manifestly inherited a distrust of workmen'.[159] There were allegations that the 'distributed profits were lower ... than the company's trading warranted',[160] – that the 'fair amount' set aside 'to reimburse capital' was anything but fair – and Holyoake was justly suspicious of the failure to provide figures on the

[153] 'Professor Fawcett M.P. and Mr. T. Hughes M.P., on co-operation', *Manchester Courier*, 4 Oct. 1866, p. 6.
[154] *Sessional Proceedings*, 1867–8, p. 328. Fawcett was chairing the discussion that followed H. C. Briggs's paper referred to in n. 152. See also Fawcett, 'Address on economy and trade', *Transactions*, 1868 p. 119.
[155] G. J. Holyoake, 'Partnerships of industry', *Transactions*, 1865, p. 486.
[156] See H. C. Briggs, 'Industrial parnerships', *Transactions*, 1872, p. 457.
[157] R. A. Church, 'Profit-sharing and labour relations in England in the nineteenth century', *International Review of Social History*, vol. 16 (1971), p. 5.
[158] J. M. Ludlow, 'Account of the West Yorkshire coal-strike and lock-out of 1858', *Trades' Societies and Strikes*, pp. 11–51.
[159] G. J. Holyoake, *The History of Cooperation*, 2 vols., (London 1906 edn), vol. 2, p. 446.
[160] Church, 'Profit-sharing and labour relations', p. 8. See also Cole, *A Century of Cooperation*, p. 160.

total profits made each year during the copartnership.[161] In 1872, the
company actually witheld the bonus of a third of the workforce who
attended the annual meeting of the miners' union at Leeds: other
employers consented to the closing of the pits for the day but the Briggs
family refused.[162] Meanwhile, Henry Briggs made no secret of his motives
in introducing the scheme. He 'admitted with disarming candour to the
Trade Union Commission that he had instituted profit-sharing to avoid
strikes, that it "infinitely" strengthened the hands of the employers, and
that the addition to wages was more "apparent than real"'.[163] Briggs
boasted that the purpose of copartnership was to 'induce them to work
more steadily and strive to promote their master's good'.[164] Above all, the
copartnership was designed to undermine the union. Archbald Briggs told
the S.S.A. in 1866 that if the scheme succeeded 'every legitimate object of
the Trades Union will be attained and it must die a natural death, or
better still, be converted into a benefit or accident club'.[165] And Henry
Briggs told the Association two years later that the local union leaders
were opposed to the scheme for fear that 'industrial cooperation will
supersede trade unions'. He agreed: 'industrial partnership grants all that
trades unionism can fairly demand. It leaves nothing more to be legitimately desired'.[166] There is thus a consensus among historians that the
Briggs's scheme was, in Sidney Pollard's words 'a cynical attempt to raise
profits by working the men harder and breaking the power of the trade
union'.[167] It lasted until late 1874 when coal prices fell and the miners
struck for four weeks against a reduction in wages. Although they
accepted a sizeable reduction after arbitration, the 'outside shareholders
interpreted the strike as a sign of the failure of industrial partnership to
solve the problems of industrial conflict', and in February 1875 it was
decided to end the payment of the bonus.[168] The scheme was not only

[161] Holyoake, *History of Cooperation*, vol. 2, p. 445.
[162] G. J. Holyoake, 'The abuse of industrial partnerships', *Transactions*, 1872, p. 459; Church, 'Profit-sharing and labour relations', p. 8.
[163] E. C. Mack and W. H. G. Armitage, *Thomas Hughes. The Life of the Author of Tom Brown's Schooldays* (London, 1952), p. 155. See the evidence from Henry and Archi- bald Briggs to the Royal Commission on Trade Unions, Sixth Report, 1868, qq. ·12486–770, P.P., 1867–8, vol. 39.
[164] B. Jones, *Co-operative Production* (2 vols., Oxford, 1894), vol. 2, p. 194.
[165] Archibald Briggs, 'The Whitwood Collieries', *Transactions*, 1866, p. 708.
[166] H. C. Briggs, 'Industrial partnership', *Sessional Proceedings*, 1867–8, p. 326.
[167] S. Pollard, 'Nineteenth Century Cooperation: from community building to shopkeep- ing', in A. Briggs and J. Saville (eds.), *Essays in Labour History* (3 vols., London, 1960), vol. 1, p. 110. See also Cole, *A Century of Cooperation*, p. 160; Church, 'Profit-sharing and labour relations', p. 5; Mack and Armitage, *Thomas Hughes*, p. 155.
[168] Church, 'Profit-sharing and labour relations', pp. 7–8. Holyoake suggested that the partnership was terminated because the owners no longer found it to be in their interests: 'It has been inferred that the company found strikes less expensive than fulfilling an honourable partnership. They may have terminated it because it was more troublesome

cynical, but also brittle: at the first hint of industrial discord it was swiftly terminated.

Evidently Fawcett cannot be held responsible for these manipulations. Nor was he the only 'friend' of the working class who was ready to support the initiative in the late 1860s. He actually chaired a meeting of the S.S.A. in London in May 1868 at which Henry Briggs explained his arrangements. And having begun the discussion by registering his support for the enterprise and the principles it supposedly embodied, he was echoed in his praise by Frederic Harrison, by William Newton of the engineers, and even by Alexander Macdonald of the miners who had also been to see for himself, 'found everyone satisfied', 'trusted the system would be extended' and pledged that the 'trades unions would offer no opposition to it' in stark contrast to the position of the local union officials at the collieries.[169] But Fawcett's public identification with a scheme that so easily degenerated – and one that was introduced in a situation of long-standing communal bitterness that Fawcett certainly knew about[170] – must call his judgement – along with that of others – into question. And it is surely important to any wider appreciation of Fawcett's politics and economics that his great panacea to the problem of reconciling organised labour and capital ended so quickly and so ignominiously. Fawcett believed he saw a 'scheme for the formation of mutuality of interest between employers and employed':[171] but he failed to look closely enough. And as Church has shown, the subsequent history of profit-sharing in the late nineteenth and early twentieth centuries constitutes a record of 'self-interested attempts on the part of the employers to improve industrial relations ... often enough through undermining the power and the influence of trade unions either explicitly or otherwise'.[172] It was an 'extension of anti-union paternalism'[173] that only interested employers in periods of industrial unrest. And after the Briggs experiment it was consistently opposed by trades unions.

VII

It would be inappropriate to accuse Fawcett of bad faith: he was limited rather than dishonest, evidently sincere in presenting himself as the

---

to them than their interest in the welfare of their men induced them to take. They have given no satisfactory explanation of the facts, financial or otherwise, involved in the case.' *History of Cooperation*, p. 445. Fawcett's account of the end of this 'very interesting experiment' is suggestively vague. *Manual* (5th edn, 1876), p. 254.

[169] *Sessional Proceedings*, 1867–8, pp. 328–9. For a fuller account, see Manfred Holyoake, 'A night at the Social Society', *The Social Economist, Industrial Partnerships Record and Cooperataive Review*, vol. 2, no. 16 (1 June 1868), p. 51.

[170] Fawcett, 'Address on economy and trade', *Transactions*, 1868 , p. 119.

[171] *Sessional Proceedings*, 1867–8, p. 328.

[172] Church, 'Profit-sharing and labour relations', p. 13.   [173] ibid., p. 16.

political ally of the working man, but unable to appreciate that the posture was compromised by an excessively rigid adherence to political economy. He was, as Mill explained to one correspondent in 1871, 'a little doctrinaire': he was able 'to see a principle in its full force', but unable 'to see the opposing principles by which it must be qualified'.[174] Bryce wrote of his 'extreme rigidity', of his 'disposition to see only the blacks and whites of a question and not to appreciate the subtler considerations which come in and must be allowed to modify the broader conclusions of economic science'.[175] Brodrick regarded him 'as a singularly honest and straightforward man' but 'with no finesse and not much delicacy of perception'.[176] And as a 'doctrinaire' he could be glib. At the Edinburgh Congress he was keen to combat the working men's 'unfortunate error' that 'competition was an enemy which oppressed them'. Competition, he declared, 'never had done, and never would do, the labourer any harm'.[177] But Ludlow's contribution to *Trades' Societies and Strikes* had demonstrated the reverse; that competition between Yorkshire coal masters in the mid-fifties had led to over-production and under-selling, and the consequent fall in the price of coal had been met by the demand for a wage cut of 15 per cent, so precipitating a strike.[178] Demonstrably, competition could and did injure the working class, though Fawcett's 'strong, but comparatively limited, intellect', as Leslie Stephen described it,[179] chose to adhere to rhetorical orthodoxies rather than confront uncomfortable and subversive information. In similar fashion, the report of the Committee on Trades' Societies and Strikes, which Fawcett signed, had concluded on the basis of its extensive research 'that the constant assertion that strikes are scarcely ever successful' was 'not at all borne out by the facts'. The various individual studies that composed the volume included many unequivocal examples of trades where strike action had achieved the unions' objectives.[180] And Frederic Harrison, referring directly to the research of the Committee, contended that 'for every argument which the economic theorist can invent to prove that unions and strikes can have no effect in raising wages, it would be easy to produce

174 Mill to George Croom Robertson, 6 Nov. 1871, in *Collected Works of John Stuart Mill*, vol. 17, p. 1850.
175 [Bryce] 'The late Mr. Fawcett', p. 457.
176 Brodrick, *Memories and Impressions*, p. 264.
177 *Transactions*, 1863, p. 754.
178 See J. M. Ludlow, 'The West Yorkshire coal-strike and lock-out of 1858', *Trades' Societies and Strikes*, pp. 20, 25–6.
179 Stephen, *Life of Fawcett*, p. 244.
180 *Trades' Societies and Strikes*, 'Report', p. xiii. For some individual examples of successful strikes, see also Godfrey Lushington, 'Miscellaneous papers arranged for the National Association for the Promotion of Social Science', ibid., pp. 287–8 (regarding the disputes of the Glasgow Carpenters and Joiners), and p. 290 (regarding disputes won by the Glasgow Master Painters' Association).

one hundred instances in which they have done so'.[181] Yet Fawcett continued to uphold the general prejudice that 'strikes have completely failed in the majority of instances'; 'that in the great majority of strikes, the workmen have failed to secure the object which they sought'.[182] It was more comfortable, no doubt, to believe this, and it was certainly in keeping with the teachings of political economy, but it was not true. Godfrey Lushington wrote in obvious frustration in *Questions for a Reformed Parliament* that 'strikes are put down as failures by persons who have not the least idea how many of them have succeeded'.[183] But Fawcett could have no excuse in ignorance: he, at least, had ready access to the facts.

It was this 'rigidity and narrowness'[184] – Leslie Stephen again – which betrayed Fawcett, and we can get a clear sense of his limitations and the consequent disjunction between his politics and economics by comparing him to another of those university Liberals who sought to influence the organised working class in the 1860s and 1870s, Frederic Harrison. Harrison 'always maintained', as he wrote in his *Memoirs*, 'that those who dogmatised about Labour problems and industrial conditions ... could only pronounce academic and doctrinaire opinions, whilst they knew nothing of how the shoe pinched the workman at home and what his working life meant. This held good of even just and generous spirits, such as those of John Stuart Mill and Henry Fawcett'.[185] If Fawcett, lecturing in Cambridge, was political economy personified, then to Harrison his subject was 'the abracadabra of McCulloch and Ricardo',[186] full of 'pedantic blindness' and 'sophisticated absurdities',[187] and the attempt to study 'the laws of wealth apart from political science as a whole' was a 'pernicious fallacy'.[188] In the year that Fawcett published his lectures on *The Economic Position of the British Labourer*, Harrison published his devastating critique on 'The limits of political economy'.[189] If Fawcett could not accept the refutation of the wage-fund doctrine, then Harrison

[181] Harrison, 'The good and evil of trade-unionism', p. 38.
[182] Fawcett, *Manual*, p. 268; idem, *The Economic Position of the British Labourer* (Cambridge and London, 1865), p. 182. Fawcett does list several examples of successful strikes in a footnote in the *Manual* but they are considered as exceptions to a general rule. See *Manual*, pp. 268–9.
[183] Godfrey Lushington, 'Workmen and trade unions', *Questions for a Reformed Parliament* (London, 1867), p. 51.
[184] ibid., pp. 178–9.   [185] Harrison, *Autobiographic Memoirs*, vol. 2, p. 217.
[186] Cited in Paul Adelman, 'Frederic Harrison and the "Positivist" attack on orthodox political economy', *History of Political Economy*, vol. 3 (1971), p. 170.
[187] Harrison, *Autobiographic Memoirs*, vol. 1, pp. 252–3.
[188] F. Harrison to E. S. Beesley (n.d.) (1858?), quoted in Harrison, *Before the Socialists*, p. 259.
[189] Frederic Harrison, 'The limits of political economy', *Fortnightly Review*, vol. 1 (1865), pp. 356–76.

had never believed in it in the first place.[190] And if Fawcett was prepared
to argue that the vast majority of strikes inevitably ended in failure, then
to Harrison, the repetition of 'old dogma respecting the inutility of strikes'
even 'in the face of unimpeachable and overwhelming testimony' to the
contrary, as provided in *Trades' Societies and Strikes*, was 'a singular
instance of the hold obtained by vicious theories, when they coincide with
the prejudices of self-interest'.[191] Harrison was 'recognised as the leading
middle-class advocate of trade unionism before the British public',[192] and
his famous manipulation of the Royal Commission on Trade Unions
between 1867 and 1869 – preparing sympathetic witnesses, directing the
questions, smoothing over the harshnesses of the Majority Report while
preparing himself a Minority Report and legislative proposals which
served as the basis of the subsequent enactments[193] – was instrumental in
changing both public and parliamentary attitudes to organised labour.
But Fawcett was ambivalent, and far more comfortable when *lecturing to*,
rather than *engaging with*, the working class: the course of history might
well have been different if Mill had been successful in his attempt to win
Fawcett a place on the Commission and Harrison had been omitted.[194]
Fawcett clearly enjoyed participating in the Social Science Association and
only ceased attending when he had consolidated his position in Parliament. But Harrison's initial enthusiasm turned to contempt and by 1863
he was railing at 'the half-crazy "ne'er-do-weels" who muddle about at
the Social Congress. Good intentions may be very well in their place. But
the social reformers who start with nothing better than good intentions
are invariably very useless and generally mischievous.'[195] And if Fawcett
welcomed the enfranchised working man into the Liberal Party, then
Harrison, from the time of the Reform agitation in the mid-sixties, flirted
with the idea of a third party and separate representation for labour.[196]
This was not a consistent position; indeed, in January 1874 Harrison
advised working-class electors, writing in the *Bee-Hive*, to vote for
Fawcett in the coming election. But it was a grudging recommendation –
'In things he has said in Parliament we may think him utterly wrong'
wrote Harrison – and the references to 'hard words' and 'differences with
Mr. Fawcett' serve only to suggest how unlike two 'advanced Liberals'
could be.[197]

190 Frederic Harrison, 'The Iron-Masters' Trade Union', *Fortnightly Review*, vol. 1 (1865),
p. 97.
191 Harrison, 'The good and evil of trade-unionism', p. 39.
192 'Frederic Harrison', in J. Saville and J. Bellamy (eds.), *Dictionary of Labour Biography*,
vol. 2 (1974), p. 163.
193 ibid., p. 164; Harrison, *Before the Socialists*, pp. 285–7.   194 See n. 87.
195 Harrison, *Autobiographic Memoirs*, vol. 1, p. 278.
196 Harrison, *Before the Socialists*, pp. 273, 299–301.
197 Frederic Harrison, 'Workmen and the elections', *Bee-Hive*, 31 Jan. 1874, p. 1.

There is a coherence to Harrison's positions – his intimate associations with the labour movement, his politics and rejection of political economy are all of a piece – which Fawcett seems to lack. But it is this very incoherence which makes Fawcett both representative and historically significant. He was one of a number of Liberal ideologues who helped consolidate the Lib-Lab politics of the later nineteenth century – a politics that tried to ignore class divisions and integrate groups whose economic interests were often opposed. Historians are so used to taking this politics for granted that the basic irrationality of the party of the masters bidding for, and winning, the votes of the organised working class is often ignored. Of course, there are some very convincing explanations as to why this politics emerged and endured, and why it fulfilled the spiritual needs and demands of both middle and working classes. As John Vincent has suggested, popular Liberalism in the mid-nineteenth century, drawing on emotional rather than rational, intellectual responses, is essentially illogical when placed in the context of a materialistic politics – 'a modern Realpolitic of bread' – and must instead be explained in terms of the 'psychic satisfaction' and 'visceral thrill' of political participation itelf. Politics, as Vincent has suggested, were akin to theatre, and the satisfaction came when the audience could believe that it was at one with the actors on the stage in playing out the great dramas of national life.[198] Thus the organised working class, seeking social and material recognition, gave enthusiastic support to politicians who were prepared to go out and meet with working men, and even lecture them, as Fawcett did at the Social Science Association, and who thereby acknowledgd their status as participants in the drama. And the desire to be accepted and to be approved was so strong that it prevented any cool appreciation of what was actually being suggested to the working class by their 'friends' from the platform. The message itself was immaterial (in more than one sense of the word); the key thing was to be recognised as legitimate players in the game of politics. It was for this reason that Fawcett could successfully stake out a political position which his economics did not fully reinforce and complement. And this particular, individual disjunction between Fawcett's politics and economics may be taken to represent all the many more unacknowledged tensions and contradictions that lay beneath the surface of this inter-class politics.

[198] J. R. Vincent, *Pollbooks. How Victorians Voted* (Cambridge, 1967), pp. 43–50.

8

Fawcett as professional politician

CHRISTOPHER HARVIE

I

Fawcett is usually discussed in the context of economics and the debate has tended to be about whether he was a second- or a third-rate economist. This may be a little unfair. I think we must also try to see him as his colleagues at Trinity Hall did in the 1860s, 1870s and 1880s. And University Liberals perceived their parliamentary political colleagues rather obliquely. As the sociologist Robert Michels noted in his study of *Political Parties* there is a greater difference between two members of the same party, one of whom is a parliamentarian, and two parliamentarians, who are members of different parties.[1] This was true of what his Cambridge contemporaries saw: Fawcett as a consummate, talented and ambitious politician.

George Brodrick of Merton, Oxford, Fawcett's friend and contemporary, a much wealthier and probably more talented man whose political career simply failed to take off, remarked in his reminiscences that Fawcett's blindness was 'not an unmixed disadvantage to him', and in this paid tribute to Fawcett's professionalism.[2] Fawcett deployed all his advantages, and his distinctive disadvantage, towards his political career. His tenure of the Political Economy Chair, from 1864, meant a more than doubling of his stipend from £250 to £550, and was, to him, a logical stepping-stone in this career, rather than an academic promotion.[3]

Fawcett took to politics with an enthusiasm which dismayed Leslie Stephen. Even at his most masculine, Stephen had misgivings about the political life. His cousin, A. V. Dicey, recollected a conversation with him, probably some time during the 1890s, when he (Dicey) was lamenting the

---

[1] R. Michels, *Political Parties*, trans. E. and C. Paul (London, 1915 edn).
[2] G. C. Brodrick, *Memories and Impressions, 1831–1900* (London, 1900), p. 264.
[3] Leslie Stephen, *Life of Henry Fawcett* (London, 1885), p. 117.

morality of his associates in the Liberal Unionist cause. 'Isn't politics', Stephen replied, 'always rather a mean pursuit?' 'I sometimes wonder', Dicey recollected gloomily, 'whether I ought not to have laid these words more to heart than I have.'[4]

Stephen's was not a sentiment with which Fawcett would have agreed. It is evident, from Mrs Fawcett's comments, interpolated in the draft of the *Life* in Trinity Hall, that Stephen expressed some disquiet at Fawcett's tolerance of the 'mean pursuit' element, only to be kept in order by Millicent.[5] At the same time it was the sense that Fawcett was 'at the centre of things', to use the words of Stephen's daughter, Virginia Woolf, that made him such a presence in the Cambridge of his day.[6] He was not alone in combining an academic with a political role. J. E. Thorold Rogers had similar ambitions at Oxford, but, after having held the Drummond Chair of Political Economy between 1862 and 1867, on offering himself for re-election he discovered that his radicalism had alienated too many members of the Convocation. Bonamy Price was elected instead and Rogers only regained the Chair in 1888 after Price had died. And Leonard Courtney, a Liberal M.P. after 1875, had held the Chair of Political Economy at University College, London, for three years preceding his entry into Parliament. But Fawcett was certainly the most successful. The Courtney – J. E. Cairnes letters show a lot of ill-concealed distaste at Fawcett's flair for politicking and somewhat cavalier attitude to his ideological *devoirs*.[7] Rogers, Courtney, Leslie and Cairnes were all performers at the British Association and Social Science Association, like Fawcett, but it is significant that once Fawcett was successful in getting into the Commons he eased off on such commitments to concentrate on his parliamentary career.[8]

Fawcett was totally absorbed in the political game. When he appeared at Cambridge for his lectures or at weekends, he talked politics. He may have talked economics of a rather primitive sort, (though 'Mill-and-water', on the level of his *Manual*, was something of a *lingua franca* among the Liberal dons and the sort of businessmen, bankers and merchants they might meet at the Political Economy Club),[9] but what

---

[4] A. V. Dicey to H. Jackson, 21 Feb. 1917, Henry Jackson MS, Trinity College, Cambridge.
[5] See the manuscript of the *Life of Fawcett* in the Trinity Hall Library, pp. 156, 240.
[6] 18 Oct. 1918, A. O. Bell (ed.), *The Diary of Virginia Woolf*, vol. 1 (London, 1977), p. 205. She is discussing her perception of the political life of her cousin, H. A. L. Fisher.
[7] J. E. Cairnes to Leonard Courtney, 15 March, 3 May 1863, 15 Oct. 1864, Courtney of Penwith MS, British Library of Political and Economic Science, London.
[8] See p. 148 above.
[9] Diary–Letter to J. A. Symonds, 11 April 1885:'The bankers come to the front. It is an exaggeration to say that they know no Political Economy: I think they read Mill some time ago, and look at him from time to time on Sundays.' Henry Sidgwick MS, Trinity College,

counted was his news from Westminster. He was part of a different world, yet while the universities remained passionately interested in London politics, in the age of the Tests Campaign (1863–71), the view into this world – who was in, who out – was absorbing. Although politics (and academia) obviously appealed less to Stephen by 1885, as he immersed himself in family life and his energetic and remarkably productive career as critic and biographer, the *Life* still graphically captures the atmosphere in the Trinity Hall senior combination room as dim, doomed little clerical dons huddled in corners while the Liberal fireworks of Fawcett and his guests flared in the centre.[10]

It was not simply the social element that mattered here. Fawcett was a recognised and respected member of the academic community; Sir William Harcourt, occupying a similar position (Liberal M.P. and Professor of International Law), was not, since he treated his Cambridge and Trinity duties with elaborate neglect. Fawcett was an oracle who expressed a necessary engagement between the university and practical politics – and he was succeeded in this public role by another 'prophet of the obvious'.

This happy phrase is from Dicey, Vinerian Professor of Constitutional Law at Oxford, whose *Law and Working of the Constitution* was the academic success of 1885.[11] Both men compensated for their physical disabilities (Dicey suffered from a spastic disorder and was severely myopic) by preaching energetically, repetitively and successfully from a restricted but deeply held conception of the fundamentals of socialisation: Dicey in the constitutional sphere, Fawcett in the economic. Both – but Fawcett more than Dicey – apprehended the essentially political lesson that the ordinary M.P. is not convinced by brilliance of argument but by the endless reiteration and illustration of a graspable proposition.[12]

II

Stephen treated his friend as a 'typical Cambridge man' but certain aspects of Fawcett's career are distinctive. He was one of a very small minority (less than 2 per cent according to Jenkins and Jones) coming to Cambridge from a background in trade and (probably even more unusual) middle-

Cambridge, and see also the membership lists of the Oxford and Cambridge Political Economy Clubs.
10 Stephen, *Life of Fawcett*, pp. 80–5.
11 Richard A. Cosgrove, *The Rule of Law: Albert Venn Dicey, Victorian Jurist* (London, 1980), p. 298.
12 A lesson taught the late earl of Stockton by David Lloyd George. See Harold Macmillan, *The Past Masters* (London, 1975), pp. 58–60.

class radical politics.[13] His father was Mayor of Salisbury and a member
of the Anti-Corn Law League. Far from sharing the public school
background of the great majority of his Cambridge contemporaries, he
attended Queenwood, a school run on the lines pioneered by Fellenberg of
Hofwyl, which were considered very advanced and 'permissive' in the
Europe of their time. Queenwood had begun as an Owenite community, a
link with the earlier provincial radicalism of George Combe, the Brays
and Herbert Spencer, which Fawcett never really lost.[14]

Fawcett's attitude to Cambridge, too, was instrumental rather than
reverential, in an age when the obstacles facing a young man intent on a
political career but without funds were all but insurmountable. Although,
on top of his Fellowship and professorial stipends, the *Manual* must have
paid quite handsomely, he needed every penny. He was debarred from
reviewing, a staple source of income for most of his colleagues, and his
marriage in 1867, to Millicent Garrett, while it gave him an essential and
formidable helpmate, did not bring him much in the way of income.
Fawcett, like his fictional contemporary Phineas Finn (John Pope-
Hennessy, said to be Finn's original, was an acquaintance of Fawcett in his
early London days), had to be on the lookout for political success, or at
the very least an income which would sustain him at Westminster.[15] His
skill in politicking was impressive. He stood for the Cambridge Chair with
a formidable slate of referees, many of whom, I would guess, were as
dubious about his attainments as Henry Sidgwick, who voted for him ('I
don't think he is the best man').[16] And he used his academic reputation –
and his blindness – to lever himself into Parliament at pretty minimal cost
to himself.[17]

Trinity Hall was important in this. It enabled him to return the
hospitality of his wealthier parliamentary colleagues, something he could
never have done from a small house in London.[18] It also emphasised his
solid, measured, academic career: he was not, unlike so many on the
Liberal left, a 'faddist', with some political *idée fixe* – temperance,
nonconformity, pacifism – that distorted his approach. He would never
allow himself to be thus sidetracked from the main route to political

---

[13] Hester Jenkins and D. Caradog Jones, 'Social class of Cambridge alumni of the eighteenth
    and nineteenth centuries', *British Journal of Sociology*, vol. 1 (1950), p. 99.

[14] Stephen, *Life of Fawcett*, pp. 9–10.   [15] ibid., pp. 34, 128.

[16] Henry to Eleanor Sidgwick, 1 Dec. 1863, in A[rthur] S[idgwick] and E[leanor] M[ildred]
    S[idgwick], *Henry Sidgwick* (London, 1906), p. 100. Fawcett's name is not given, but
    from the date he seems the obvious choice.

[17] Stephen, *Life of Fawcett*, pp. 205, 216. Fawcett's Cambridge contest cost his supporters
    £600 in 1863; his successful Brighton candidacy in 1865 cost £900. These sums are on
    the low side for 'large borough' contests. See H. J. Hanham, *Elections and Party
    Management. Politics in the Time of Disraeli and Gladstone* (London, 1959), pp. 250–8.

[18] Stephen, *Life of Fawcett*, p. 82.

power. His practicality had, to his more idealistic colleagues, its ironic side. In 1873 John Morley, then editor of the *Fortnightly Review*, wrote to Frederic Harrison:

And his hypocrisy in calling himself a moderate churchman! Why he is a notorious freethinker and religious indifferent. Some years ago he electrified Fitzjames Stephen, as they were walking together, and the latter was airing his logic on the question of the existence of God, – by saying in his noisy way – 'Well, you know, Stephen, the question of the existence of God is a thing *I never could take the slightest interest in*!' Very laudably positive, but hardly the view of a moderate churchman.[19]

Fawcett was careful to keep this sort of opinion to his immediate colleagues, and to take studious, although selective, note of the opinions of his constituents and the groups, like Indian reformers, for whom he spoke at Westminster, and who paid for his election campaigns. In this he represented a notable example of the transition in political ethics which seems to have accompanied household suffrage and the ballot. Leslie Stephen includes in the *Life* a lengthy section on Fawcett's electioneering and in particular his relationship with his agent, the enigmatic Mr Dredge, in the mid-1860s, which was certainly derived from his (Stephen's) own recollections:

The ordinary code of political morality admits of manoeuvres of which it may be said that their adroitness is more conspicuous than their lofty morality. Fawcett would never at any time have lent himself to any such manoeuvre which was tainted by a want of generosity. But I may say frankly that at this period his own shrewdness and his hearty appreciation of shrewdness in others led him to take rather a lenient view of some ingenious devices. His sense of humour was tickled, and he could not help enjoying a strategem which was free from malevolence. He looked at it rather in the light of a good practical joke, and could not find it in his heart to be over-severe on the contriver.[20]

I think that this passage suffered some modification at the hands of Mrs Fawcett, but it shows how much Fawcett (and, for that matter, Stephen) fitted into the world that we know, quite vividly, from Trollope's political novels. It was a world he was, in the 1870s, careful to discard for scrupulous relations with his constituency caucus.

III

Fawcett's political approach has, in fact, much of the tentative quality of a blind man feeling his way along a street, testing out with his stick the way he should take, and then acting quite decisively. He was, for example, the

19 John Morley to Frederic Harrison, 25 July 1873, Frederic Harrison MS, British Library of Political and Economic Science, London.
20 Stephen, *Life of Fawcett*, p. 196.

founder of the Cambridge Republican Club in the early 1870s, but he was also – with the rapidity of a snail retreating into its shell – the first to quit the republican cause when the limitations of its political support became apparent.[21] Having determined on a line, however, he could be counted on to push it through. In the issue of manhood suffrage, his views in the early 1860s were anything but radical, but under pressure of the public anti-Adullamite agitation of 1865–7 they moved robustly in a universal suffrage direction.[22] Unlike other academic reformers, such as A. O. Rutson, editor of *Essays on Reform*, 1867, and Professor Goldwin Smith, who retreated from manhood suffrage when Disraeli seemed likely to embrace it,[23] Fawcett was one of the 'Tea-Room radicals' who were determined to push Disraeli much further than he wanted to go.[24]

Fawcett was, at the same time, no less robust on university reform. Already one of the founders in 1864 of the Ad Eundem dining club, an important forum for the coordination of the Liberal movement at Oxford and Cambridge,[25] in April 1867 he moved an instruction in committee which summarily amalgamated the two Test Reform Bills hitherto promoted by Liberals at the separate universities. This caused an immediate furore within the ranks of the academic reformers, but the principle of a single measure succeeded and endured. He was also responsible in 1867 with William Ewart, M.P., for the Select Committee into University Extension which presented probably the most cogent case for the urgency of a settlement.[26]

The more Fawcett immersed himself in politics, I would argue, the more he diverged from his economic dogmatism. He was, for example, one of the stalwarts of the Commons Preservation Movement, which Dicey saw as 'a decisive reaction against the policy ardently favoured by Bentham of converting common land into private property'.[27] This makes him, with Sir Robert Hunter and Octavia Hill, a forerunner of the National Trust – whose origins thus became an ironic combination of individualism and Ruskinian collectivism. In 1867 he spoke strongly in favour of the Factory Acts being extended to agriculture – to farmers and landowners doubtless an almost surrealistic threat. This antedated by six years the Liberals' support for Joseph Arch's unionisation of the farm labourers.[28]

There is also his support for the rights of India. Obviously this was

21 Roy Jenkins, *Sir Charles Dilke. A Victorian Tragedy* (London, 1958), p. 76.
22 Stephen, *Life of Fawcett*, p. 186.
23 *Daily News*, 9 April 1867; *Manchester Examiner*, 5 April 1867.
24 Asa Briggs, *Victorian People* (Harmondsworth, 1965 edn) p. 189.
25 Stephen, *Life of Fawcett*, p. 80.
26 ibid., p. 236. *Hansard*, clxxxvi, 10 April 1867, clxxxv, 12 March 1867, 1631.
27 A. V. Dicey, *Law and Public Opinion* (London, 1906), p. 249.
28 Stephen, *Life of Fawcett*, p. 230.

cemented by the retainers from the Indians which he received, but it was
also regarded by establishment opinion as subversive, and it led Fawcett
to make a partial breach in his laissez-faire, to sanction India's right to
impose a duty on British exports, defending this exception with arguments
which, as Phyllis Deane has shown, were political rather than economic.[29]
One implication of his death in 1884 was almost certainly the founding in
1885 of the Indian Congress as a means of formalising the expression of
Indian opinions; this was organised by another product of British radicalism, Allan Octavian Hume, the son of Joseph Hume M.P. 'By encouraging state interference in cases where he approved, he actually encouraged it in cases where he disapproved', was how Stephen tried to explain
the paradox that Fawcett, whose individualism became more distinctive
in his later career – as others moved away from it – was, at the Post Office,
a familiarly pragmatic, empire-building minister. Theoretically, he would
certainly have applauded the privatisation of the telephone service, but his
was the regime which set up the first state-run telephone exchanges, and
extended post office services – in parcels post, telegraphs and savings
banks – as well![30]

In his support for women's suffrage, meanwhile, he was considerably in
advance of the university Liberalism of his time, and certainly more
advanced than the Positivists, to whom he has been compared adversely.
In the 1880s there was an intellectual backlash against the democratic
idea, expressing itself even more forcibly in anti-women's suffrage propa-
ganda than in, say, Unionism. And in her campaign against this, Millicent
made good use of her husband's memory and example.[31]

IV

How do we sum up Fawcett as a politician? Was he, in the early 1880s, a
surviving dinosaur of mid-nineteenth-century laissez-faire, or was he of
that pretty recognisable breed, a politician's politician, more interested in
the great game than in ideology? I have spent most of my adult life as an
academic on the fringes of politics, and know something of the privacy of
the political world, the sense in which at a party, you will always see the
eyes of parliamentarians flickering around the room, looking for other
parliamentarians to talk to. Fawcett was obviously disqualified from the
physical element of this, but otherwise he belongs here, as does his
operative ideology, which is the politician's one of the repetition, illustra-

[29] See pp. 104–5 above.   [30] Stephen, *Life of Fawcett*, pp. 170, 402.
[31] See 'An appeal against female suffrage', *Nineteenth Century*, vol. 25 (June 1889),
    pp. 781–8; Millicent Garrett Fawcett, 'The appeal against female suffrage: a reply', ibid.,
    vol. 26 (July 1889), pp. 86–96. For Millicent's references to Henry Fawcett see esp.
    pp. 92–3.

tion and elaboration of a simple thesis rather than the academic's more speculative and tentative approach. In this sense Fawcett used the labour question with political – not theoretical – consistency as an *entrée* into one of Liberalism's new client groups, and thereafter played the political game by its own rules. Fawcett thus remained relevant as a politician – relevant enough to make it far from straightforward to conjecture how he would have jumped in the Home Rule crisis of 1886. Millicent became a militant Liberal Unionist, and claimed to be the inheritor of her husband's views. Fawcett, like practically every other Liberal in 1884 (the Positivists excepted) was against Home Rule, yet he had defended Irish Land Leaguers from W. E. Forster's coercion policy in 1881; he was associated with Irish Nationalist M.P.s in his fight for Indian rights.[32] What would he have done in 1886, when his Hackney constituents plumped, without serious exception, for Gladstone? On most domestic issues he had less in common with Joseph Chamberlain – and would have loathed a Birmingham captivity – than he had with Gladstone. Faced with the alternatives: collapse of his political career, or a reasonably rosy future – the Local Government Board, Education, the Board of Trade – in a future Gladstonian cabinet purged of Chamberlainite collectivism, what course would he have taken?

Fawcett enjoyed a useful career, and he provides an object lesson in the transition from an academic to political life. Obviously, aspects of this robust, hard-working, insensitive but kindly man would jar on his Cambridge colleagues, but the best of them valued him for the qualities his strenuous ambition brought out. This was recognised by two men who scarcely fall into the 'masculine' stereotype. Writing to John Addington Symonds on 6 November 1884, Henry Sidgwick paid a moving tribute to Fawcett, a fitting note, perhaps, on which to end:

Just now I think most of the wonderful success and example of this life, which is now beyond the reach of time and change. Some lines of Tennyson run in my head.

> O well for him whose will is strong
> He suffers *but shall not suffer long*
> For him,
> Not all calamities hugest waves confound,
> He seems a promontory of rock,
> Tempest-buffeted, citadel crowned.

He was a hero of a peculiar type, without any outward air of self-sacrifice or suggestion of idealism in his ordinary talk: and yet one felt his determination to live the ordinary life of a man, and a successful man, who gives pity and aid more than he takes it, required a continual sustained effort which did not draw its force

---

[32] See H. V. Brasted, 'India and Irish Home Rule Politics, 1873–86: F. H. O'Donnell and Other Irish Friends of India' (unpublished Ph.D. thesis, University of Edinburgh, 1975).

from self-love alone; it continually demanded and obtained further force given by consciousness of the power of serving others: and the needs of this struggle gave to a nature which, though large, healthy and generous was not originally characterised by high aspiration, an elevation it would not otherwise have had. In spite of all that I have read of saints and sages I feel that if great physical calamity came upon me, yet one that left the springs of physical energy unimpaired, I should turn for strength to this example. I wonder how many blind feel that he has opened the door of their prison-house and shown them the way back to ordinary life: steep, yet one that may be trodden by a steady and trustful step.[33]

[33] Henry Sidgwick to J. A. Symonds, 6 Nov. 1884, Sidgwick MS.

Henry Fawcett, 1833–1884: a bibliography

1 PRIMARY SOURCES

Fawcett's papers have not survived but a selection of his letters can be found in a number of collections. The following list does not comprise all the extant letters but includes some of the more important items.

LETTERS FROM FAWCETT TO:

Lady Amberley. One letter, 7 Nov. 1866. Bertrand Russell Papers, McMaster University, Rec. Acq. 754.

Henry Broadhurst. Two letters, 1877–8. Broadhurst Collection, vol. 1, letters 19, 46, British Library of Political and Economic Science, London School of Economics.

Henry Peter Brougham, first baron Brougham and Vaux. Four letters, 1860–1. Brougham Papers, University College, London.

Sir Francis Joseph Campbell. several letters in the Campbell Papers, Library of Congress, Washington D.C.
(Campbell was born in Tennessee in 1832. Trained as a musician, he became a teacher of the blind and first Principal of the Royal Normal College and Academy of Music for the Blind, Norwood, London, between 1872 and 1912.)

Edwin Chadwick. Five letters, 1874–80. University College, London.

Charles Darwin. One letter, 16 July 186[1]. Darwin Papers, Cambridge University Library.

Sir Charles Dilke. Ten letters, 1868–80. British Library, Add. MSS 43909–10.

Louisa Garrett. One letter, 24 Dec. 1869. Elizabeth Garrett Anderson Papers, held by Mrs C. G. Williams, St Brelade, Jersey.

William Ewart Gladstone. A volume of letters, 1865–84. Gladstone Papers, British Library, Add. MS 44156.

Henry George, third earl Grey. Five letters, 1860–79, and copies of two letters from Grey to Fawcett, 1872. Grey of Howick MSS, Dept of Palaeography and Diplomatic, University of Durham.

Sir William Harcourt. Twelve letters, 1873–83. Harcourt Papers, General Correspondence, Bodleian Library, Oxford.

Frederic Harrison. One letter, 19 June 1884. Harrison Collection, file 1.32, British Library of Political and Economic Science, London School of Economics.

Fanny Hertz. Eight letters, 1859–64. Miscellaneous letters, Marshall Library, University of Cambridge.

George Jacob Holyoake. Four letters, 1865–78. Holyoake Collection, Co-operative Union Ltd, Manchester.

Richard Monckton Milnes, first Baron Houghton. Four letters, 1862–81. Houghton Collection, Trinity College, Cambridge.

George Howell. Eight letters, 1866–84. Howell Papers, Bishopsgate Institute, London.

Henry Jackson. Three letters, 1873. Cambridge University Library, Add. MS 5944.

John Neville Keynes. Eight letters, 1875–84. Cambridge University Library, Add. MS 7562.

Macmillan's (Fawcett's publisher). Several letters. The Macmillan Archive, British Library, B.M. Add. MS 55206.

Anthony John Mundella. Twelve letters, 1873–9. Mundella Papers, Sheffield University Library.

Bessie Rayner Parkes. One letter, 23 October 1859. B. R. Parkes, Papers, IX 21, Girton College, Cambridge.

Charles Henry Pearson. Three letters, 1879–83. Bodleian Library, Oxford, MS Eng. lett. d. 187.

James Edwin Thorold Rogers. Four letters, 1862–84. Thorold Rogers papers, Bodleian Library, Oxford.

Sedley Taylor. Seventeen letters, 1873–84. Cambridge University Library, Add. MS 6258.

William Whewell. One letter, 21 May 1864. Whewell Collection, Trinity College, Cambridge.

There are forty-one letters from J. S. Mill to Fawcett, 1860–70, and one letter from W. T. Thornton to Fawcett (1862) in the Mill–Taylor Collection, vol. lvii. A. 1–41, British Library of Political and Economic Science, London School of Economics.

There is also an album of Fawcett's speeches in the Fawcett Library at the City of London Polytechnic. It contains cuttings from newspapers of Fawcett's speeches (mainly parliamentary), letters, addresses and articles, 1870–84.

2 SEPARATE PUBLICATIONS

Mr Hare's Reform Bill, Simplified and Explained (London, 1860).
The Leading Clauses of a New Reform Bill (London, 1860).
Manual of Political Economy (Cambridge and London, 1863).
   (Eight editions were published, six during Fawcett's lifetime.)
The Economic Position of the British Labourer (Cambridge and London, 1865).
   ('a portion of a course of lectures which I delivered in the University of Cambridge in the autumn of 1864' – preface.)
Pauperism: Its Causes and Remedies (Cambridge and London, 1871).
   ('the substance of a course of lectures which I delivered in the University of Cambridge during the October term of 1870' – preface.)
Essays and Lectures on Social and Political Subjects (Cambridge and London, 1872).

(Eight of the pieces were by Millicent and six were by Henry Fawcett.)
The Present Position of the Government (London, 1872).
(Reprinted from the *Fortnightly Review*, with a postscript in reference to recent ministerial statements.)
Speeches on some Current Political Questions (Cambridge and London, 1873).
Free Trade and Protection. An Inquiry into the Causes which have Retarded the General Adoption of Free Trade since its Introduction into England (London, 1878).
(A course of lectures delivered in Cambridge in the autumn of 1877. A sixth edition was published in 1885.)
Indian Finance. Three Essays (London, 1880).
(Republished from the *Nineteenth Century* with an introduction and appendix.)
The Post Office and Aids to Thrift (London, 1881).
State Socialism and the Nationalisation of Land (Cambridge and London, 1883).
(Reprinted from *Macmillan's Magazine* for July 1883, it also appeared as a chapter in the sixth edition of the *Manual* which was published in the same year.)
Labour and Wages. Chapters Reprinted from the Manual of Political Economy (London, 1884).
(A reprint of five chapters from the sixth edition of the *Manual*. A French edition, edited by A. Raffalovich, was published in Paris in 1885.)

3 ARTICLES

Macmillan's Magazine
'On the social and economical influence of the new gold', vol. 2, July 1860, pp. 186–91.
'Co-operative societies; their social and economical aspects', vol. 2, Oct. 1860, pp. 434–41.
'A popular exposition of Mr. Darwin on the origin of species', vol. 3, Dec. 1860, pp. 81–92.
'On the exclusion of those who are not members of the Established Church from Fellowships and other privileges of the English Universities', vol. 3, March 1861, pp. 411–16.
'Mr. Mill's Treatise On Representative Government', vol. 4, June 1861, pp. 97–103.
'On the present prospects of co-operative societies', vol. 5, Feb. 1862, pp. 335–42.
'Inaugural lecture on political economy', vol. 9, April 1864, pp. 495–503.
'What can be done for the agricultural labourers?', vol. 18, Oct. 1868, pp. 515–25.
'State socialism and the nationalisation of the land', vol. 48, July 1883, pp. 182–94.

Fortnightly Review
'To what extent is England prosperous?', vol. 15 (old series), vol. 9 (new series), Jan. 1871, pp. 40–52.
'The boarding-out of pauper children', vol. 15 (o.s.), vol. 9 (n.s.), Feb. 1871, pp. 255–61.
'The House of Lords', vol. 16 (o.s.), vol. 10 (n.s.), Oct. 1871, pp. 491–504.

'The present position of the government', vol. 16 (o.s.), vol. 10 (n.s.), Nov. 1871,
    pp. 544–58.
'The nationalisation of the land', vol. 18 (o.s.), vol. 12 (n.s.), Dec. 1872,
    pp. 627–43.
'The incidence of local taxation', vol. 19 (o.s.), vol. 13 (n.s.), May 1873,
    pp. 549–63.
'The effect of an increased production of wealth on wages', vol. 21 (o.s.), vol. 15
    (n.s.), Jan. 1874, pp. 75–81.
'The position and prospects of cooperation', vol. 21 (o.s.), vol 15 (n.s.), Feb. 1874,
    pp. 190–208.
'Professor Cairnes', vol. 24 (o.s.), vol. 18 (n.s.), Aug. 1875, pp. 149–54.
'The recent development of socialism in Germany and the United States', vol. 30,
    (o.s.), vol. 24 (n.s.), Nov. 1878, pp. 605–15.

Fraser's Magazine
'The enclosure of commons', vol. 81 (o.s.), vol. 1 (n.s.), Feb. 1870, pp. 185–96.
'The Indian Deficit', vol. 83 (o.s.), vol. 3 (n.s.), Jan. 1871, pp. 14–27.

Nineteenth Century
'The financial condition of India', vol. 5, Feb. 1879, pp. 193–218.
'The proposed loans to India', vol. 5, May 1879, pp. 872–89.
'The new departure in Indian finance', vol. 6, Oct. 1879, pp. 639–63.
'The next reform bill', vol. 7, March 1880, pp. 443–63.

Westminster Review
'Strikes: their tendencies and remedies', vol. 74 (o.s.), vol. 18 (n.s.), July 1860,
    pp. 1–23.

British Quarterly Review
'Pauperism', vol. 49, April 1869, pp. 487–509.

Cassell's Magazine
'The condition of the agricultural population of England', June 1872, Pt 1,
    pp. 142–4; Pt 2, pp. 146–8; Pt 3, pp. 174–6.
'The Poor Law and the poor', Oct. 1872, Pt 1, pp. 8–12; Pt 2, pp. 18–21.
'Increasing prosperity and advancing prices', Feb. 1873, Pt 1, pp. 258–61; Pt 2,
    pp. 277–80.
'Local taxation', April 1873, Pt 1, pp. 30–2; Pt 2, pp. 34–7.
'Our present national expenditure', Aug. 1873, Pt 1, pp.242–4; Pt 2,
    pp. 261–3.
'The income tax and small incomes', Nov. 1873, pp. 434–7.

British Association for the Advancement of Science, Reports
1859 (Aberdeen)
'On the social and economical influences of the new gold', Transactions of the
    Sections, pp. 205–9.
1861 (Manchester)
'On the method of Mr. Darwin in his treatise on the Origin of Species',
    Transactions of the Sections, pp. 141–3.
1864 (Bath)

'On the causes which produce the present high rate of discount', Transactions of the Sections, p. 165.

Transactions of the National Association for the Promotion of Social Science
1859 (Bradford)
'The theory and tendency of strikes', pp. 635–40.
'The protection of labour against immigration', pp. 704–5.
1860 (Glasgow)
'How the condition of the labouring classes may be raised by cooperation', pp. 871–3.
1868 (Birmingham)
'Address on economy and trade', pp. 113–24.

The Association's *Transactions* also include many of Fawcett's verbatim contributions to discussions.

4 MISCELLANEOUS SPEECHES PRINTED SEPARATELY

Speech on Indian finance. Delivered in the House of Commons in the debate on the Indian budget, 6 Aug. 1872. Reprinted with a few explanatory notes (London, 1872).
Debate on the Women's Disabilities Bill. House of Commons, 30 April 1873. Speech of Professor Fawcett (London and Manchester, 1873).
Factory Acts Amendment Bill. Speeches of Professor Fawcett, M.P., and Sir Thomas Bazley, M.P., on the adjourned debate on Wednesday, 30 July 1873 (with a letter to the editor of *The Times* from Mrs Fawcett) (London, 1873).
Government Factory Bill. Speech on the second reading of the Bill, 11 June 1874 (Manchester, 1874).
The Endowed Schools Act Amendment Bill. Speech delivered in the House of Commons, 20 July 1874 (Manchester Nonconformist Association, 1874).
Address delivered (on education) on 18 Oct. 1875. Birmingham and Midland Institute, Presidential Addresses (Birmingham, 1875).
Speech delivered to his constituents at Hackney on 13 Oct. 1884 by Henry Fawcett. Reprinted from *The Times* (Glasgow, 1884).

5 BIOGRAPHICAL MATERIAL

[Anon.], *In Memoriam. Life and Labours of Henry Fawcett* (London, Nov. 1884).
(A short pamphlet published soon after Fawcett's death.)
George Hugh Bourne, *'The King Taking Account of his Servants'. A Sermon Preached in Salisbury Cathedral on the Sunday following the Death of the Rt. Hon. H. Fawcett* (Salisbury, 1885).
Winifred Holt, *A Beacon for the Blind. Being a Life of Henry Fawcett, the Blind Postmaster General.* With a Foreword by Viscount Bryce (London, 1915).
Henry Peto, *The Late Right Hon. H. Fawcett, M.P.* (London, 1886).
(A lecture delivered to the Weymouth Working Men's Club, largely based on Stephen's *Life*.)
Leslie Stephen, *Life of Henry Fawcett* (London, 1885).
(Stephen's two-volume manuscript of the *Life* is kept in the Trinity Hall Library, Cambridge.)

Index

(1865), 6, 18; *Life of Henry Fawcett* (1885), 8, 17, 42–3, 181–2
Sumner, John Bird, 60
Sunmner, William Graham, 104

Taylor, Harriet, 134
Taylor, Helen, 10, 80, 82, 136,
Taylor, Peter, 11
Thackeray, J. M., 5
Thornton, W. T., 8, 99–100, 137–8
Tooke, Thomas, 112
Toynbee, Arnold, 121
Trades Union Congress, 13, 159
Trevelyan, G. O., 16, 17, 33
Trinity College, Dublin, 24–8
Trinity Hall, Cambridge, 3, 6–9, 180–3

University Liberalism, 7, 11, 37–8, 156–7
Utilitarianism, 44–5, 61,

Vaughan, C.J., 66

Walras, Léon, 108, 110
Webb, Sidney and Beatrice, 151
Wedderburn, Sir David, 16
Wells, David Ames, 104
Westminster Abbey, memorial to Fawcett in, 36
Whewell, William, 125, 167, 168n
Wicksteed, Philip, 117
Wilberforce, Bishop Samuel, 94

For EU product safety concerns, contact us at Calle de José Abascal, 56–1°,
28003 Madrid, Spain or eugpsr@cambridge.org.

www.ingramcontent.com/pod-product-compliance
Ingram Content Group UK Ltd.
Pitfield, Milton Keynes, MK11 3LW, UK
UKHW010045140625
459647UK00012BB/1619